PARASOMNIA

BUNN ◆ MUTTI ◆ BOWLAND

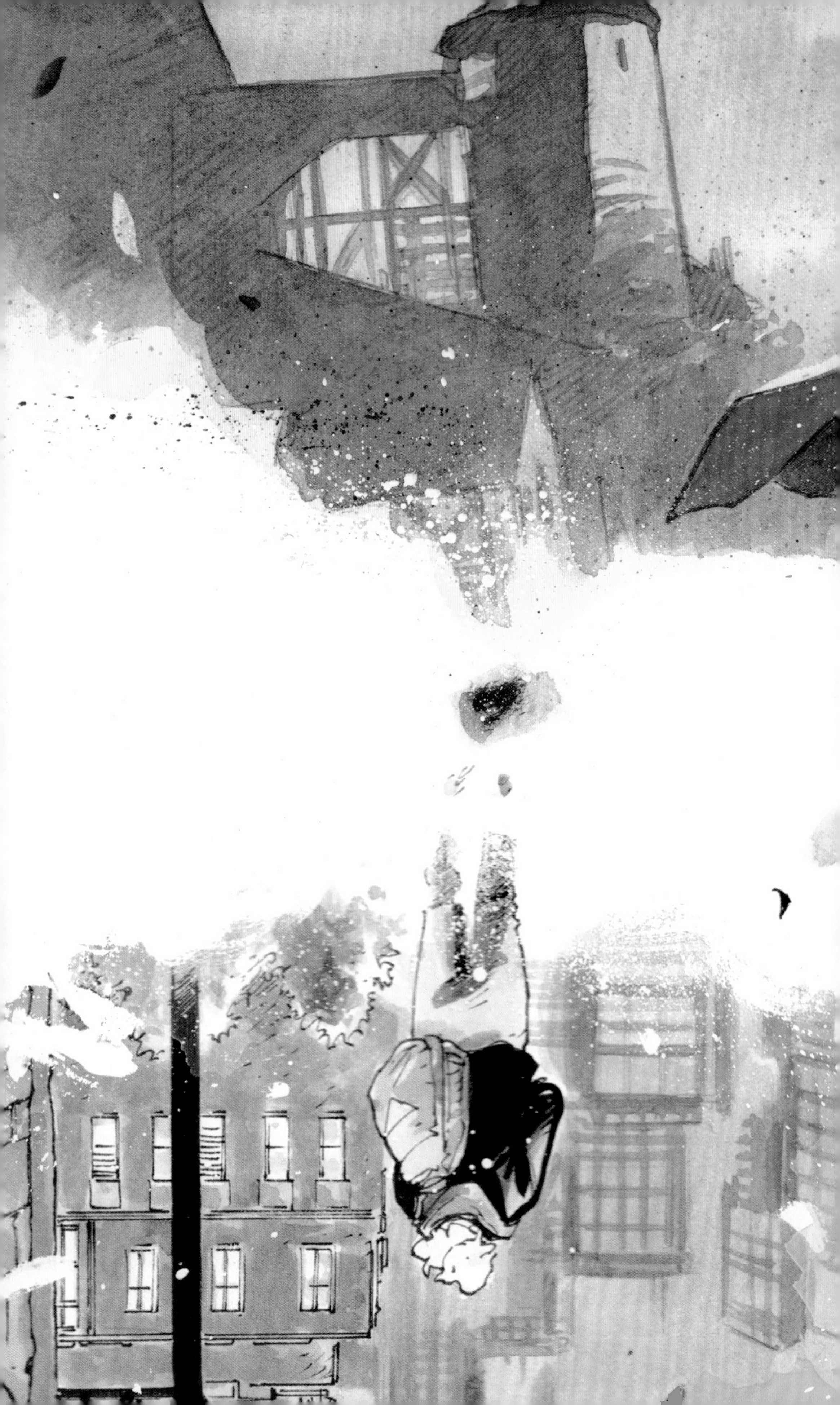

PARASOMNIA ™

BUNN ◆ MUTTI ◆ BOWLAND

Script
CULLEN BUNN

Art and Colors
ANDREA MUTTI

Lettering
SIMON BOWLAND

Cover Artist
ANDREA MUTTI

Parasomnia created by
CULLEN BUNN AND ANDREA MUTTI

DARK HORSE BOOKS

President & Publisher **MIKE RICHARDSON** · Editor **DANIEL CHABON**
Assistant Editors **CHUCK HOWITT AND KONNER KNUDSEN**
Designer **DIEGO MORALES-PORTILLO** · Digital Art Technician **ADAM PRUETT**

NEIL HANKERSON Executive Vice President · TOM WEDDLE Chief Financial Officer · DALE LₐFOUNTAIN Chief Information Officer TIM WIESCH Vice President of Licensing · MATT PARKINSON Vice President of Marketing · VANESSA TODD-HOLMES Vice President of Production and Scheduling · MARK BERNARDI Vice President of Book Trade and Digital Sales · RANDY LAHRMAN Vice President of Product Development · KEN LIZZI General Counsel · DAVE MARSHALL Editor in Chief · DAVEY ESTRADA Editorial Director · CHRIS WARNER Senior Books Editor · CARY GRAZZINI Director of Specialty Projects · LIA RIBACCHI Art Director · MATT DRYER Director of Digital Art and Prepress · MICHAEL GOMBOS Senior Director of Licensed Publications · KARI YADRO Director of Custom Programs KARI TORSON Director of International Licensing

Parasomnia

Collects Parasomnia #1–#4.

Published by
Dark Horse Books
A division of Dark Horse Comics LLC
10956 SE Main Street
Milwaukie, OR 97222

DarkHorse.com

To find a comics shop in your area, visit comicshoplocator.com

First edition: February 2022
Ebook ISBN 978-1-50672-051-7
Trade paperback ISBN 978-1-50672-042-5
10 9 8 7 6 5 4 3 2 1
Printed in China

Library of Congress Cataloging-in-Publication Data

Names: Bunn, Cullen, author. | Mutti, Andrea, 1973- artist. | Bowland, Simon, letterer.
Title: Parasomnia / script, Cullen Bunn ; art and colors, Andrea Mutti ; lettering, Simon Bowland.
Description: First edition. | Milwaukie, OR : Dark Horse Books, 2022. | "Collects Parasomnia #1-#4, including all covers and bonus material." | Summary: "After his son disappears, a broken-down man braves a nightmarish dreamscape in order to find him--and battle the ruthless cult that seeks to rule the land of dreams as the barrier between realities starts to collapse."-- Provided by publisher.
Identifiers: LCCN 2021034594 (print) | LCCN 2021034595 (ebook) | ISBN 9781506720425 (trade paperback) | ISBN 9781506720517 (ebook)
Subjects: LCGFT: Fantasy comics.
Classification: LCC PN6728.P369 B86 2022 (print) | LCC PN6728.P369 (ebook) | DDC 741.5/973--dc23
LC record available at https://lccn.loc.gov/2021034594
LC ebook record available at https://lccn.loc.gov/2021034595

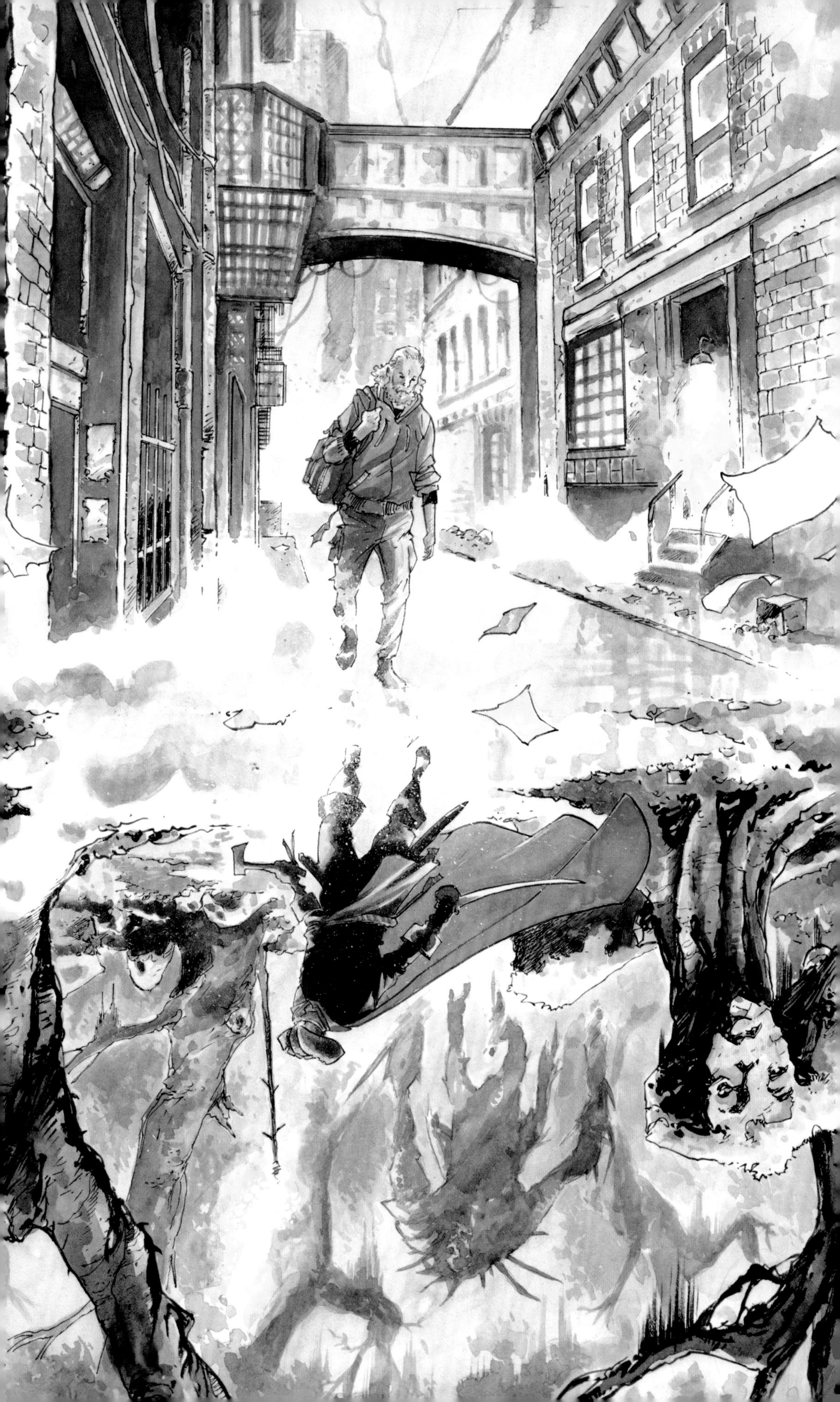

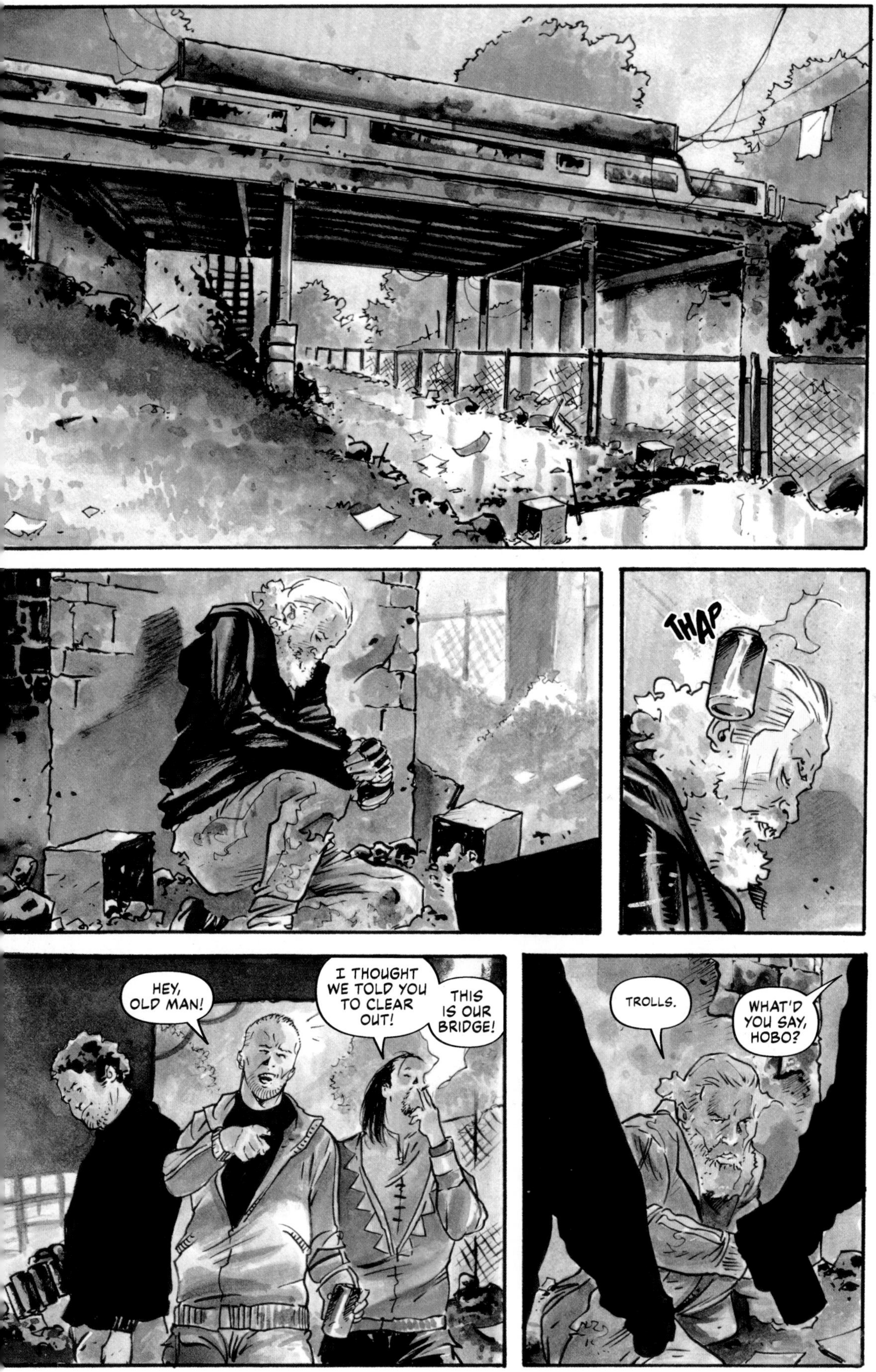
THAP
HEY, OLD MAN!
I THOUGHT WE TOLD YOU TO CLEAR OUT!
THIS IS OUR BRIDGE!
TROLLS.
WHAT'D YOU SAY, HOBO?

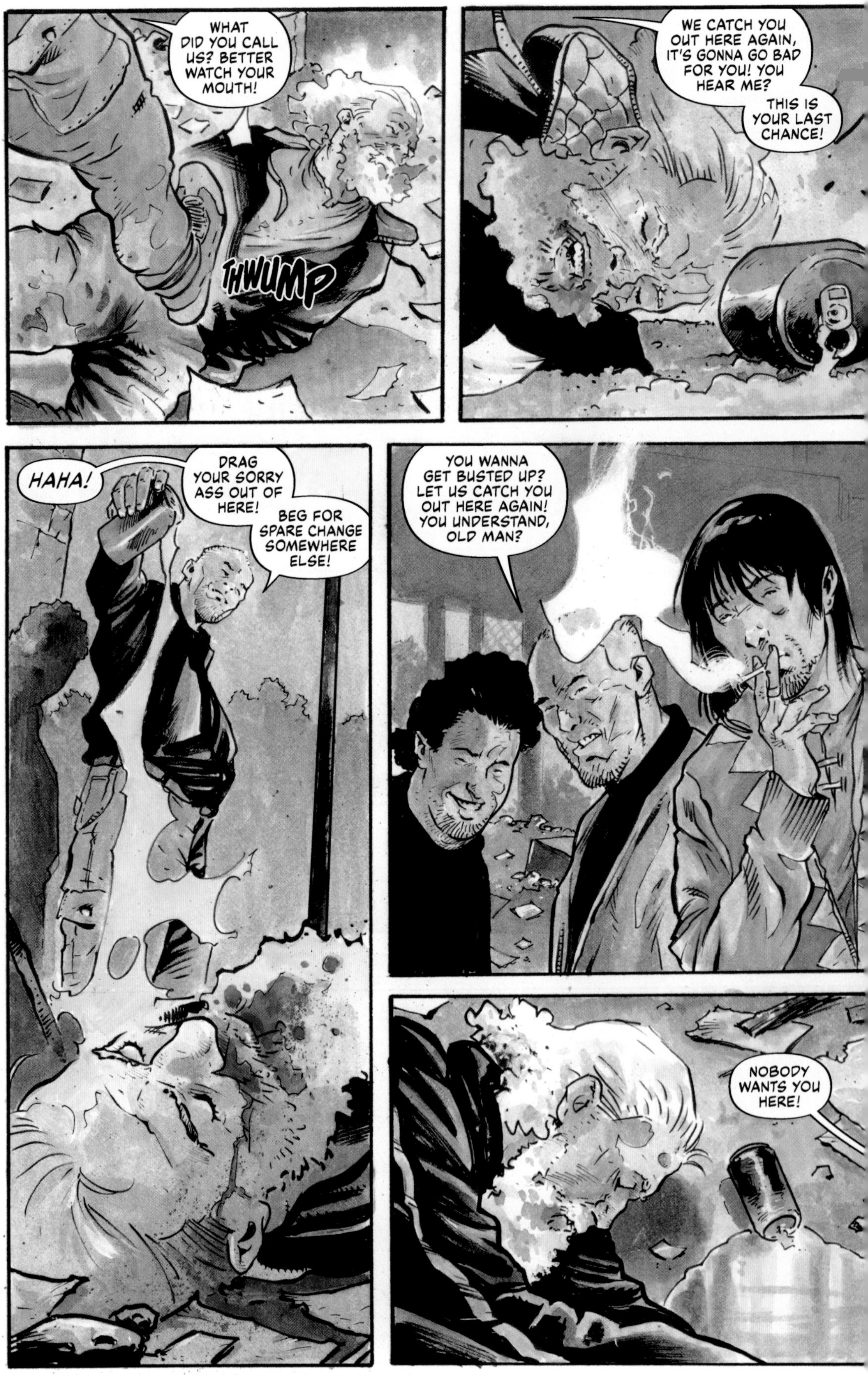
WHAT DID YOU CALL US? BETTER WATCH YOUR MOUTH!
THWUMP
WE CATCH YOU OUT HERE AGAIN, IT'S GONNA GO BAD FOR YOU! YOU HEAR ME?
THIS IS YOUR LAST CHANCE!
HAHA!
DRAG YOUR SORRY ASS OUT OF HERE!
BEG FOR SPARE CHANGE SOMEWHERE ELSE!
YOU WANNA GET BUSTED UP? LET US CATCH YOU OUT HERE AGAIN! YOU UNDERSTAND, OLD MAN?
NOBODY WANTS YOU HERE!

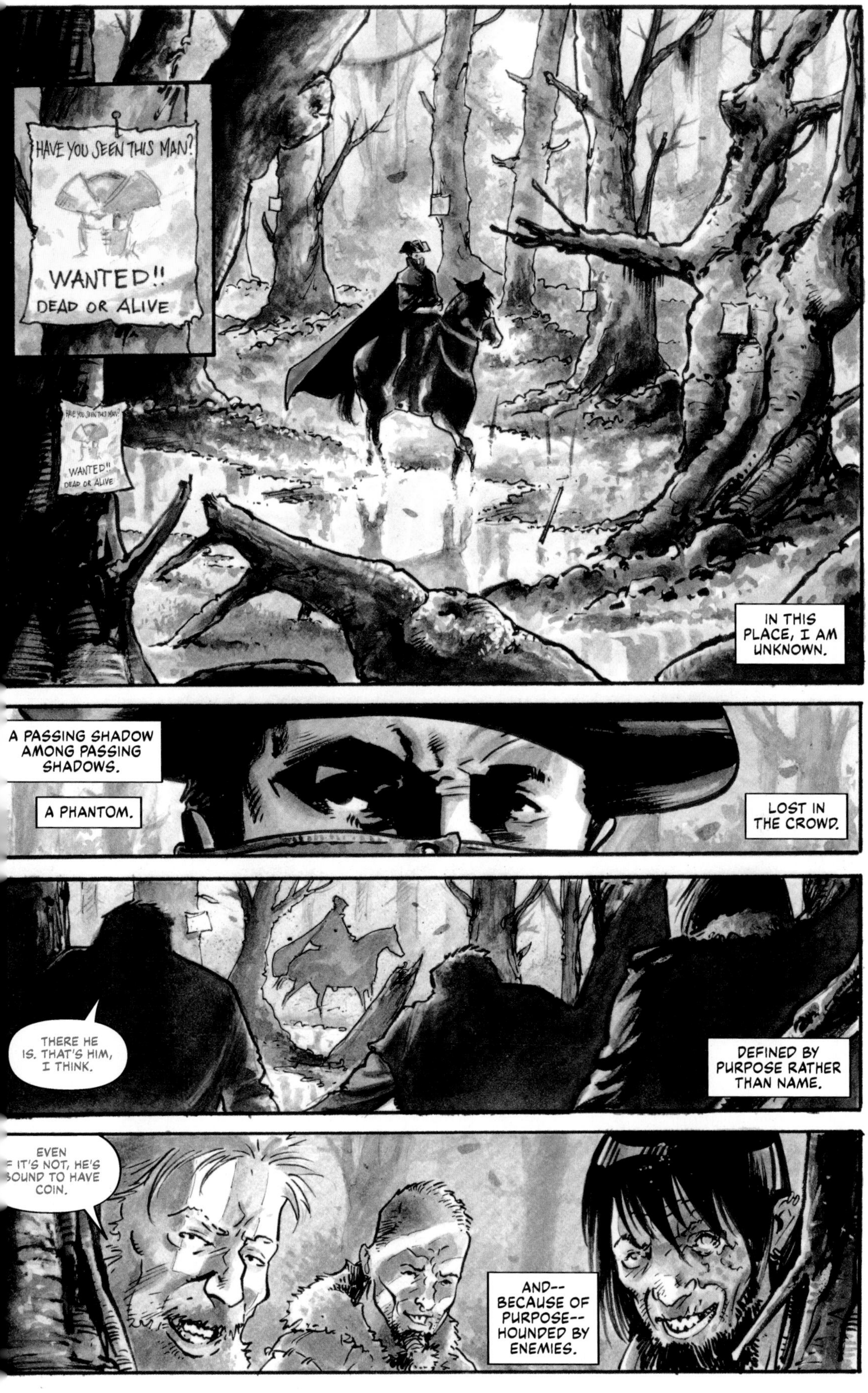
HAVE YOU SEEN THIS MAN?
WANTED!!
DEAD OR ALIVE
HAVE YOU SEEN THIS MAN?
WANTED!!
DEAD OR ALIVE
IN THIS PLACE, I AM UNKNOWN.
A PASSING SHADOW AMONG PASSING SHADOWS.
A PHANTOM.
LOST IN THE CROWD.
THERE HE IS. THAT'S HIM, I THINK.
DEFINED BY PURPOSE RATHER THAN NAME.
EVEN IF IT'S NOT, HE'S BOUND TO HAVE COIN.
AND-- BECAUSE OF PURPOSE-- HOUNDED BY ENEMIES.

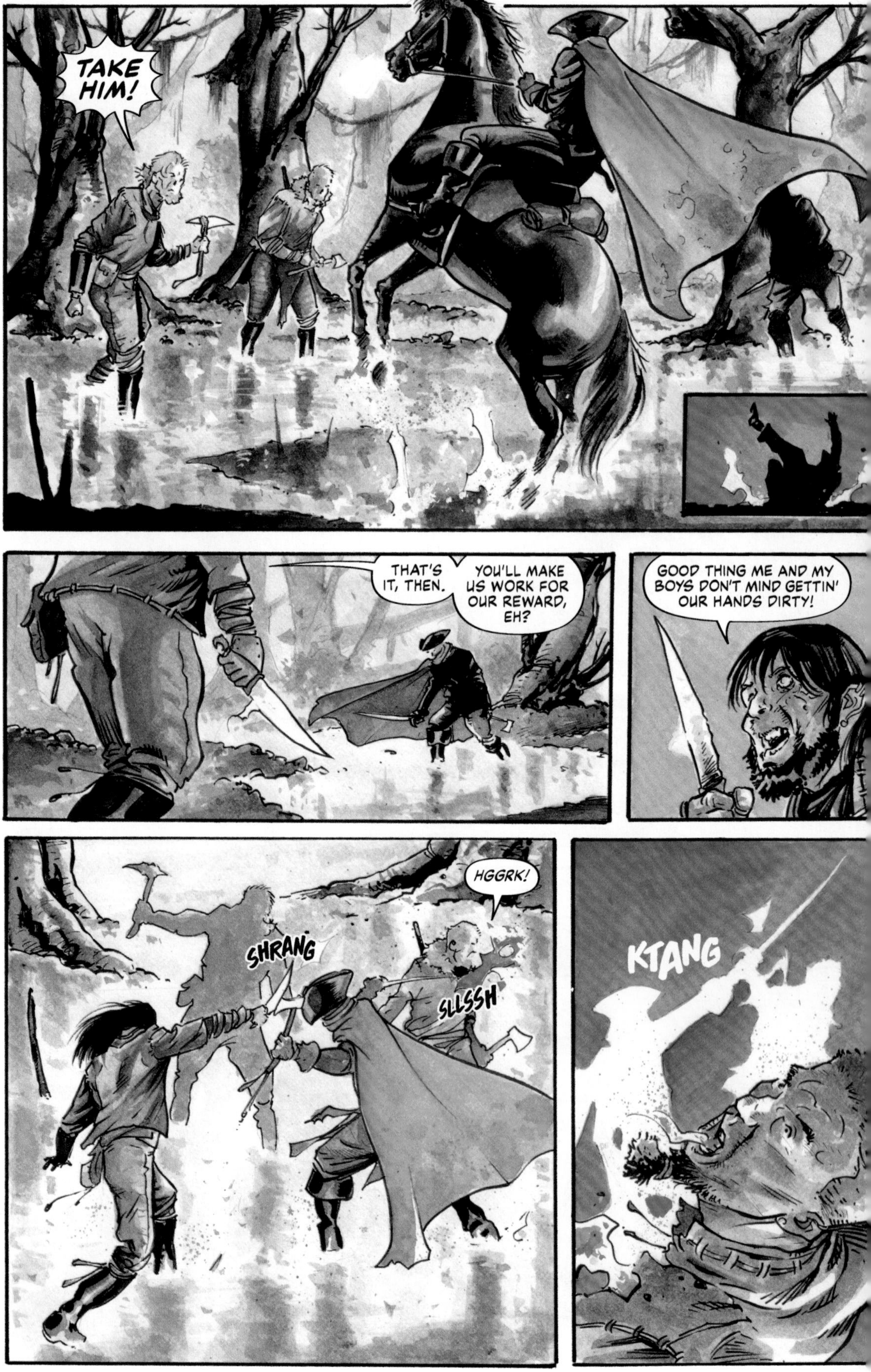
TAKE HIM!
THAT'S IT, THEN.
YOU'LL MAKE US WORK FOR OUR REWARD, EH?
GOOD THING ME AND MY BOYS DON'T MIND GETTIN' OUR HANDS DIRTY!
HGGRK!
SHRANG
SLLSSH
KTANG

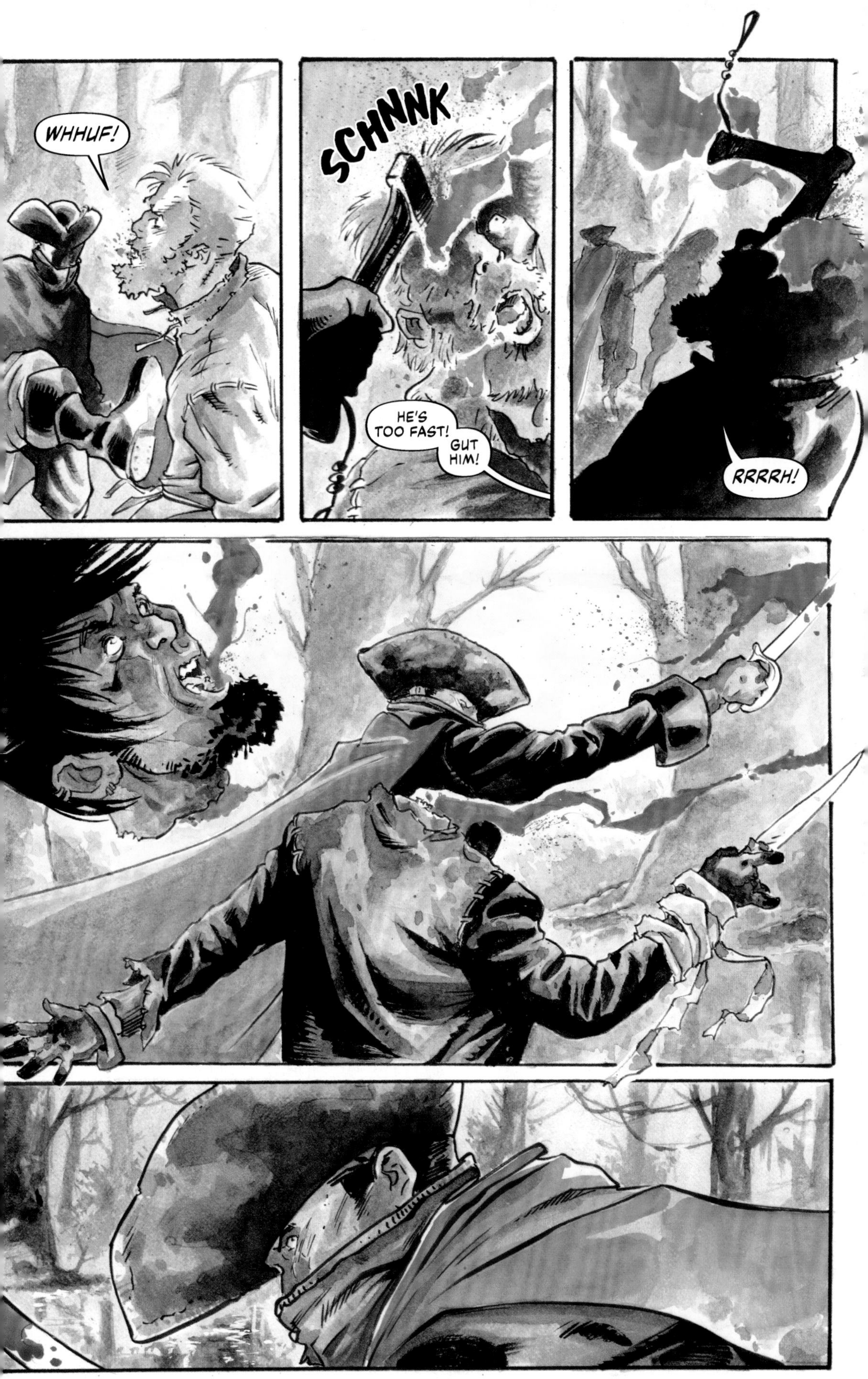
WHHUF!
SCHNNK
HE'S TOO FAST!
GUT HIM!
RRRRH!

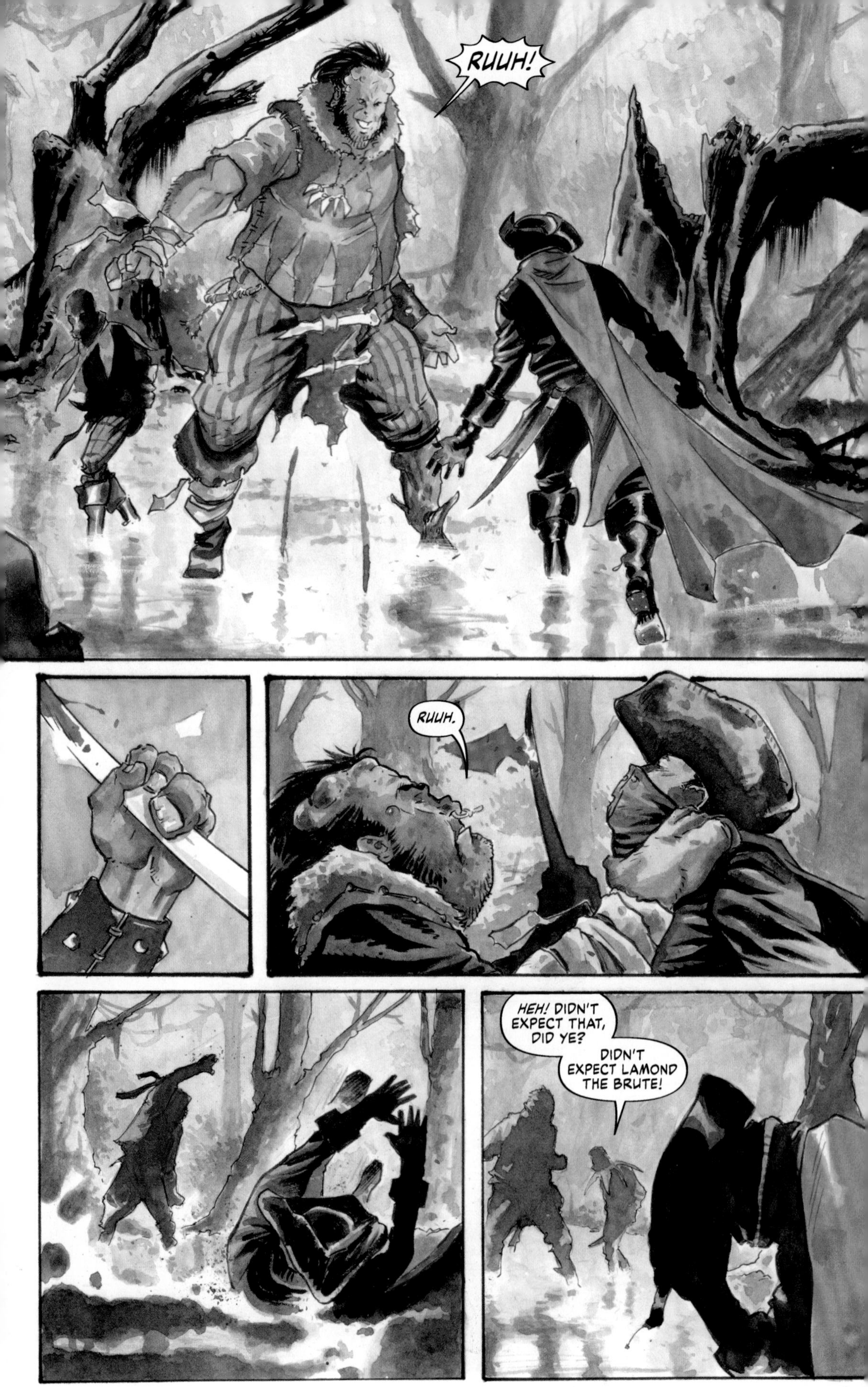
RUUH!
RUUH.
HEH! DIDN'T EXPECT THAT, DID YE?
DIDN'T EXPECT LAMOND THE BRUTE!

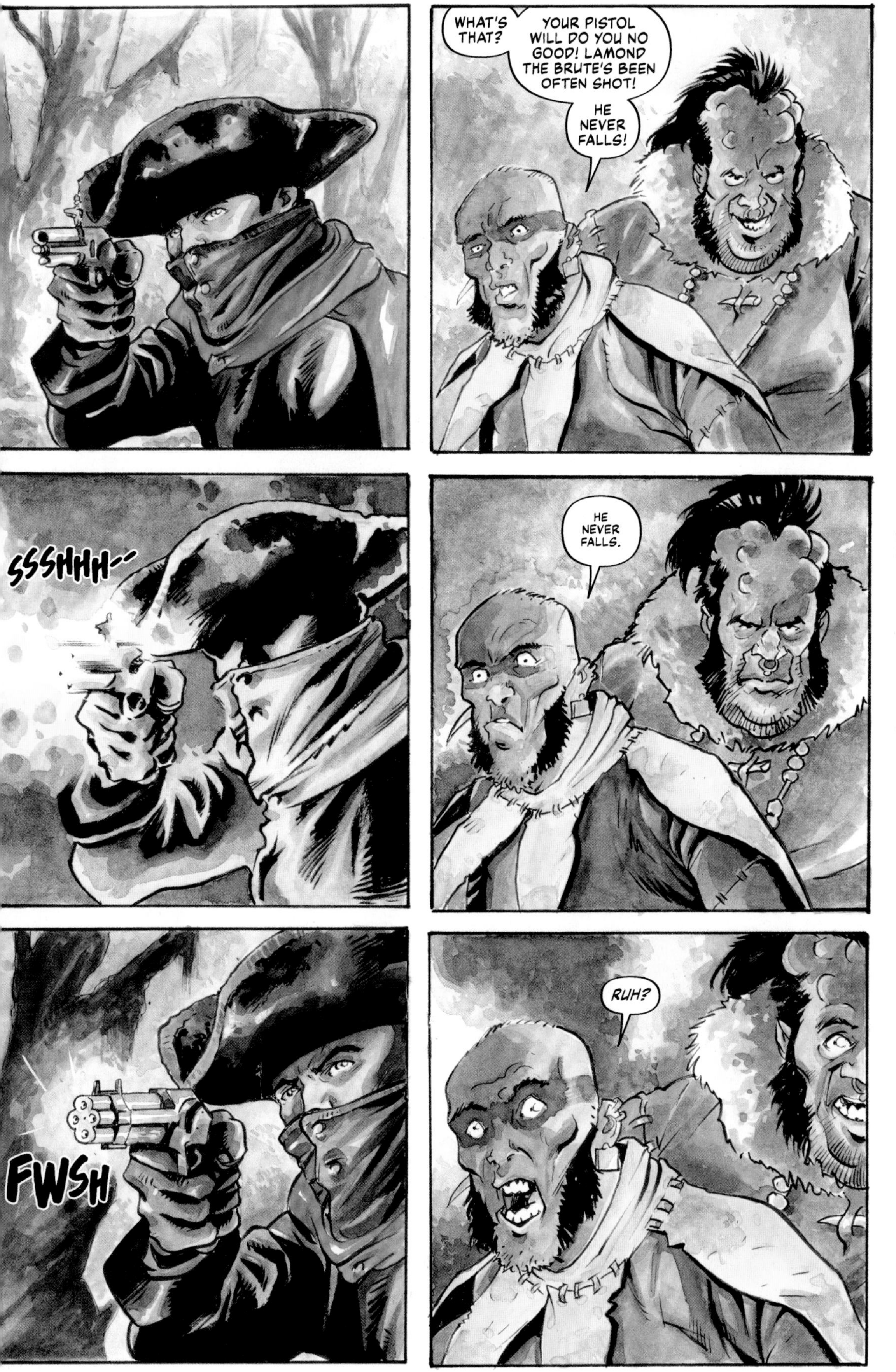
WHAT'S THAT?
YOUR PISTOL WILL DO YOU NO GOOD! LAMOND THE BRUTE'S BEEN OFTEN SHOT!
HE NEVER FALLS!
SSSHHH--
HE NEVER FALLS.
FWSH
RUH?

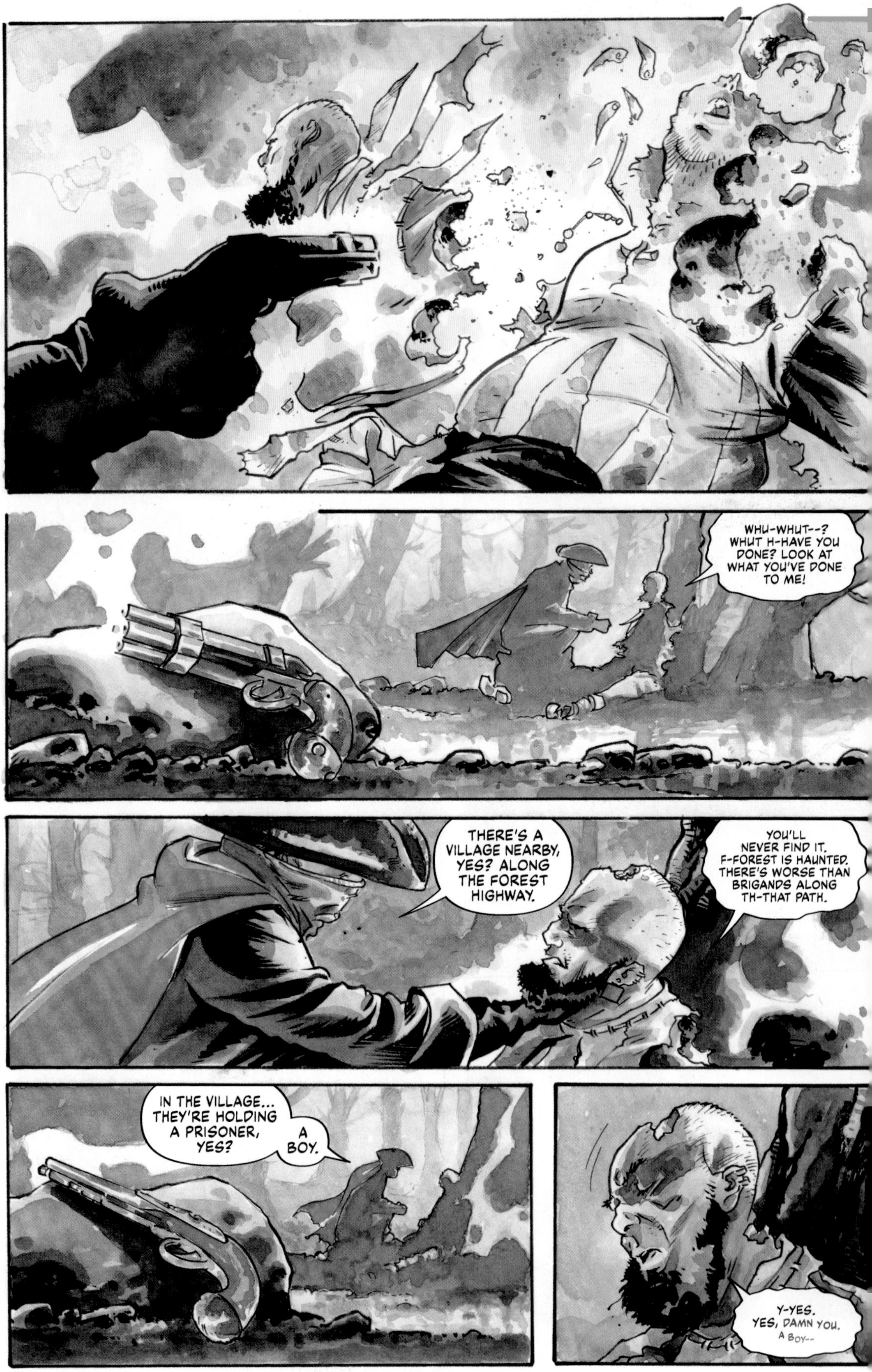
WHU-WHUT--? WHUT H-HAVE YOU DONE? LOOK AT WHAT YOU'VE DONE TO ME!
THERE'S A VILLAGE NEARBY, YES? ALONG THE FOREST HIGHWAY.
YOU'LL NEVER FIND IT. F-FOREST IS HAUNTED. THERE'S WORSE THAN BRIGANDS ALONG TH-THAT PATH.
IN THE VILLAGE... THEY'RE HOLDING A PRISONER, YES?
A BOY.
Y-YES. YES, DAMN YOU. A BOY--

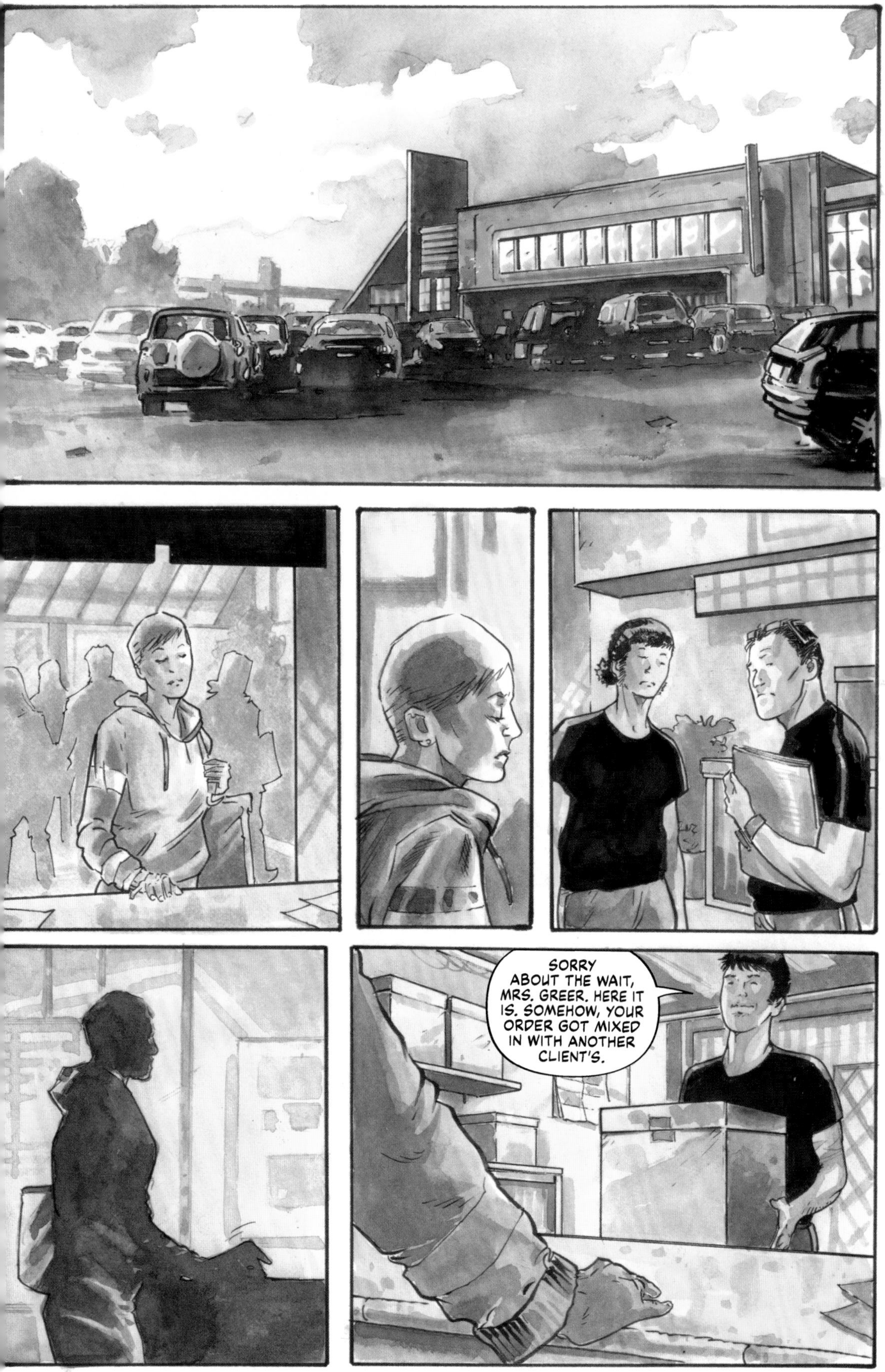
SORRY ABOUT THE WAIT, MRS. GREER. HERE IT IS. SOMEHOW, YOUR ORDER GOT MIXED IN WITH ANOTHER CLIENT'S.

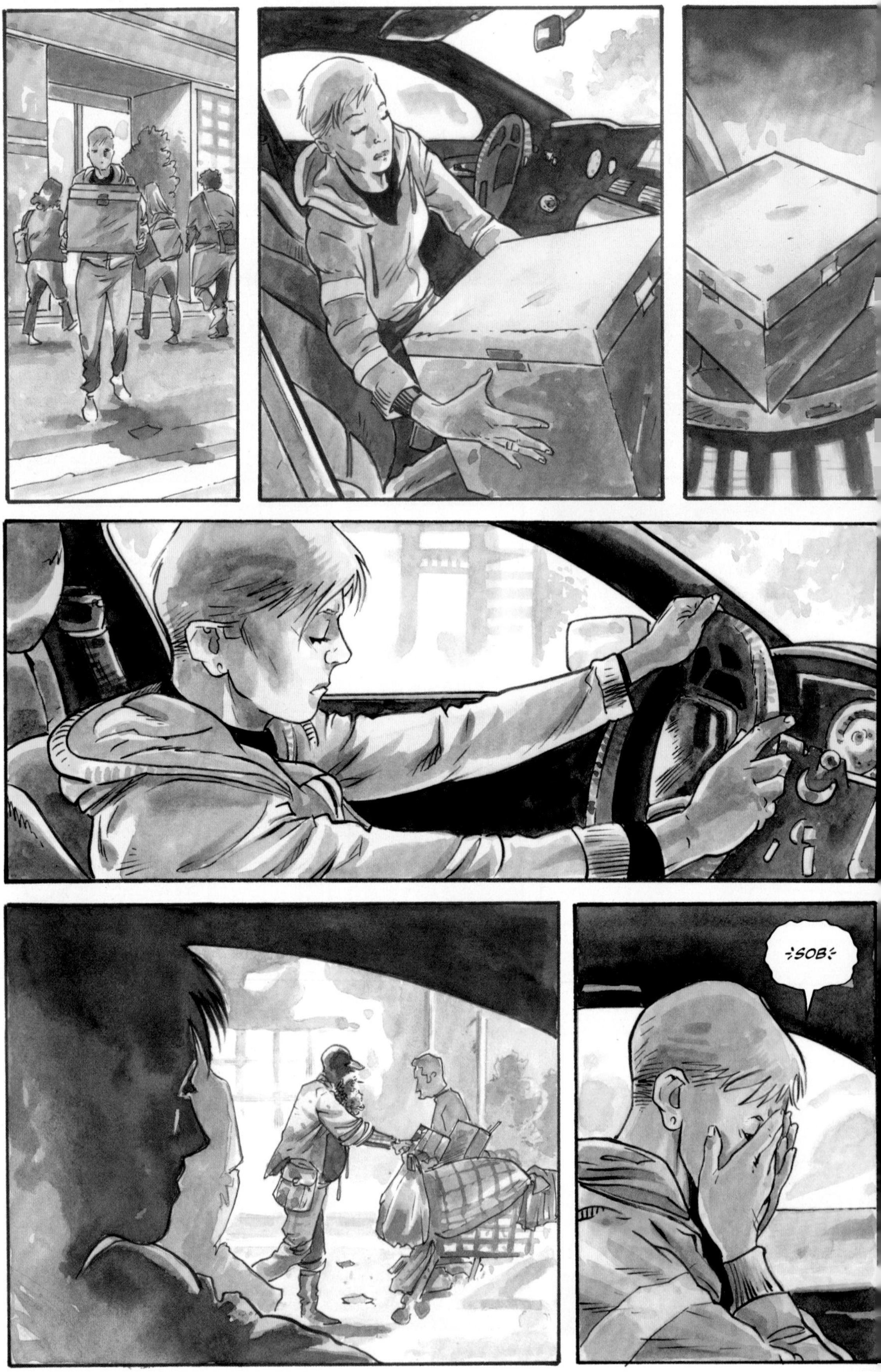
SOB

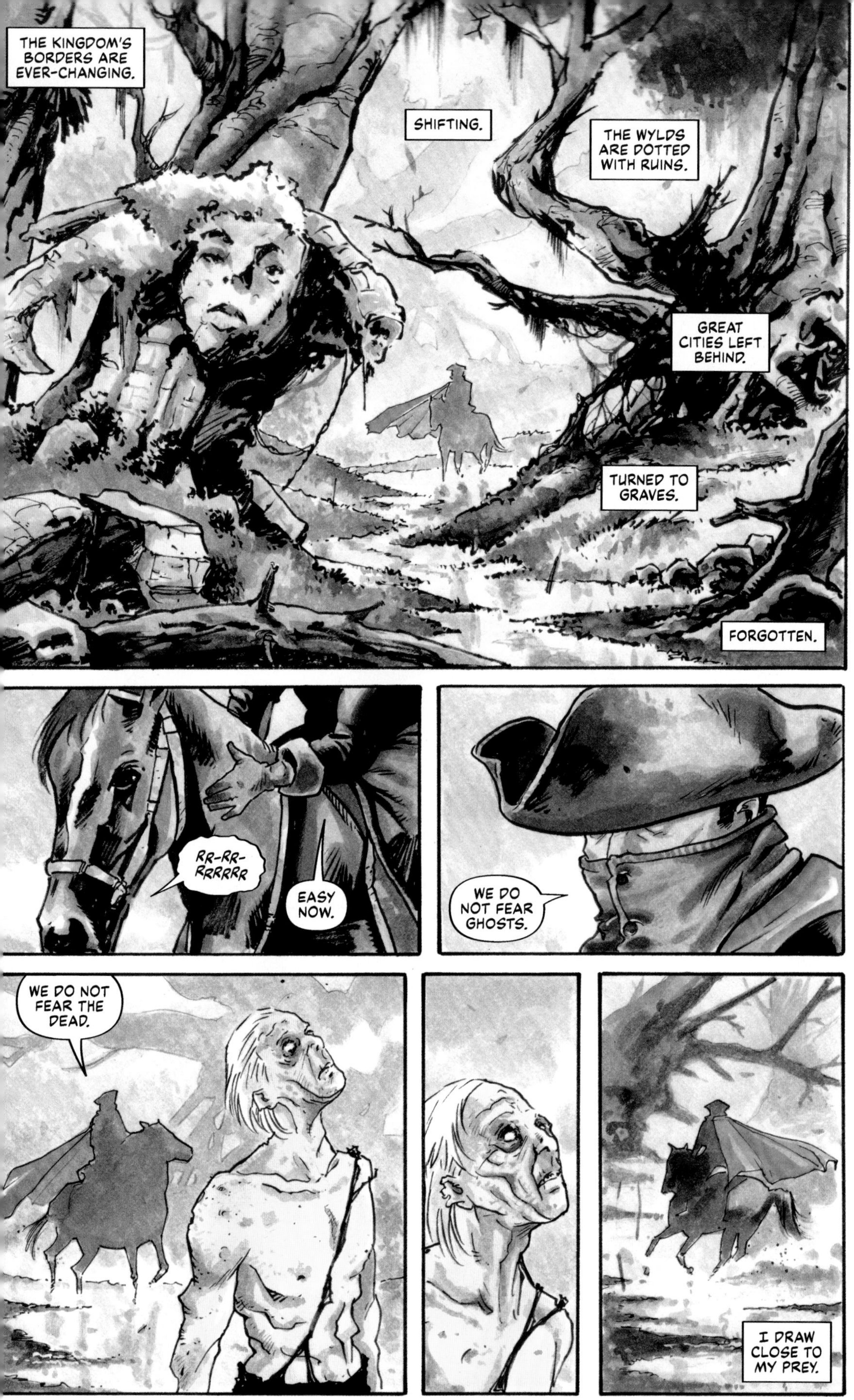
THE KINGDOM'S BORDERS ARE EVER-CHANGING.
SHIFTING.
THE WYLDS ARE DOTTED WITH RUINS.
GREAT CITIES LEFT BEHIND.
TURNED TO GRAVES.
FORGOTTEN.
RR-RR-RRRRRR
EASY NOW.
WE DO NOT FEAR GHOSTS.
WE DO NOT FEAR THE DEAD.
I DRAW CLOSE TO MY PREY.

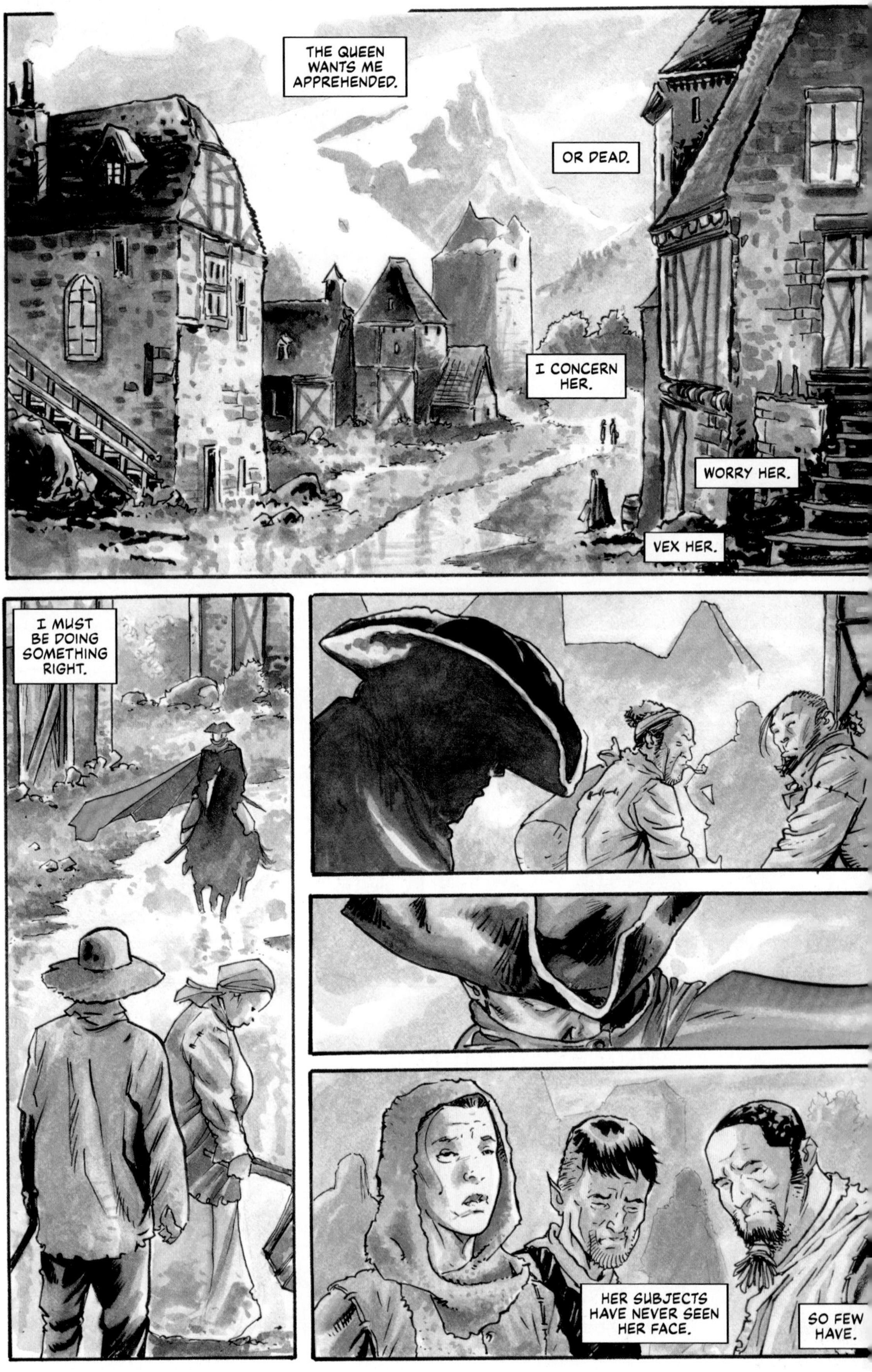
THE QUEEN WANTS ME APPREHENDED.
OR DEAD.
I CONCERN HER.
WORRY HER.
VEX HER.
I MUST BE DOING SOMETHING RIGHT.
HER SUBJECTS HAVE NEVER SEEN HER FACE.
SO FEW HAVE.

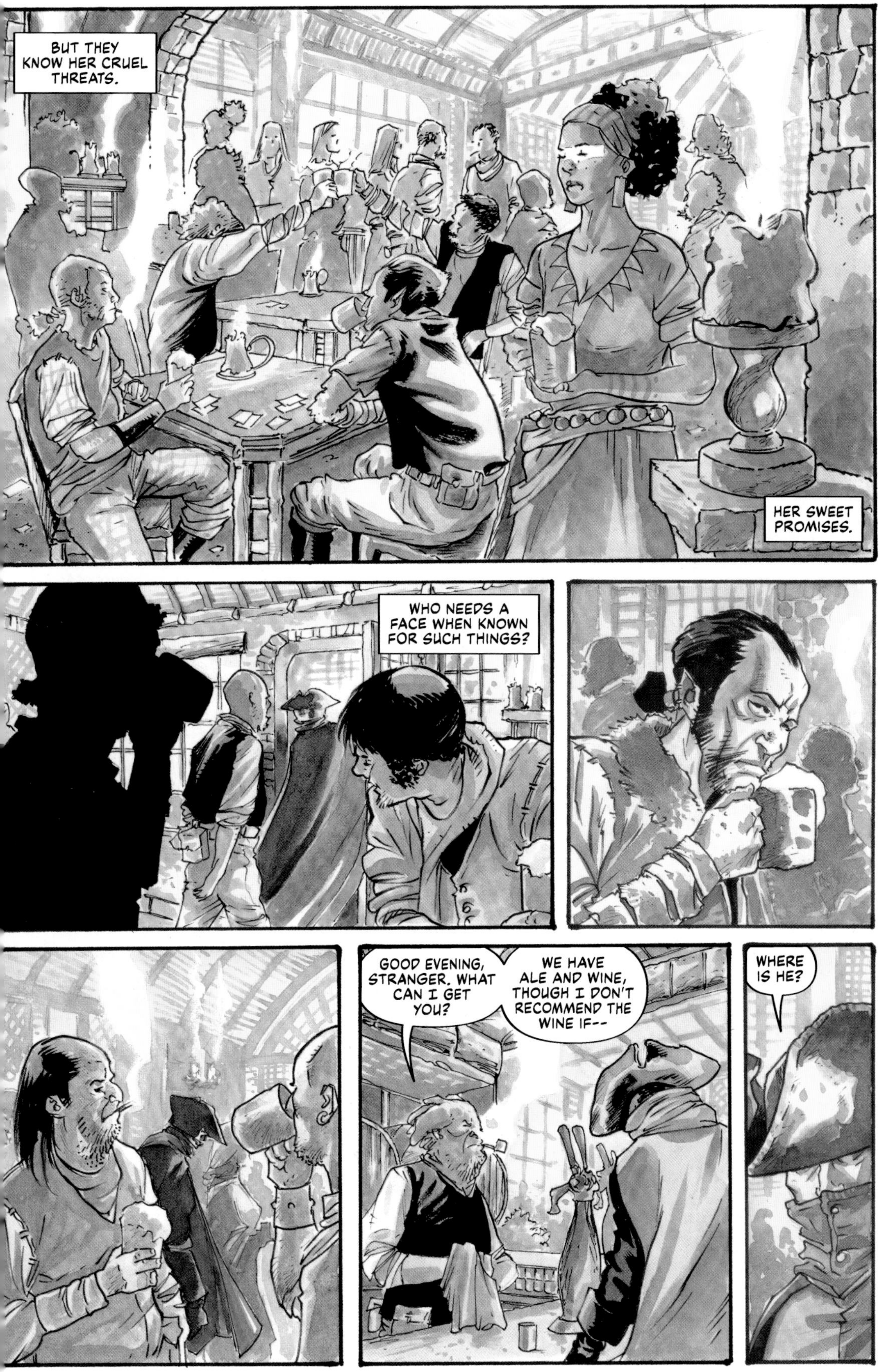
BUT THEY KNOW HER CRUEL THREATS.
HER SWEET PROMISES.
WHO NEEDS A FACE WHEN KNOWN FOR SUCH THINGS?
GOOD EVENING, STRANGER. WHAT CAN I GET YOU?
WE HAVE ALE AND WINE, THOUGH I DON'T RECOMMEND THE WINE IF--
WHERE IS HE?

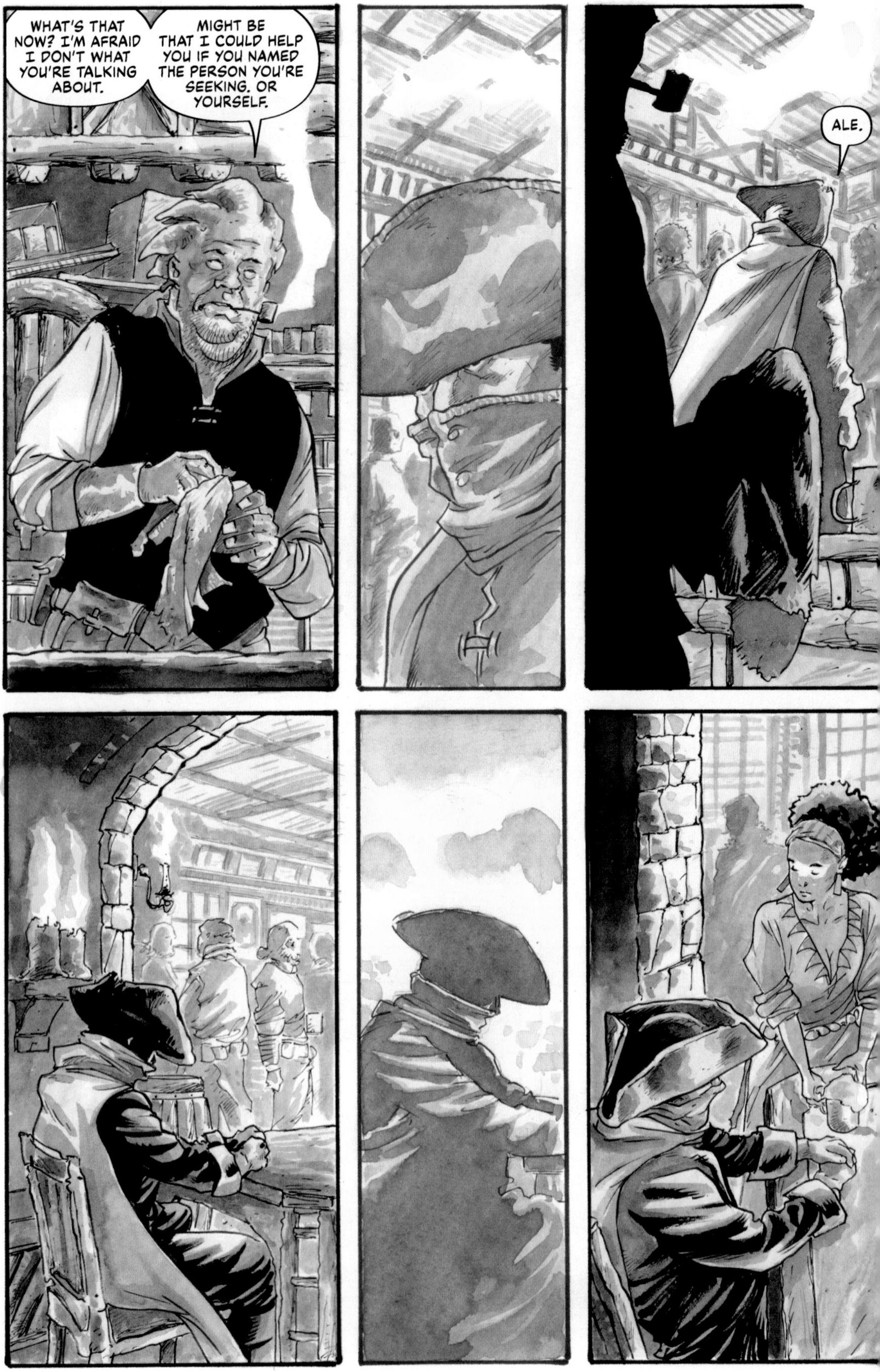

WHAT'S THAT NOW? I'M AFRAID I DON'T WHAT YOU'RE TALKING ABOUT.
MIGHT BE THAT I COULD HELP YOU IF YOU NAMED THE PERSON YOU'RE SEEKING. OR YOURSELF.
ALE.

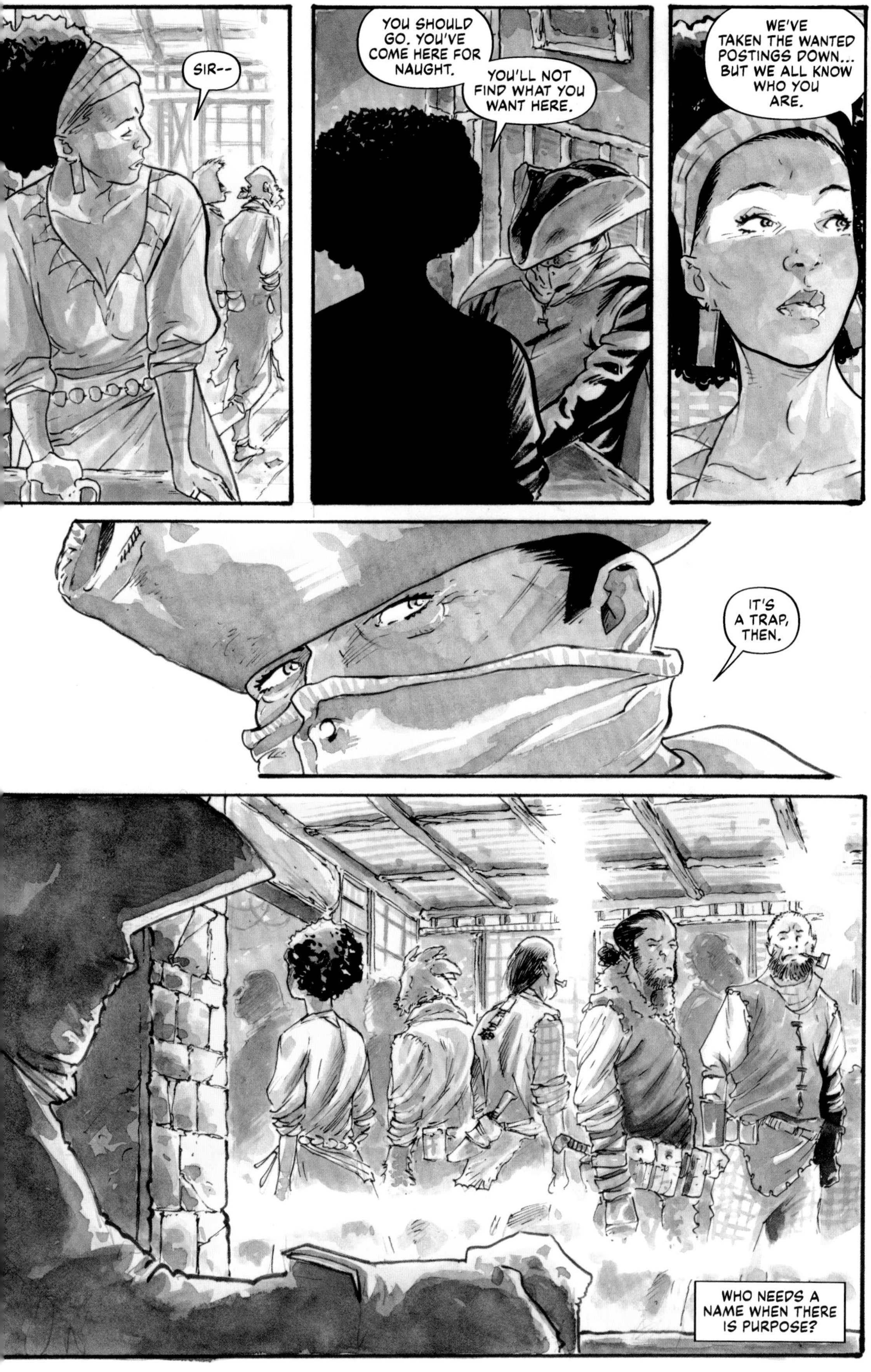
SIR--
YOU SHOULD GO. YOU'VE COME HERE FOR NAUGHT.
YOU'LL NOT FIND WHAT YOU WANT HERE.
WE'VE TAKEN THE WANTED POSTINGS DOWN... BUT WE ALL KNOW WHO YOU ARE.
IT'S A TRAP, THEN.
WHO NEEDS A NAME WHEN THERE IS PURPOSE?

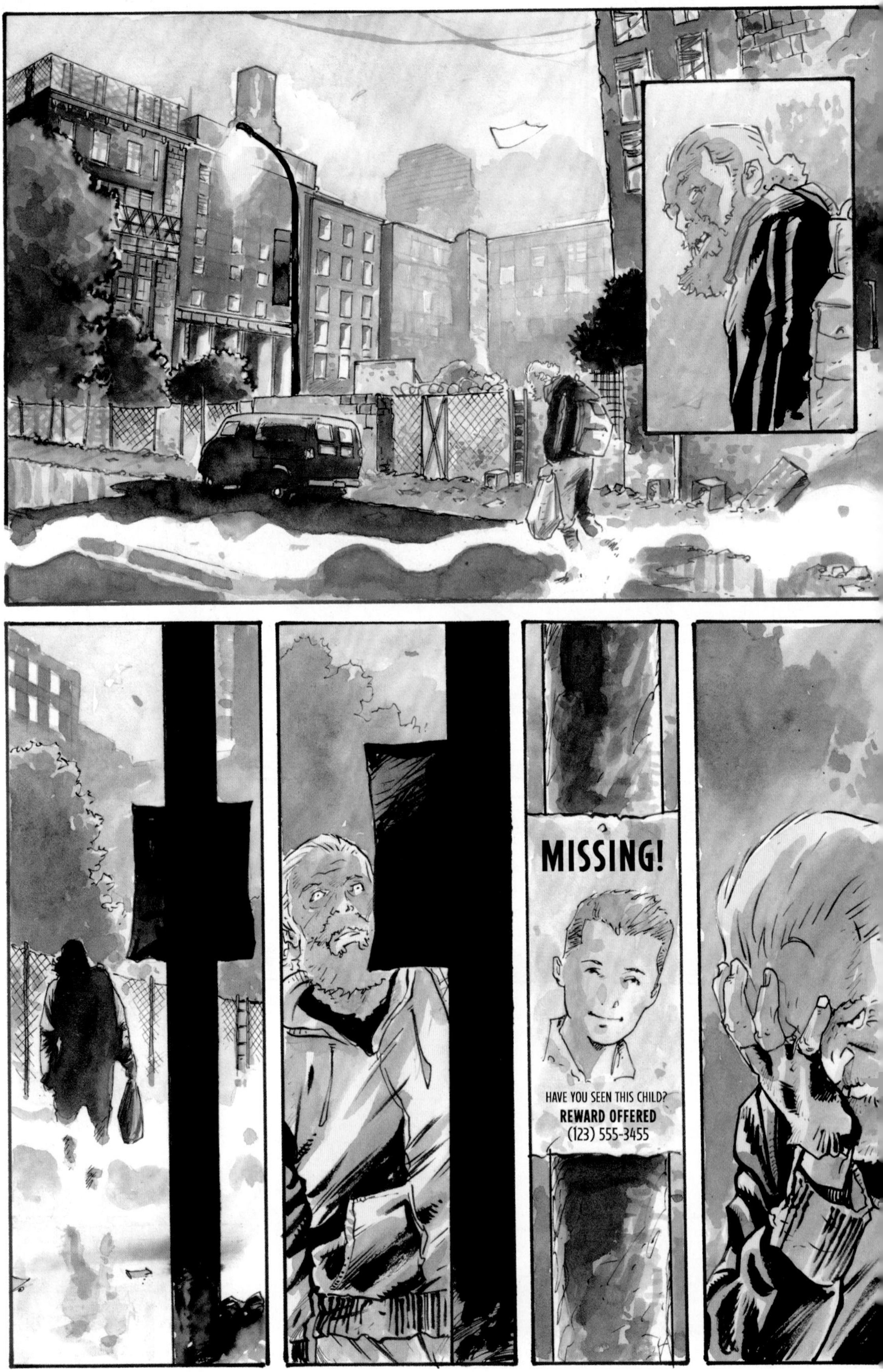
MISSING!
HAVE YOU SEEN THIS CHILD?
REWARD OFFERED
(123) 555-3455

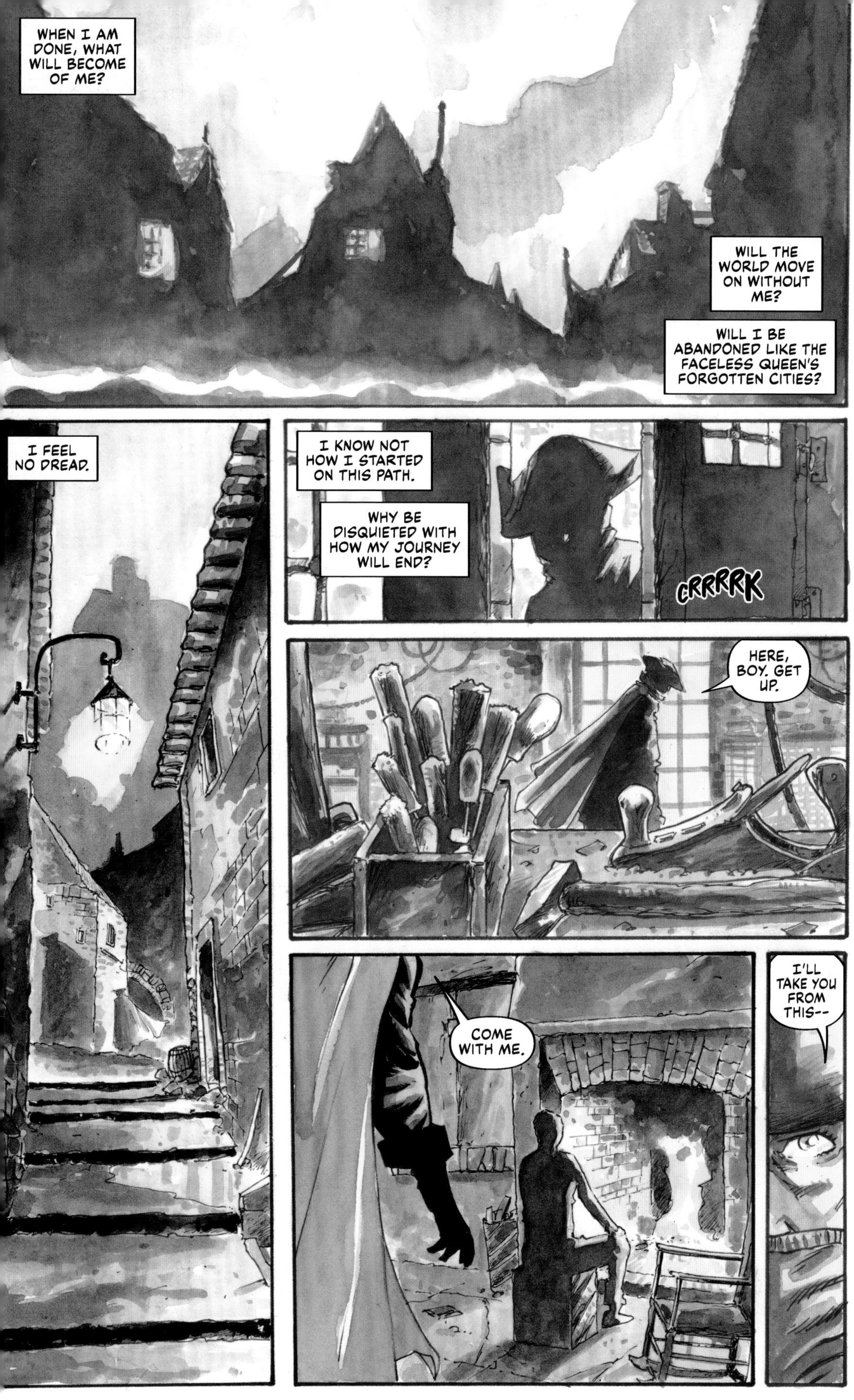
WHEN I AM DONE, WHAT WILL BECOME OF ME?
WILL THE WORLD MOVE ON WITHOUT ME?
WILL I BE ABANDONED LIKE THE FACELESS QUEEN'S FORGOTTEN CITIES?
I FEEL NO DREAD.
I KNOW NOT HOW I STARTED ON THIS PATH.
WHY BE DISQUIETED WITH HOW MY JOURNEY WILL END?
CRRRRK
HERE, BOY. GET UP.
COME WITH ME.
I'LL TAKE YOU FROM THIS--

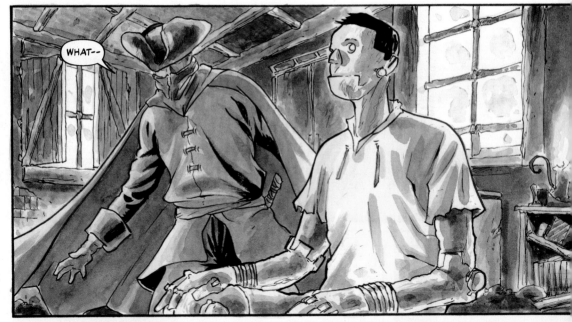

WHAT--

I TRIED TO WARN YOU. YOU SHOULD HAVE LISTENED. BUT I KNEW YOU WOULDN'T.

AAAGH!
SLAAASH
CURSE HIM!
SHHHK
KRNCH
WHERE IS HE?
THUNK
UNNNF!

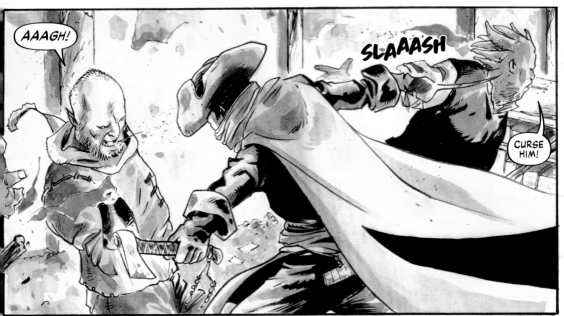

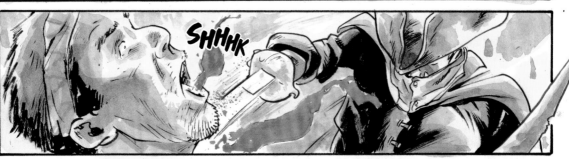

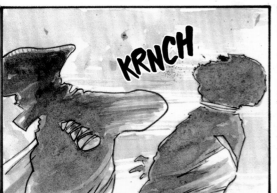

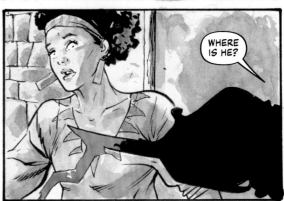

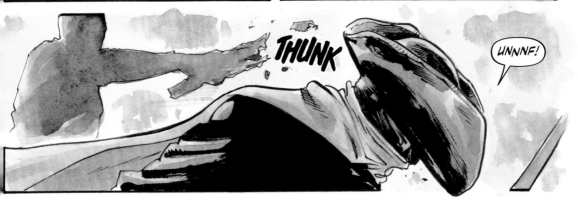

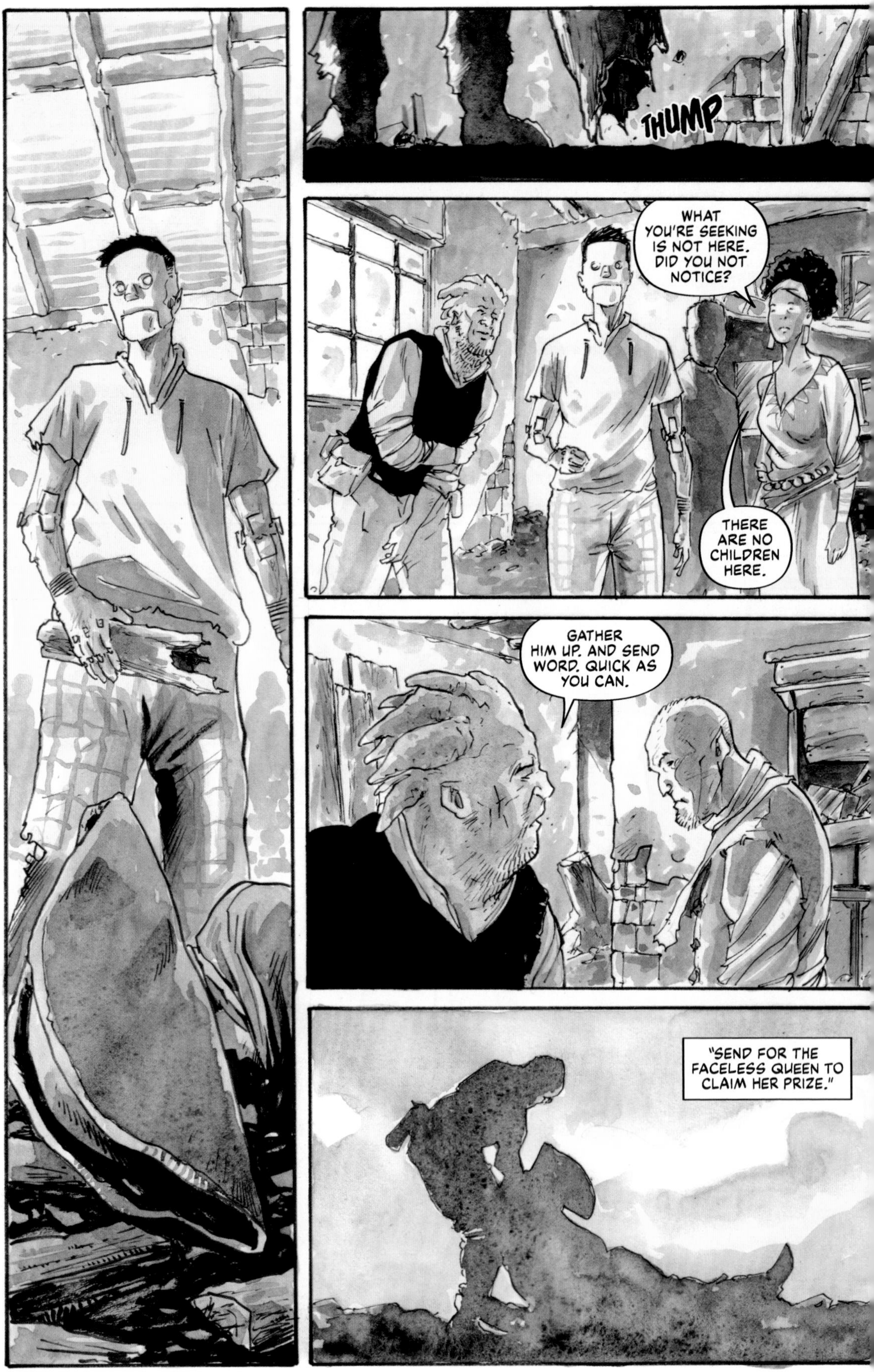
THUMP
WHAT YOU'RE SEEKING IS NOT HERE. DID YOU NOT NOTICE?
THERE ARE NO CHILDREN HERE.
GATHER HIM UP. AND SEND WORD. QUICK AS YOU CAN.
"SEND FOR THE FACELESS QUEEN TO CLAIM HER PRIZE."

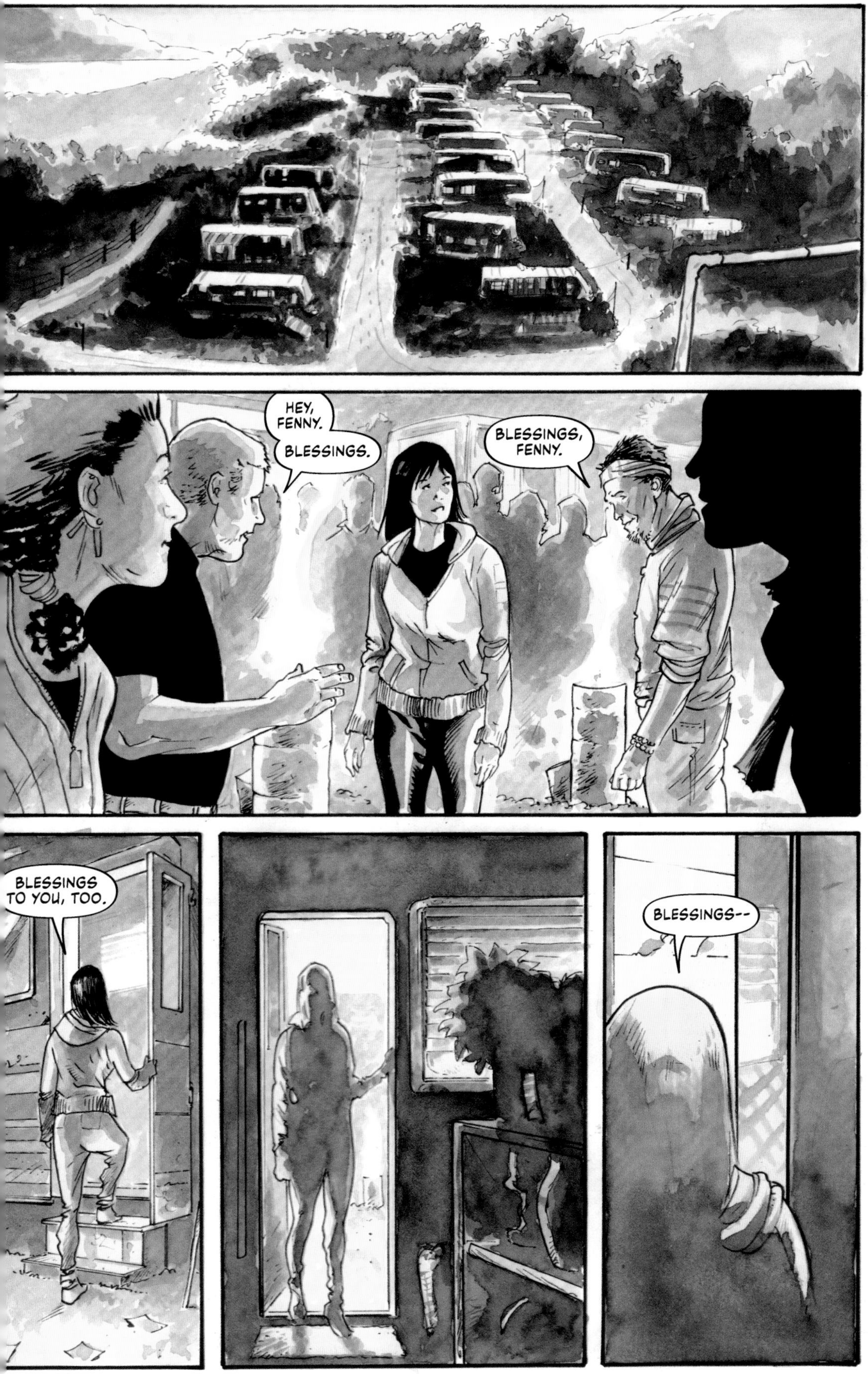
HEY, FENNY.
BLESSINGS.
BLESSINGS, FENNY.
BLESSINGS TO YOU, TOO.
BLESSINGS--

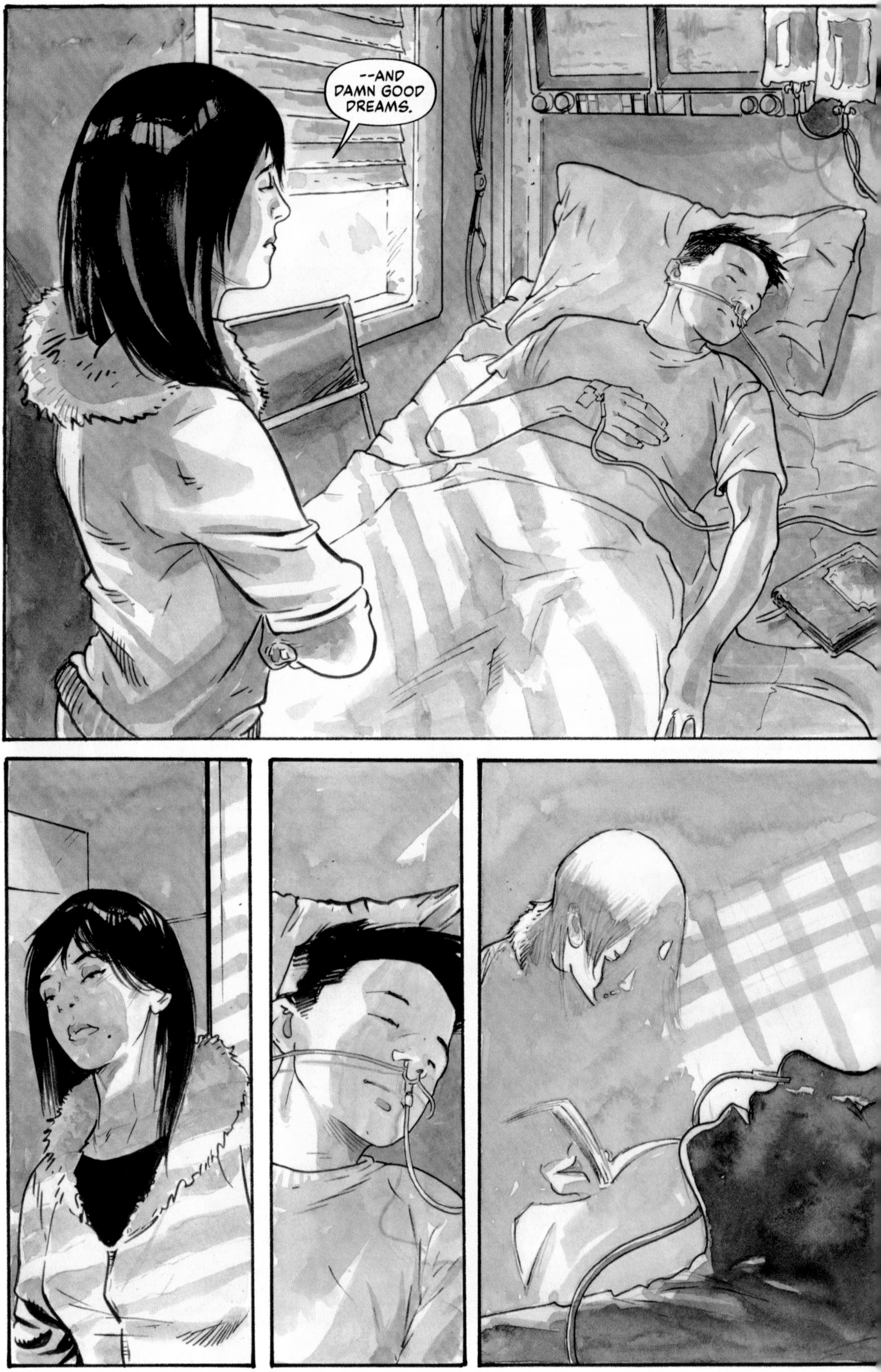
--AND DAMN GOOD DREAMS.

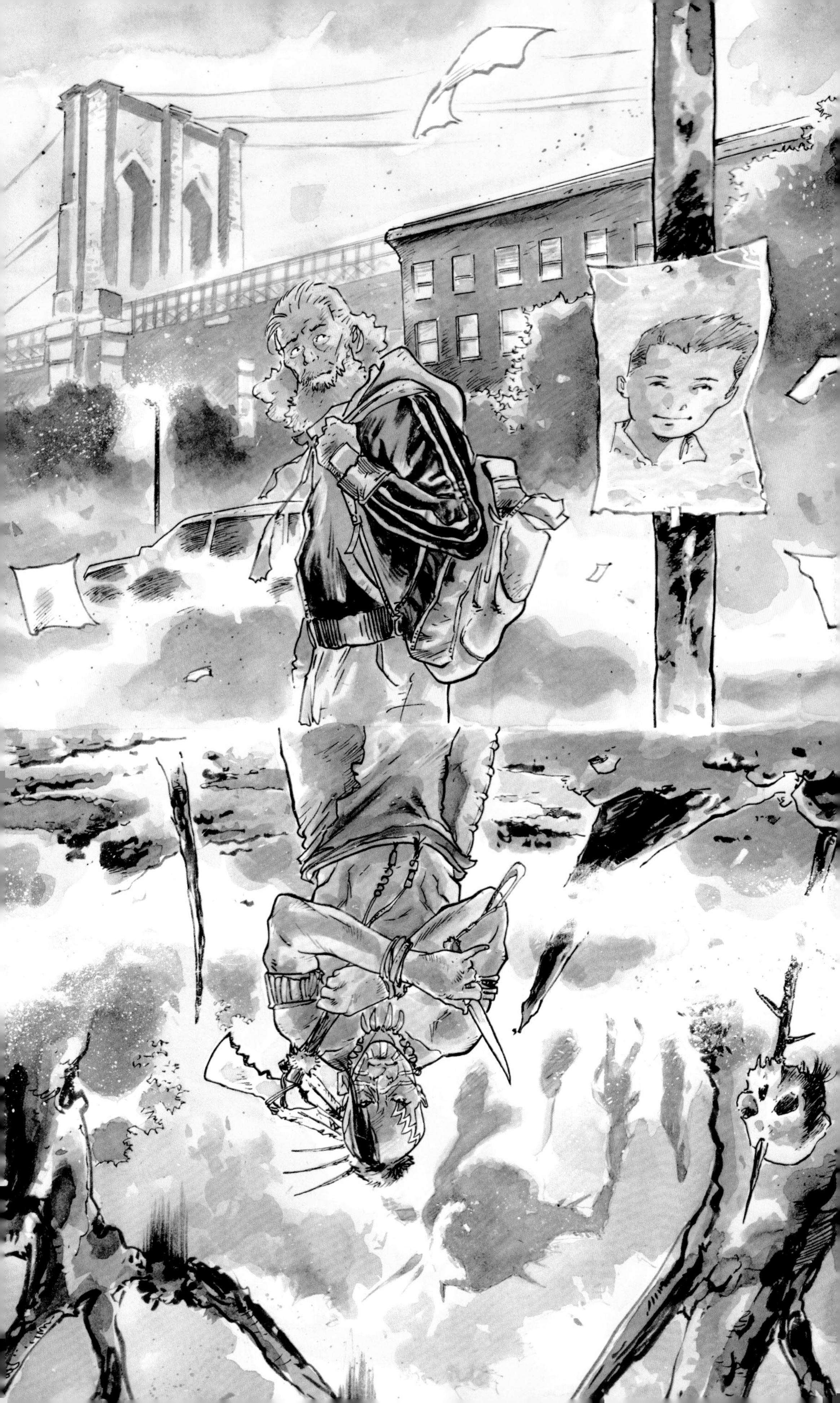

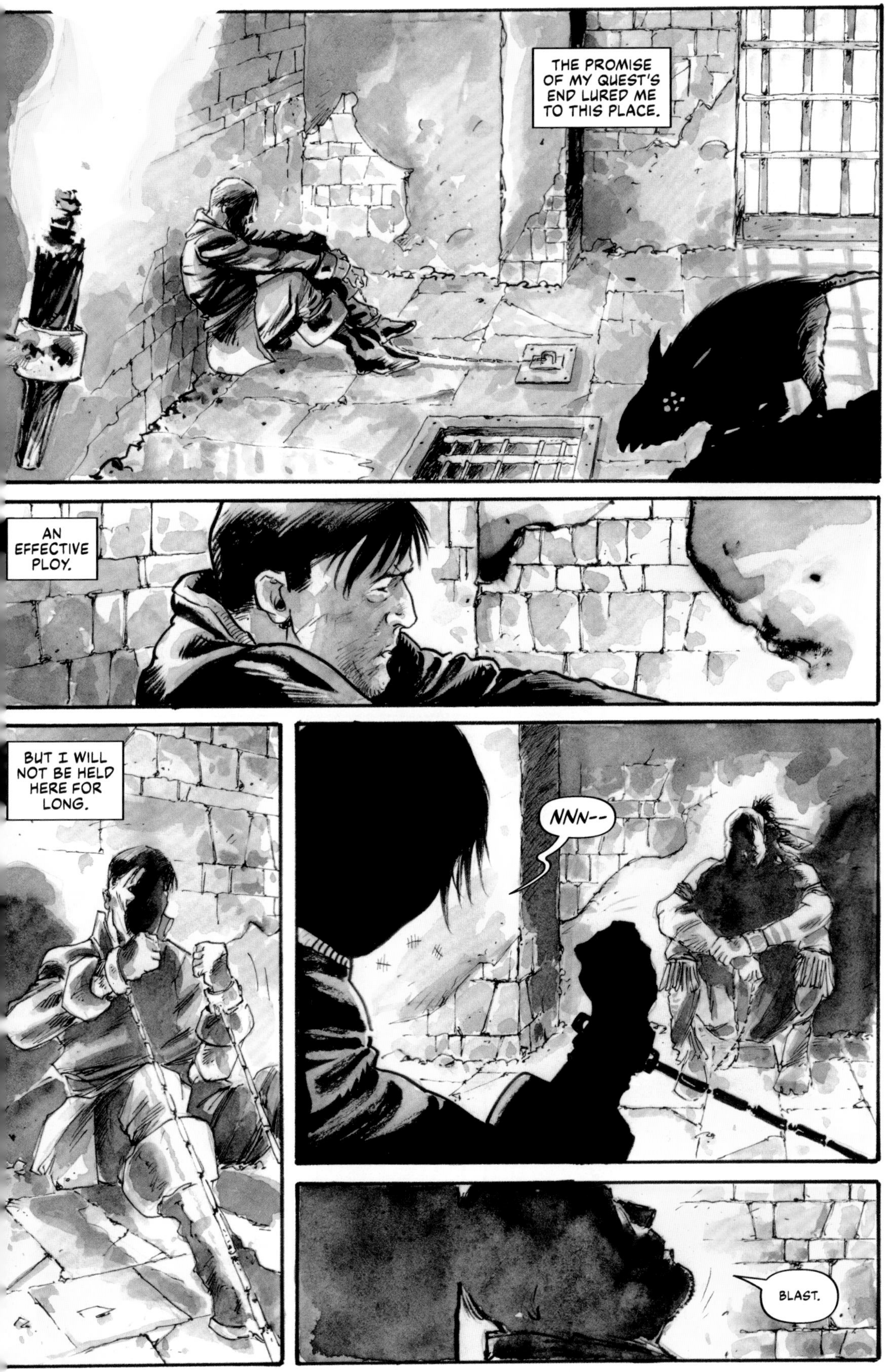
THE PROMISE OF MY QUEST'S END LURED ME TO THIS PLACE.
AN EFFECTIVE PLOY.
BUT I WILL NOT BE HELD HERE FOR LONG.
NNN--
BLAST.

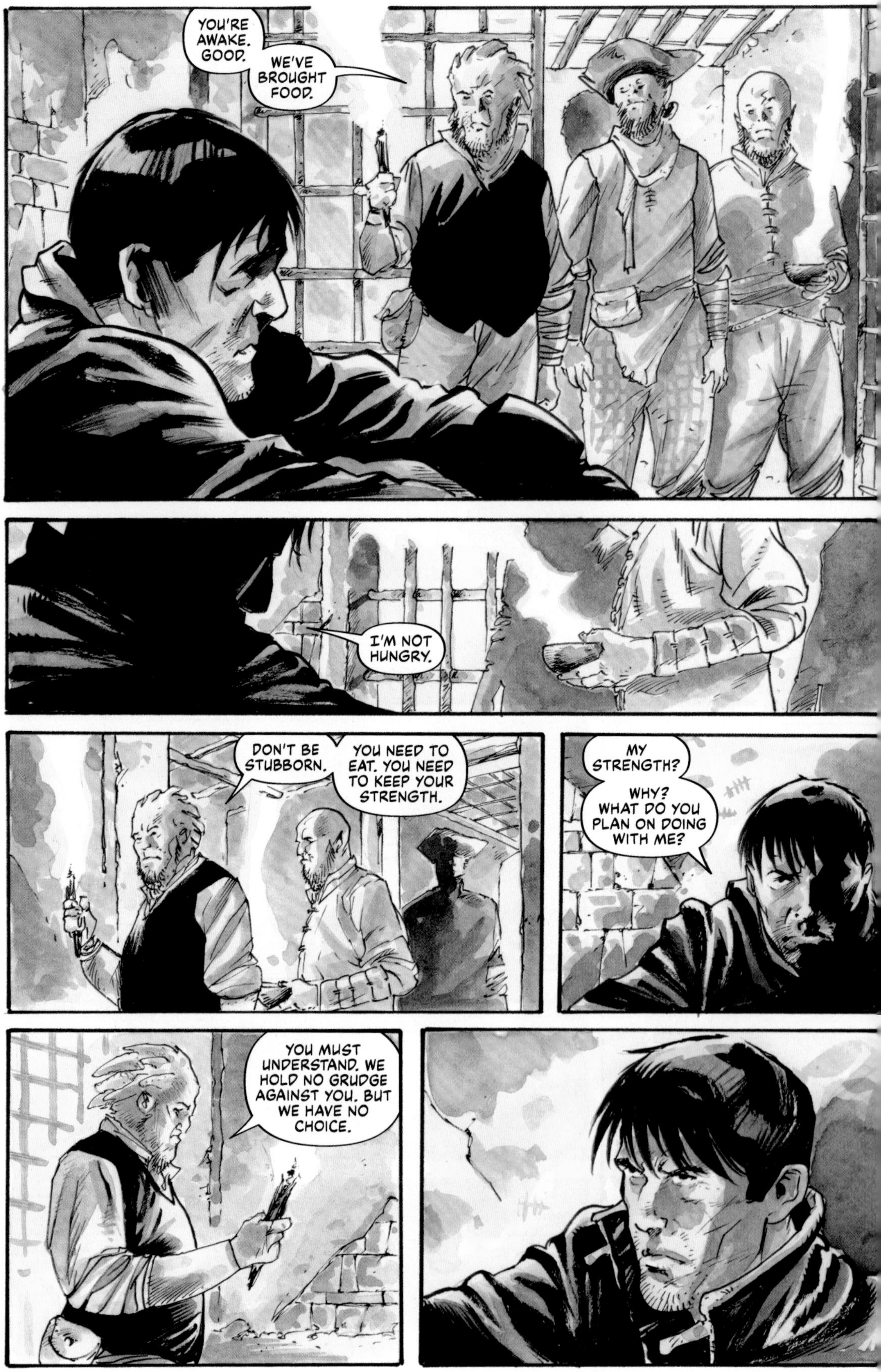
YOU'RE AWAKE. GOOD.
WE'VE BROUGHT FOOD.
I'M NOT HUNGRY.
DON'T BE STUBBORN.
YOU NEED TO EAT. YOU NEED TO KEEP YOUR STRENGTH.
MY STRENGTH?
WHY? WHAT DO YOU PLAN ON DOING WITH ME?
YOU MUST UNDERSTAND. WE HOLD NO GRUDGE AGAINST YOU. BUT WE HAVE NO CHOICE.

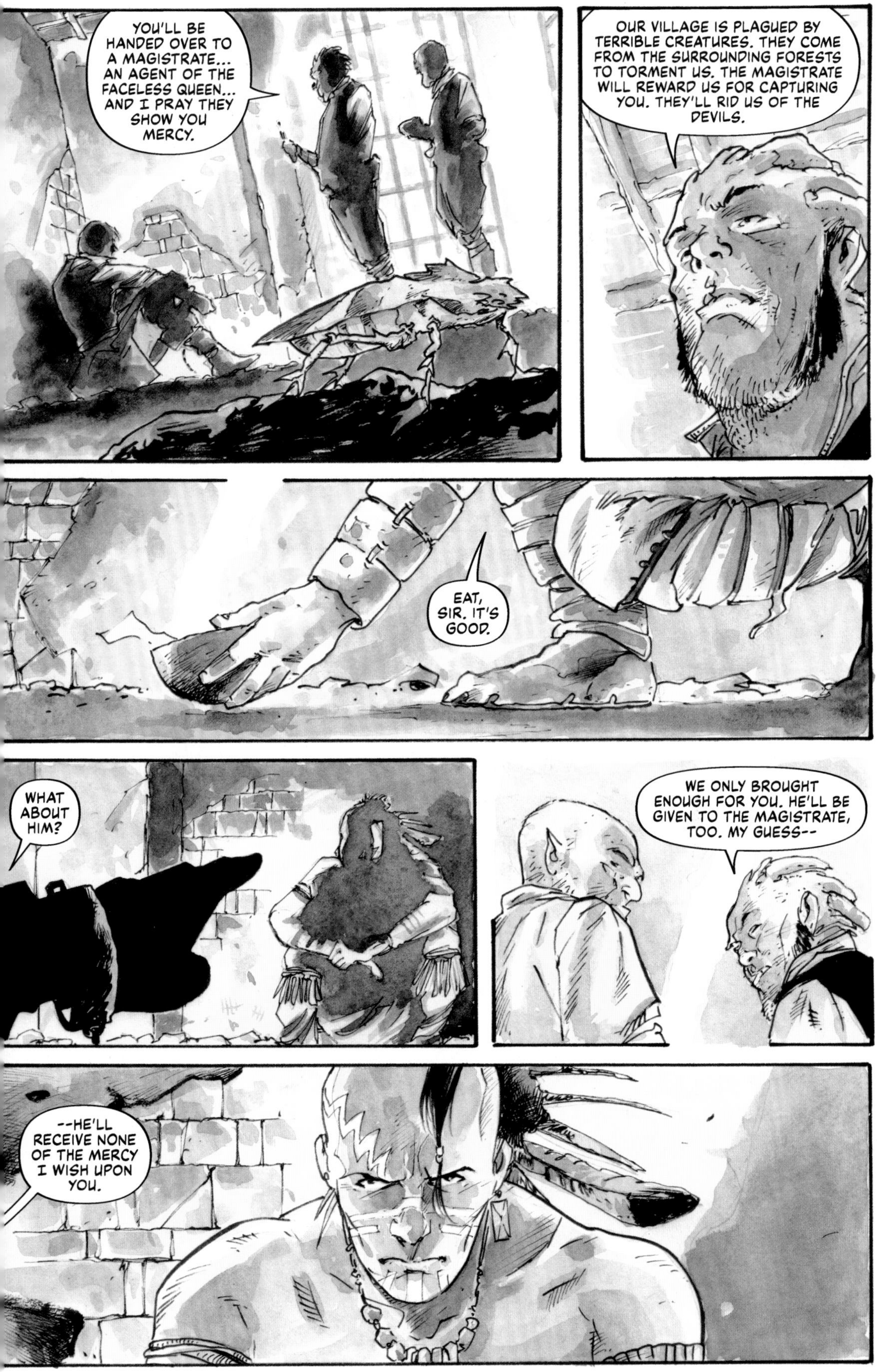
YOU'LL BE HANDED OVER TO A MAGISTRATE... AN AGENT OF THE FACELESS QUEEN... AND I PRAY THEY SHOW YOU MERCY.
OUR VILLAGE IS PLAGUED BY TERRIBLE CREATURES. THEY COME FROM THE SURROUNDING FORESTS TO TORMENT US. THE MAGISTRATE WILL REWARD US FOR CAPTURING YOU. THEY'LL RID US OF THE DEVILS.
EAT, SIR. IT'S GOOD.
WHAT ABOUT HIM?
WE ONLY BROUGHT ENOUGH FOR YOU. HE'LL BE GIVEN TO THE MAGISTRATE, TOO. MY GUESS--
--HE'LL RECEIVE NONE OF THE MERCY I WISH UPON YOU.

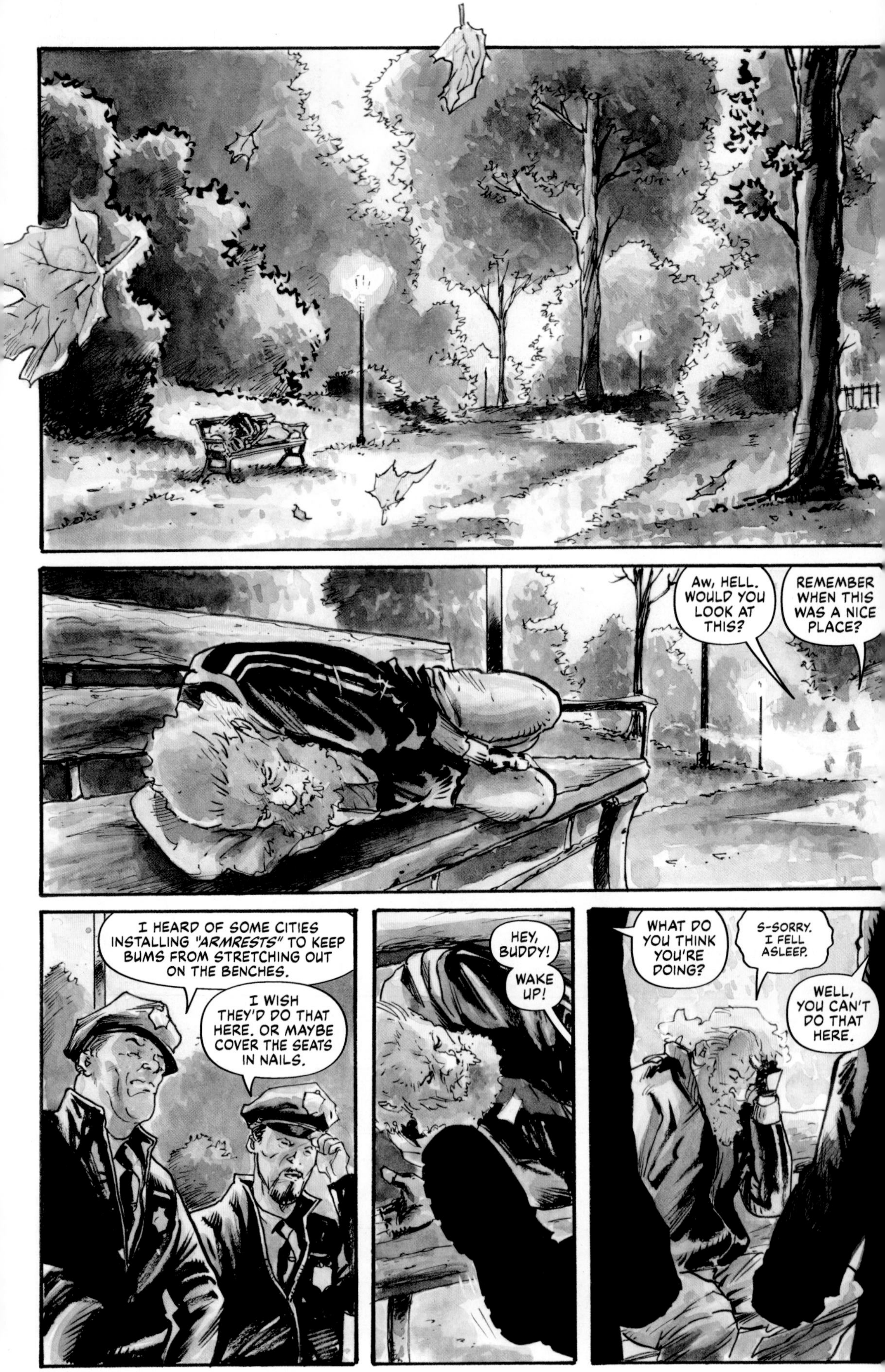
AW, HELL. WOULD YOU LOOK AT THIS?
REMEMBER WHEN THIS WAS A NICE PLACE?
I HEARD OF SOME CITIES INSTALLING "ARMRESTS" TO KEEP BUMS FROM STRETCHING OUT ON THE BENCHES.
I WISH THEY'D DO THAT HERE. OR MAYBE COVER THE SEATS IN NAILS.
HEY, BUDDY!
WAKE UP!
WHAT DO YOU THINK YOU'RE DOING?
S-SORRY. I FELL ASLEEP.
WELL, YOU CAN'T DO THAT HERE.

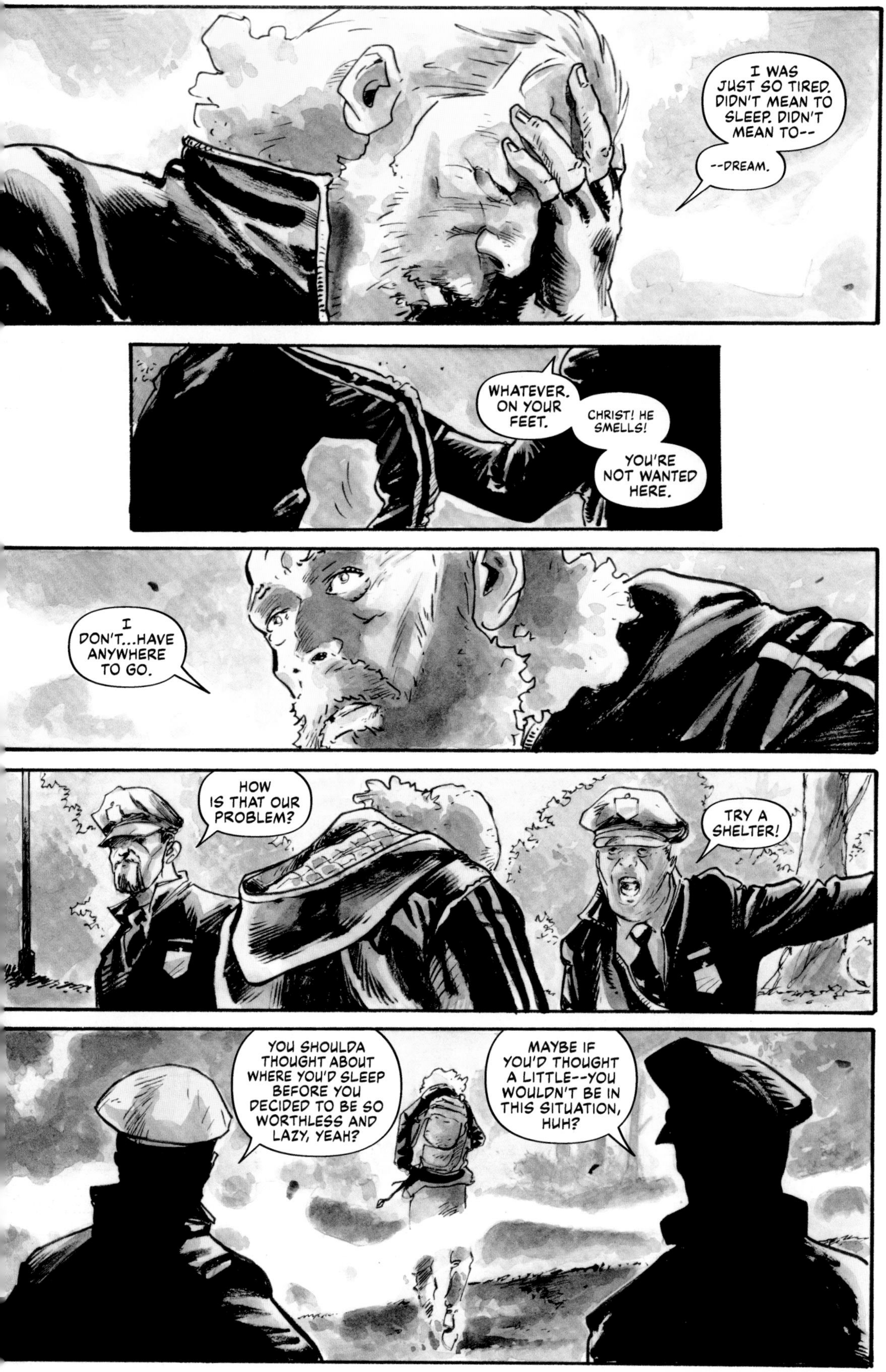
I WAS JUST SO TIRED. DIDN'T MEAN TO SLEEP. DIDN'T MEAN TO--
--DREAM.
WHATEVER. ON YOUR FEET.
CHRIST! HE SMELLS!
YOU'RE NOT WANTED HERE.
I DON'T...HAVE ANYWHERE TO GO.
HOW IS THAT OUR PROBLEM?
TRY A SHELTER!
YOU SHOULDA THOUGHT ABOUT WHERE YOU'D SLEEP BEFORE YOU DECIDED TO BE SO WORTHLESS AND LAZY, YEAH?
MAYBE IF YOU'D THOUGHT A LITTLE--YOU WOULDN'T BE IN THIS SITUATION, HUH?

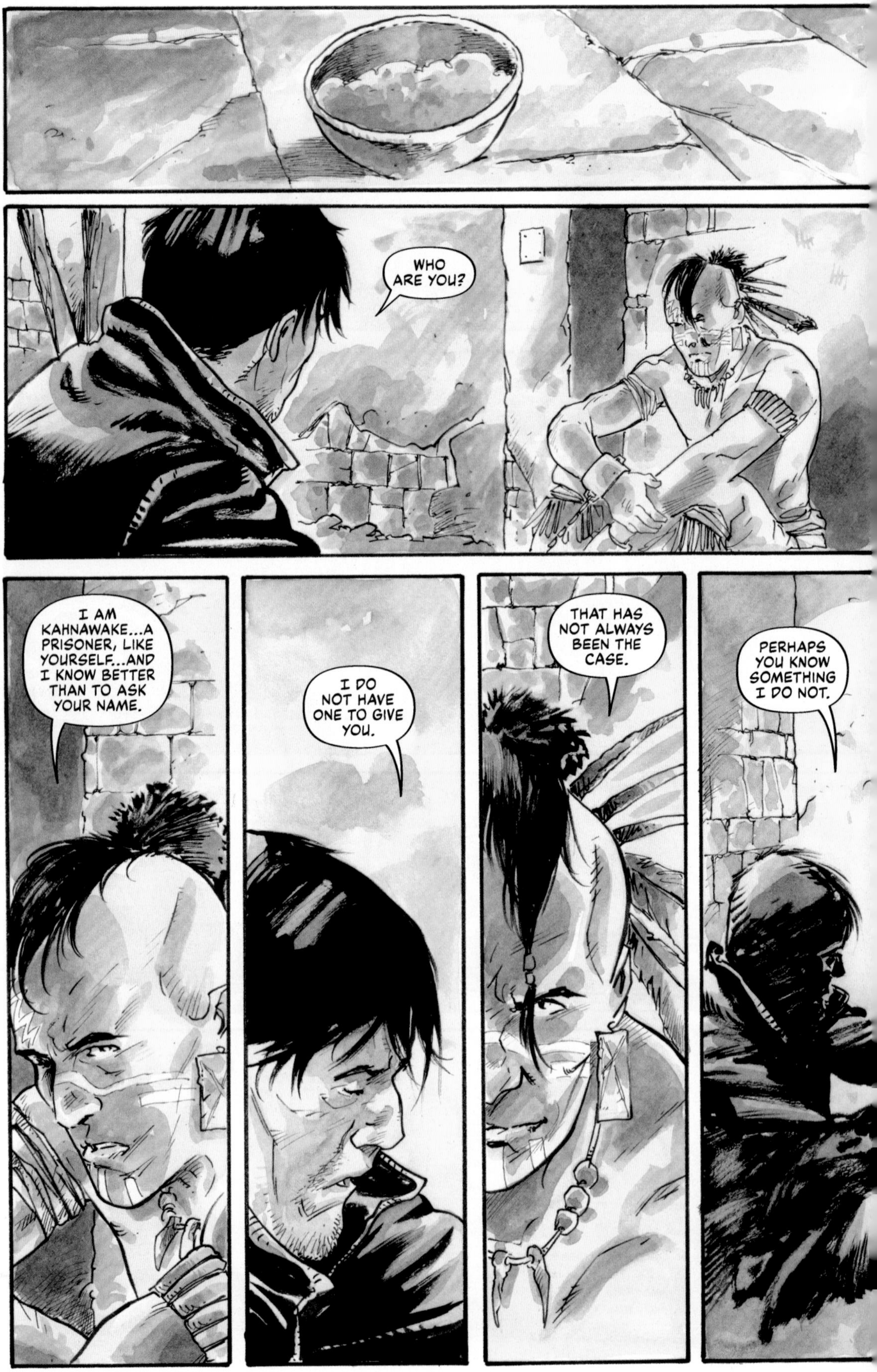
WHO ARE YOU?
I AM KAHNAWAKE...A PRISONER, LIKE YOURSELF...AND I KNOW BETTER THAN TO ASK YOUR NAME.
I DO NOT HAVE ONE TO GIVE YOU.
THAT HAS NOT ALWAYS BEEN THE CASE.
PERHAPS YOU KNOW SOMETHING I DO NOT.

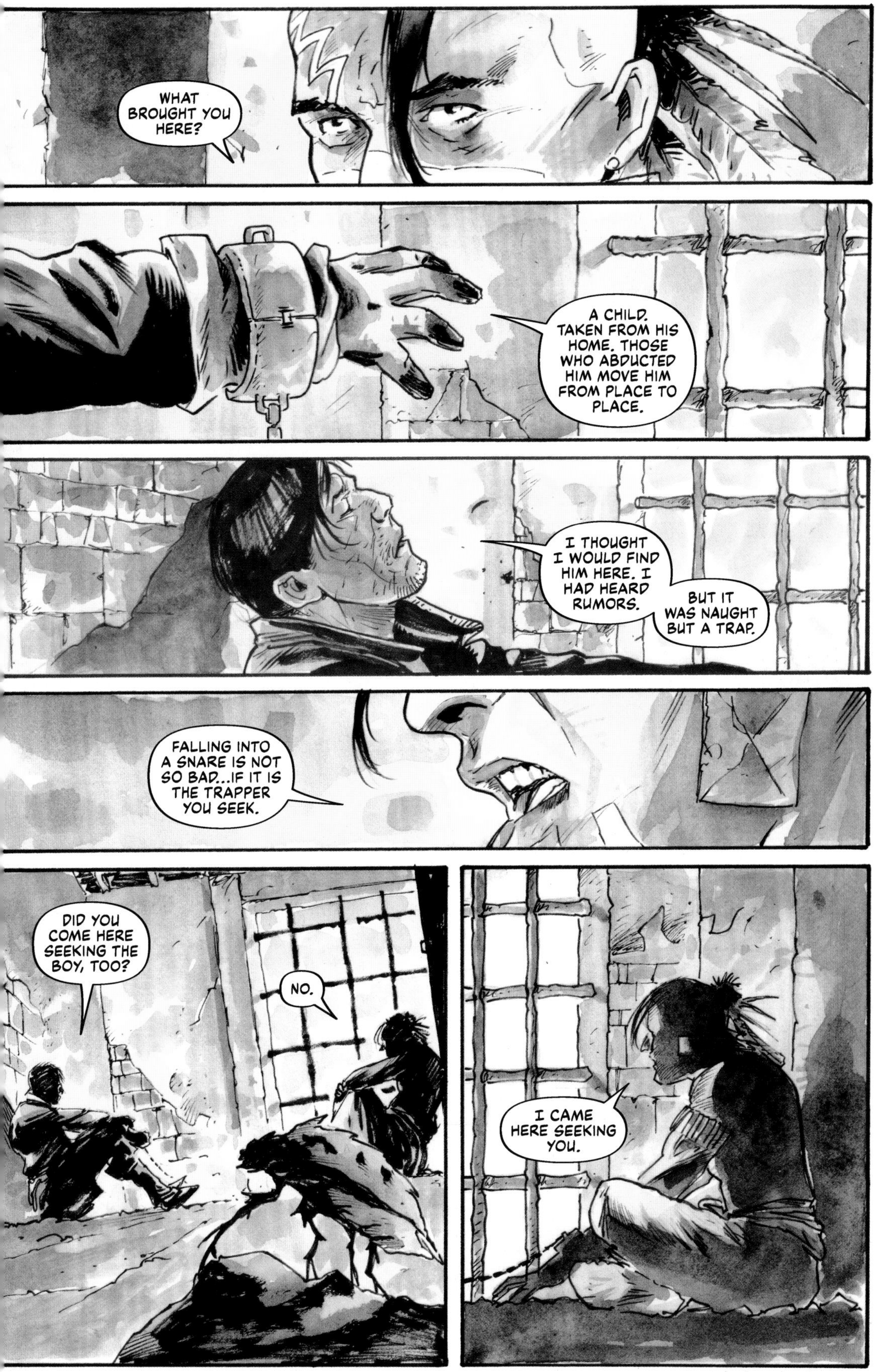
WHAT BROUGHT YOU HERE?
A CHILD. TAKEN FROM HIS HOME. THOSE WHO ABDUCTED HIM MOVE HIM FROM PLACE TO PLACE.
I THOUGHT I WOULD FIND HIM HERE. I HAD HEARD RUMORS.
BUT IT WAS NAUGHT BUT A TRAP.
FALLING INTO A SNARE IS NOT SO BAD...IF IT IS THE TRAPPER YOU SEEK.
DID YOU COME HERE SEEKING THE BOY, TOO?
NO.
I CAME HERE SEEKING YOU.

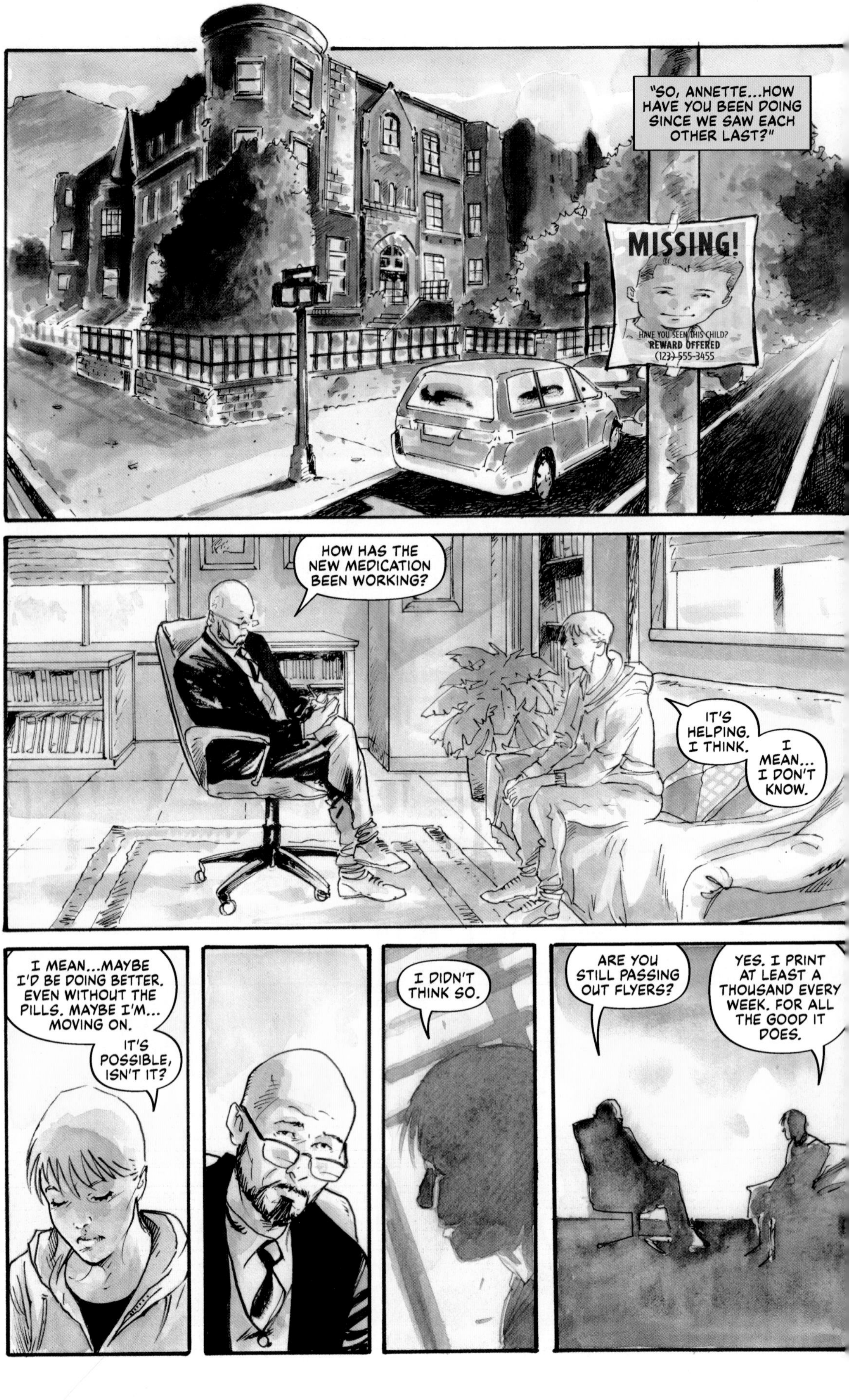
"SO, ANNETTE...HOW HAVE YOU BEEN DOING SINCE WE SAW EACH OTHER LAST?"
MISSING!
HAVE YOU SEEN THIS CHILD?
REWARD OFFERED
(123) 555-3455
HOW HAS THE NEW MEDICATION BEEN WORKING?
IT'S HELPING. I THINK.
I MEAN... I DON'T KNOW.
I MEAN...MAYBE I'D BE DOING BETTER. EVEN WITHOUT THE PILLS. MAYBE I'M... MOVING ON.
IT'S POSSIBLE, ISN'T IT?
I DIDN'T THINK SO.
ARE YOU STILL PASSING OUT FLYERS?
YES. I PRINT AT LEAST A THOUSAND EVERY WEEK. FOR ALL THE GOOD IT DOES.

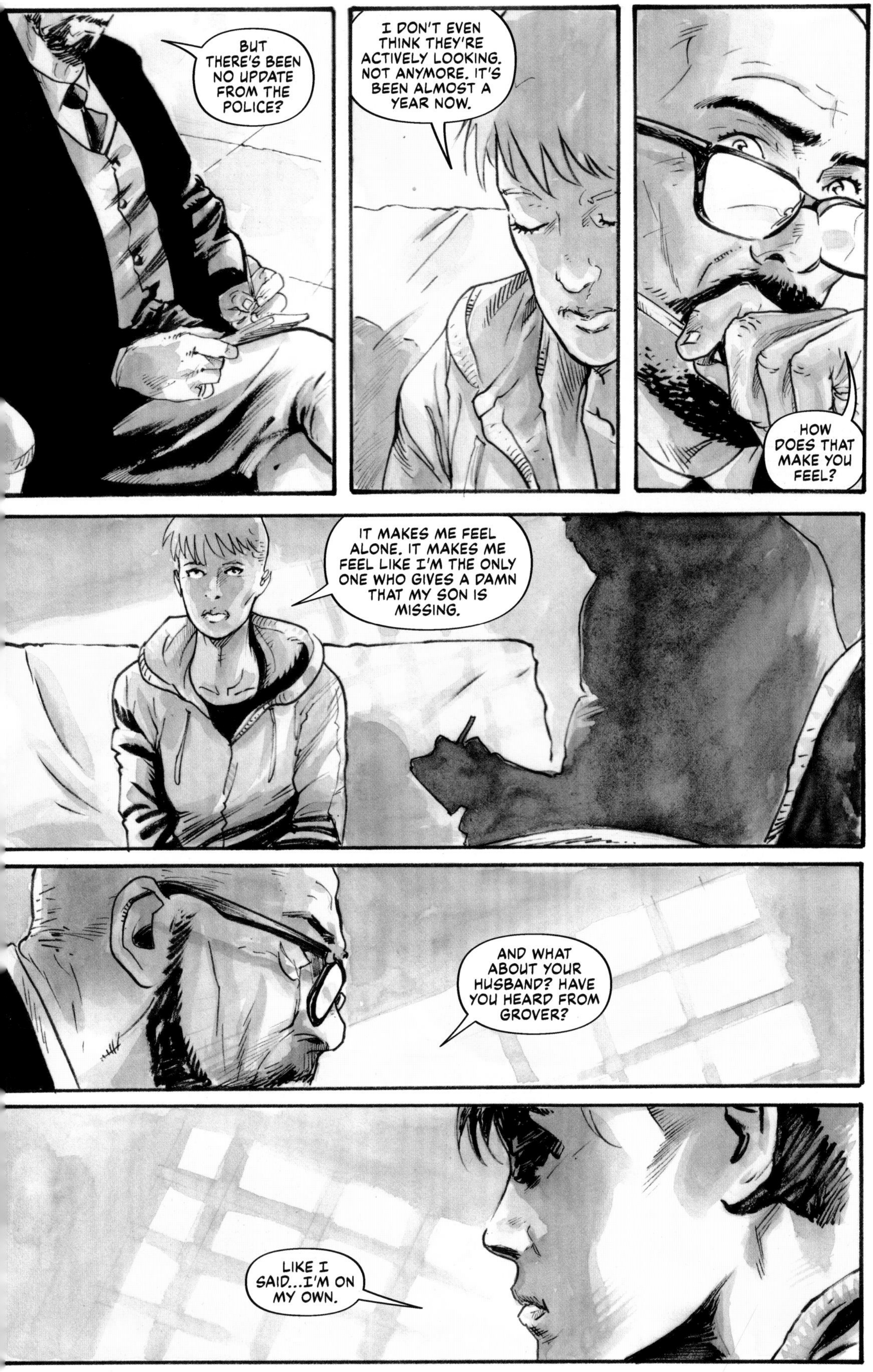
BUT THERE'S BEEN NO UPDATE FROM THE POLICE?
I DON'T EVEN THINK THEY'RE ACTIVELY LOOKING. NOT ANYMORE. IT'S BEEN ALMOST A YEAR NOW.
HOW DOES THAT MAKE YOU FEEL?
IT MAKES ME FEEL ALONE. IT MAKES ME FEEL LIKE I'M THE ONLY ONE WHO GIVES A DAMN THAT MY SON IS MISSING.
AND WHAT ABOUT YOUR HUSBAND? HAVE YOU HEARD FROM GROVER?
LIKE I SAID...I'M ON MY OWN.

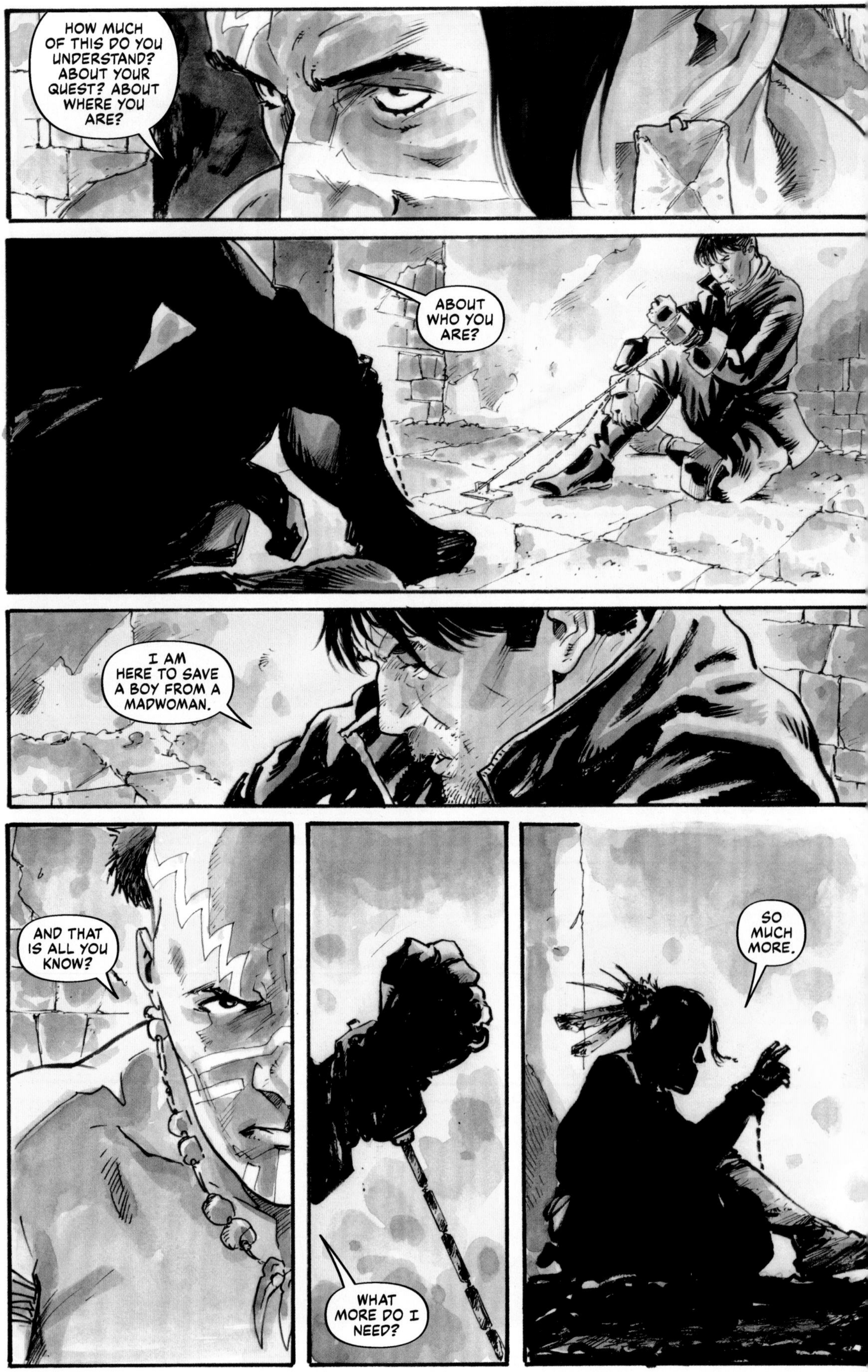
HOW MUCH OF THIS DO YOU UNDERSTAND? ABOUT YOUR QUEST? ABOUT WHERE YOU ARE?
ABOUT WHO YOU ARE?
I AM HERE TO SAVE A BOY FROM A MADWOMAN.
AND THAT IS ALL YOU KNOW?
WHAT MORE DO I NEED?
SO MUCH MORE.

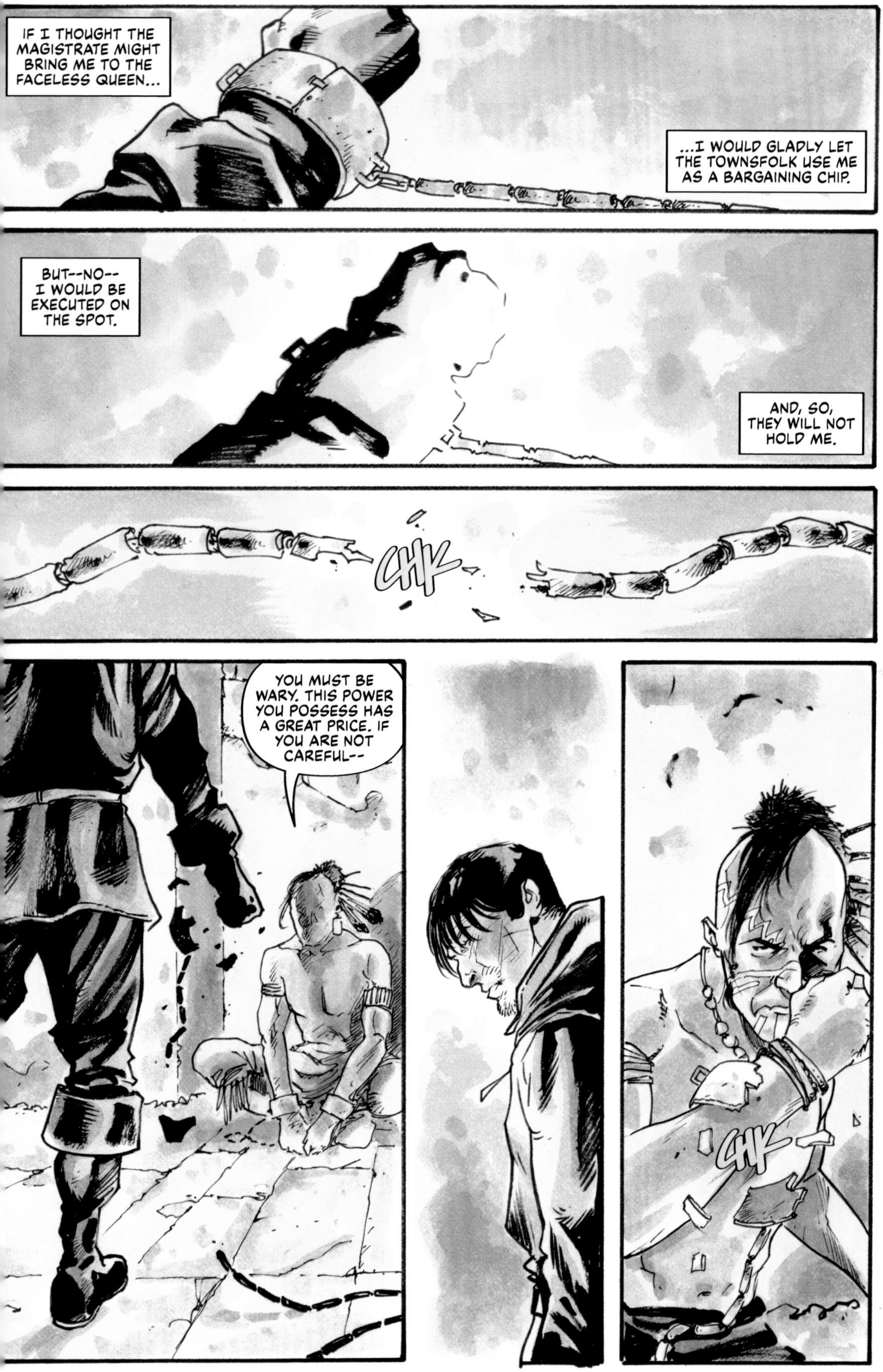
IF I THOUGHT THE MAGISTRATE MIGHT BRING ME TO THE FACELESS QUEEN...
...I WOULD GLADLY LET THE TOWNSFOLK USE ME AS A BARGAINING CHIP.
BUT--NO-- I WOULD BE EXECUTED ON THE SPOT.
AND, SO, THEY WILL NOT HOLD ME.
CHK
YOU MUST BE WARY. THIS POWER YOU POSSESS HAS A GREAT PRICE. IF YOU ARE NOT CAREFUL--
CHK

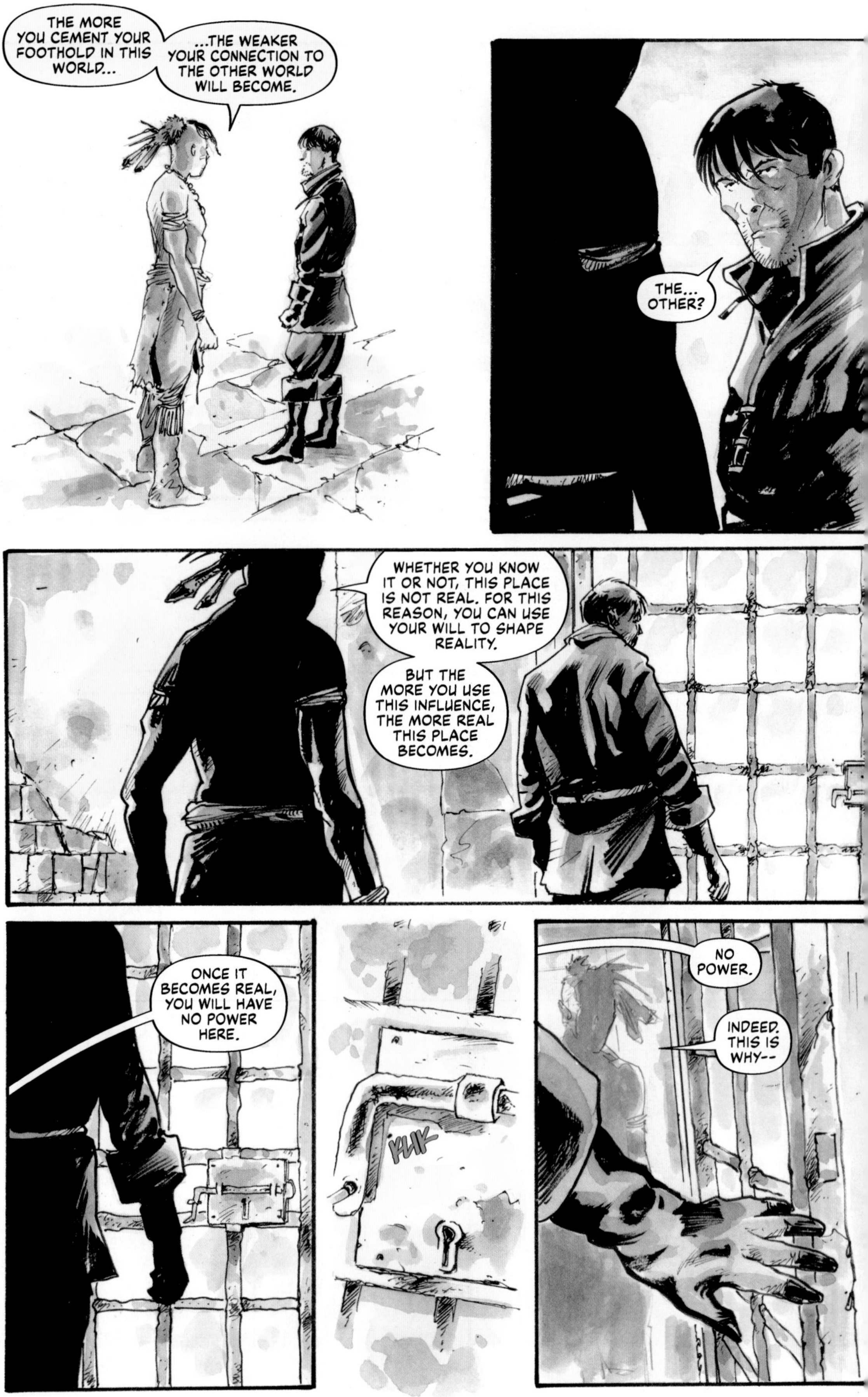
THE MORE YOU CEMENT YOUR FOOTHOLD IN THIS WORLD...
...THE WEAKER YOUR CONNECTION TO THE OTHER WORLD WILL BECOME.
THE... OTHER?
WHETHER YOU KNOW IT OR NOT, THIS PLACE IS NOT REAL. FOR THIS REASON, YOU CAN USE YOUR WILL TO SHAPE REALITY.
BUT THE MORE YOU USE THIS INFLUENCE, THE MORE REAL THIS PLACE BECOMES.
ONCE IT BECOMES REAL, YOU WILL HAVE NO POWER HERE.
KLIK
NO POWER.
INDEED. THIS IS WHY--

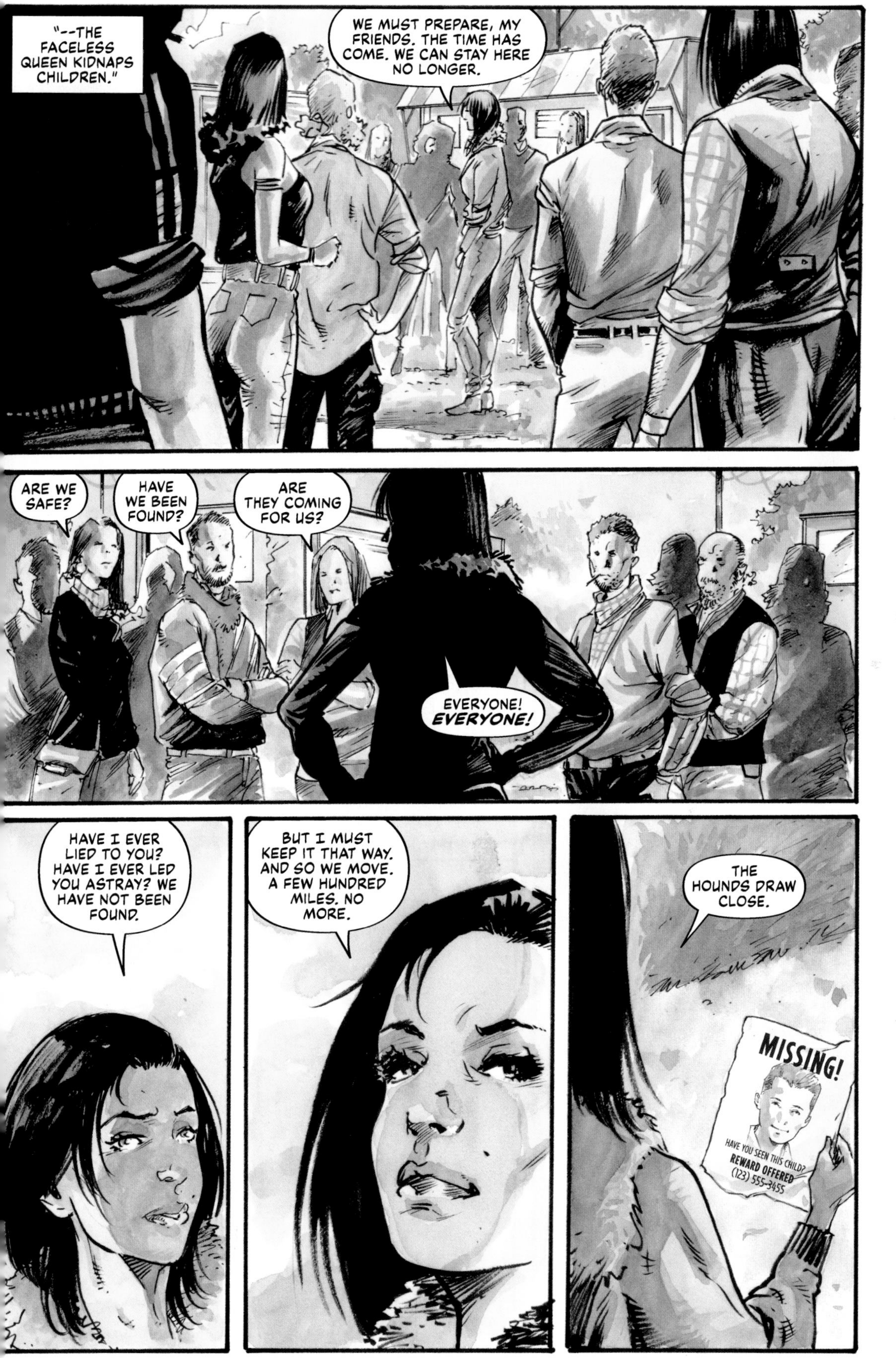
"--THE FACELESS QUEEN KIDNAPS CHILDREN."
WE MUST PREPARE, MY FRIENDS. THE TIME HAS COME. WE CAN STAY HERE NO LONGER.
ARE WE SAFE?
HAVE WE BEEN FOUND?
ARE THEY COMING FOR US?
EVERYONE! *EVERYONE!*
HAVE I EVER LIED TO YOU? HAVE I EVER LED YOU ASTRAY? WE HAVE NOT BEEN FOUND.
BUT I MUST KEEP IT THAT WAY. AND SO WE MOVE. A FEW HUNDRED MILES. NO MORE.
THE HOUNDS DRAW CLOSE.
MISSING!
HAVE YOU SEEN THIS CHILD?
REWARD OFFERED
(123) 555-3455

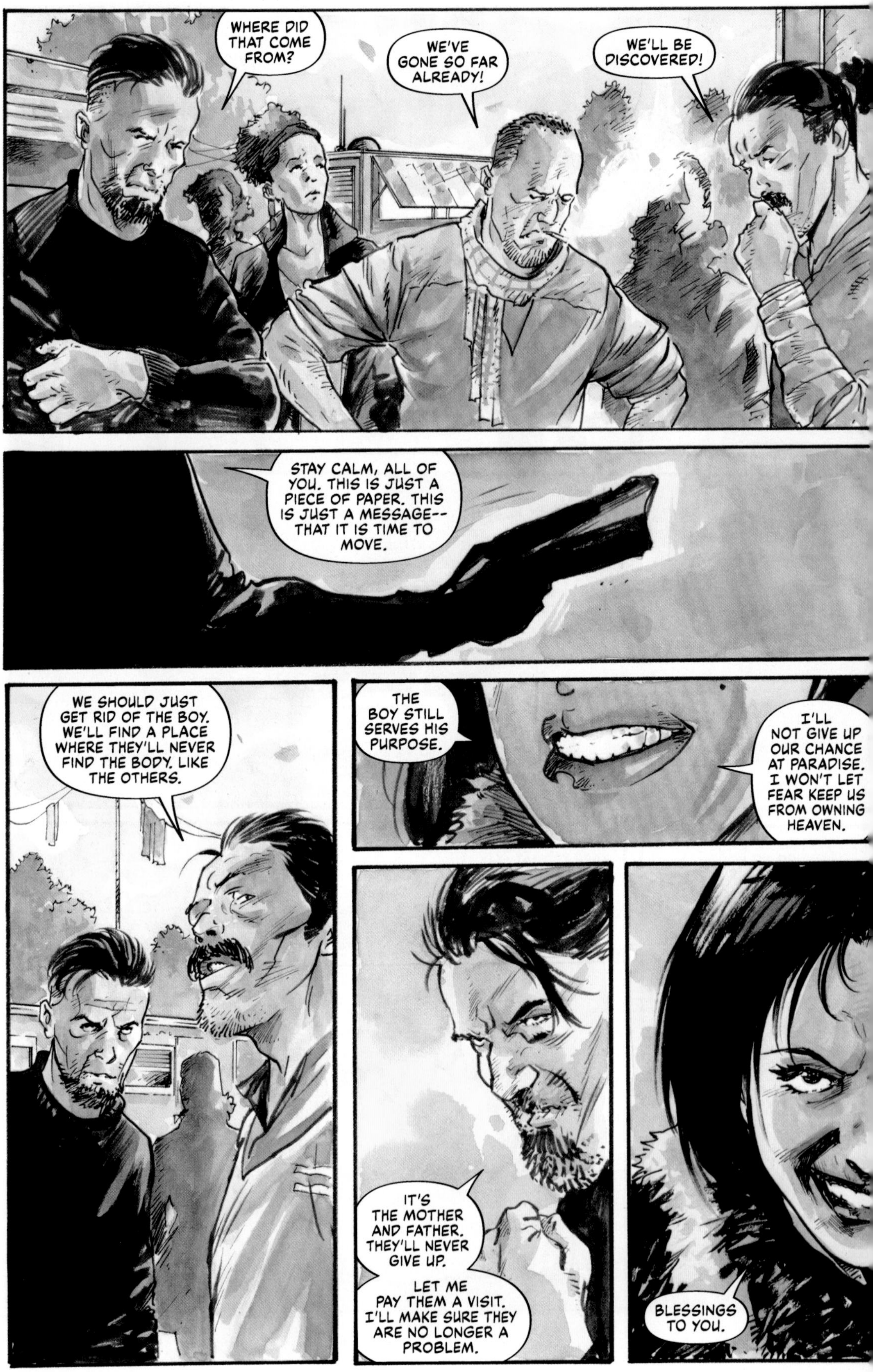
WHERE DID THAT COME FROM?
WE'VE GONE SO FAR ALREADY!
WE'LL BE DISCOVERED!
STAY CALM, ALL OF YOU. THIS IS JUST A PIECE OF PAPER. THIS IS JUST A MESSAGE-- THAT IT IS TIME TO MOVE.
WE SHOULD JUST GET RID OF THE BOY. WE'LL FIND A PLACE WHERE THEY'LL NEVER FIND THE BODY. LIKE THE OTHERS.
THE BOY STILL SERVES HIS PURPOSE.
I'LL NOT GIVE UP OUR CHANCE AT PARADISE. I WON'T LET FEAR KEEP US FROM OWNING HEAVEN.
IT'S THE MOTHER AND FATHER. THEY'LL NEVER GIVE UP.
LET ME PAY THEM A VISIT. I'LL MAKE SURE THEY ARE NO LONGER A PROBLEM.
BLESSINGS TO YOU.

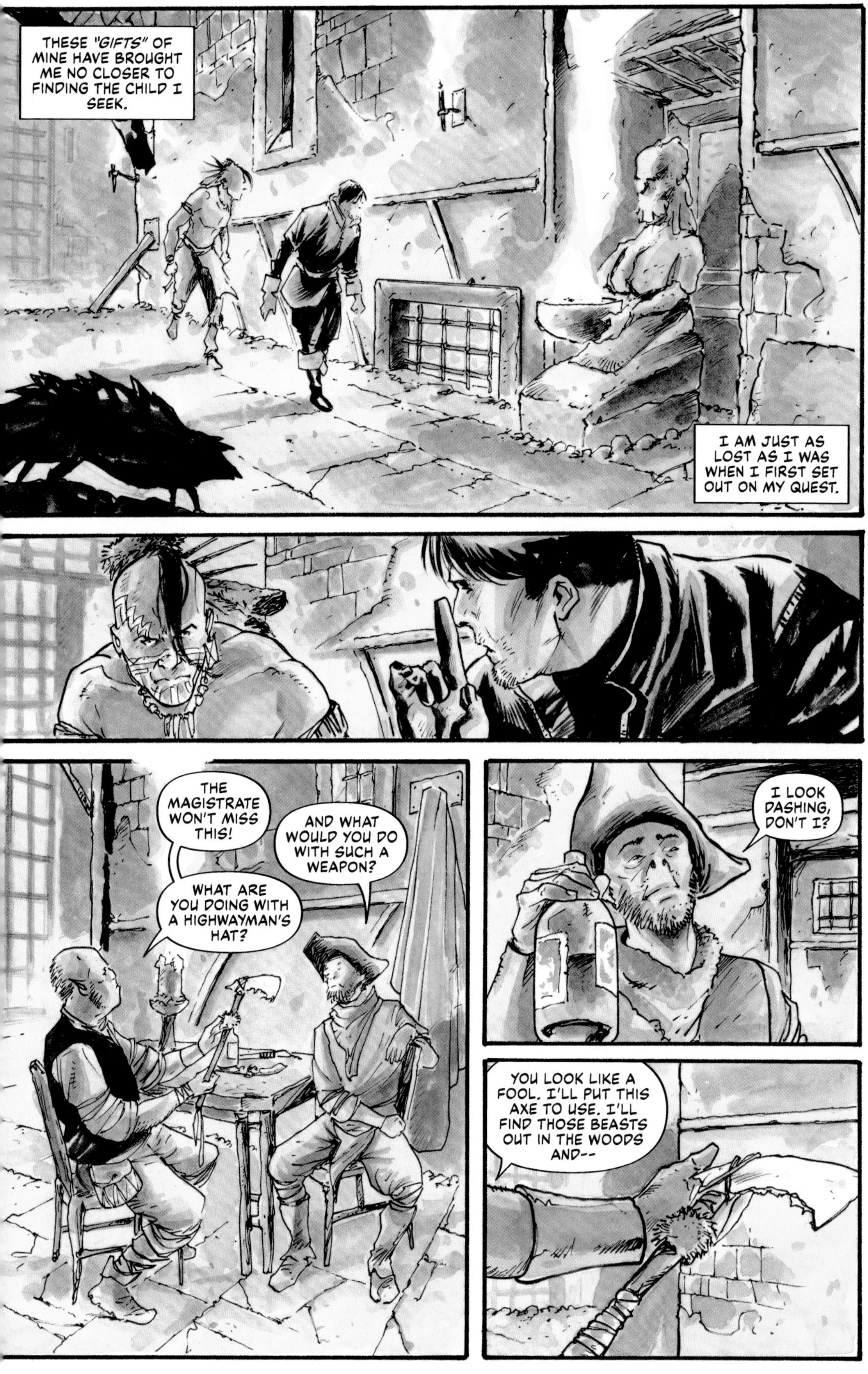
THESE "GIFTS" OF MINE HAVE BROUGHT ME NO CLOSER TO FINDING THE CHILD I SEEK.
I AM JUST AS LOST AS I WAS WHEN I FIRST SET OUT ON MY QUEST.
THE MAGISTRATE WON'T MISS THIS!
WHAT ARE YOU DOING WITH A HIGHWAYMAN'S HAT?
AND WHAT WOULD YOU DO WITH SUCH A WEAPON?
I LOOK DASHING, DON'T I?
YOU LOOK LIKE A FOOL. I'LL PUT THIS AXE TO USE. I'LL FIND THOSE BEASTS OUT IN THE WOODS AND--

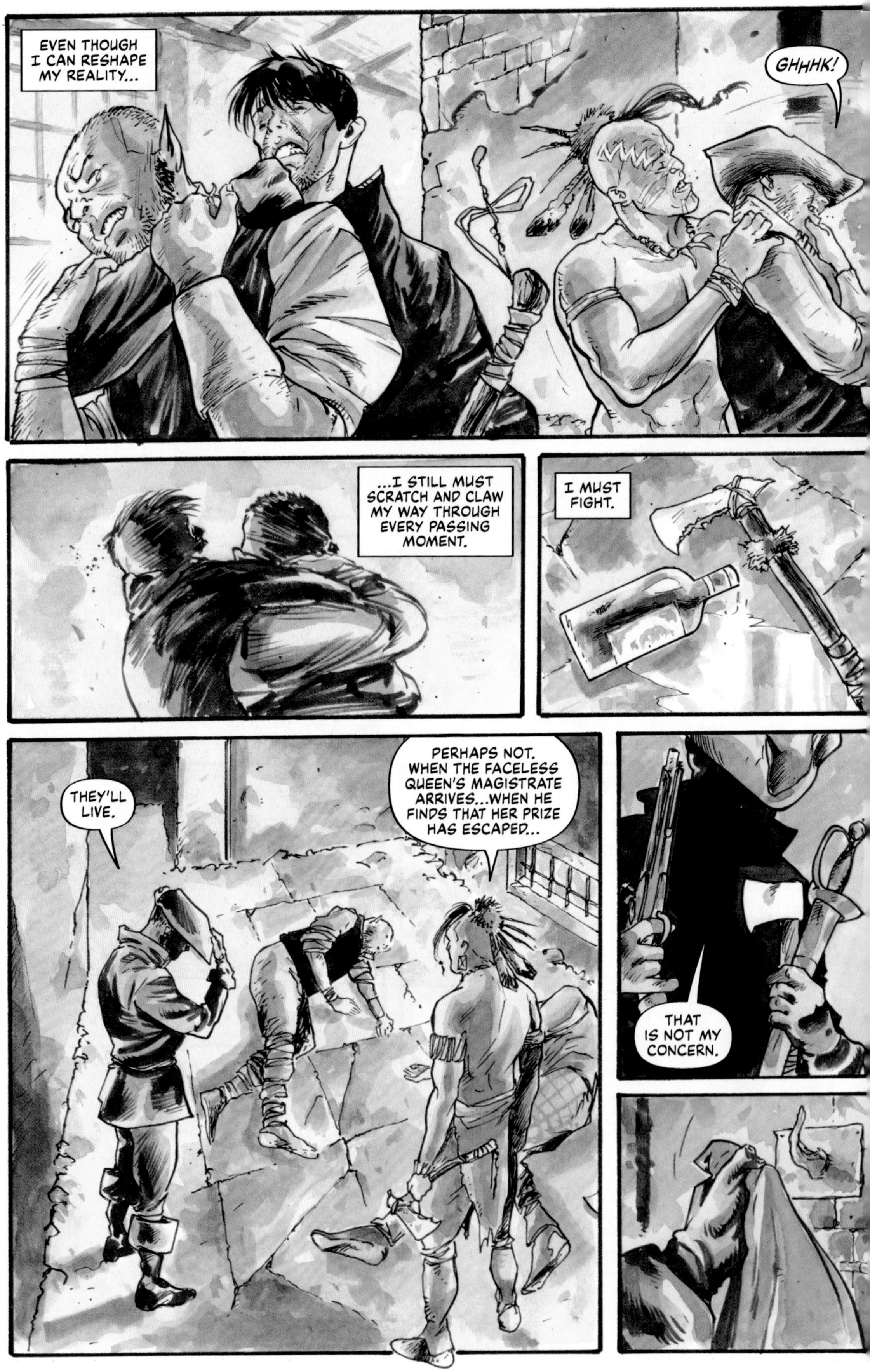
EVEN THOUGH I CAN RESHAPE MY REALITY...
GHHHK!
...I STILL MUST SCRATCH AND CLAW MY WAY THROUGH EVERY PASSING MOMENT.
I MUST FIGHT.
THEY'LL LIVE.
PERHAPS NOT. WHEN THE FACELESS QUEEN'S MAGISTRATE ARRIVES...WHEN HE FINDS THAT HER PRIZE HAS ESCAPED...
THAT IS NOT MY CONCERN.

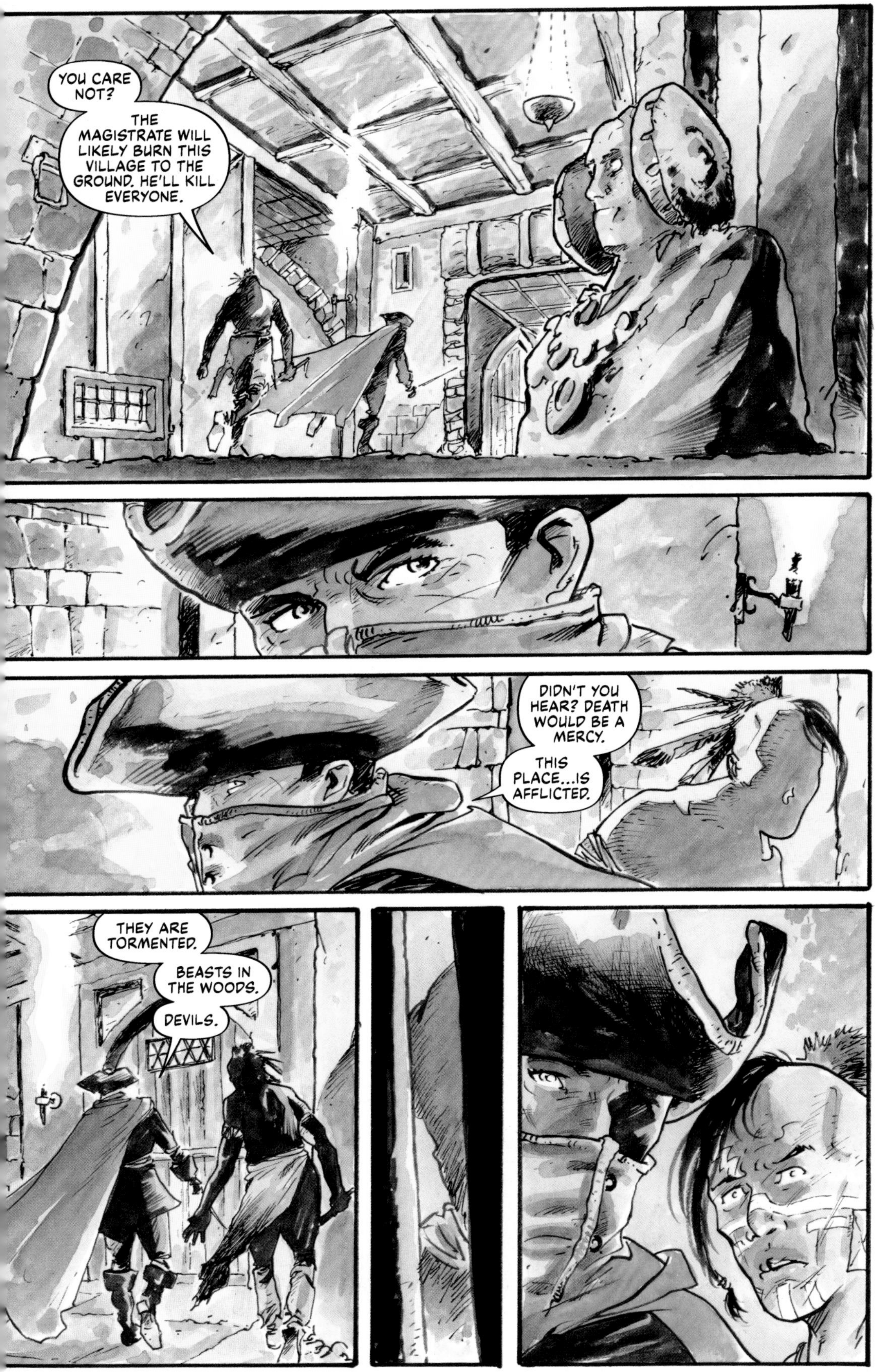
YOU CARE NOT?
THE MAGISTRATE WILL LIKELY BURN THIS VILLAGE TO THE GROUND. HE'LL KILL EVERYONE.
DIDN'T YOU HEAR? DEATH WOULD BE A MERCY.
THIS PLACE...IS AFFLICTED.
THEY ARE TORMENTED.
BEASTS IN THE WOODS.
DEVILS.

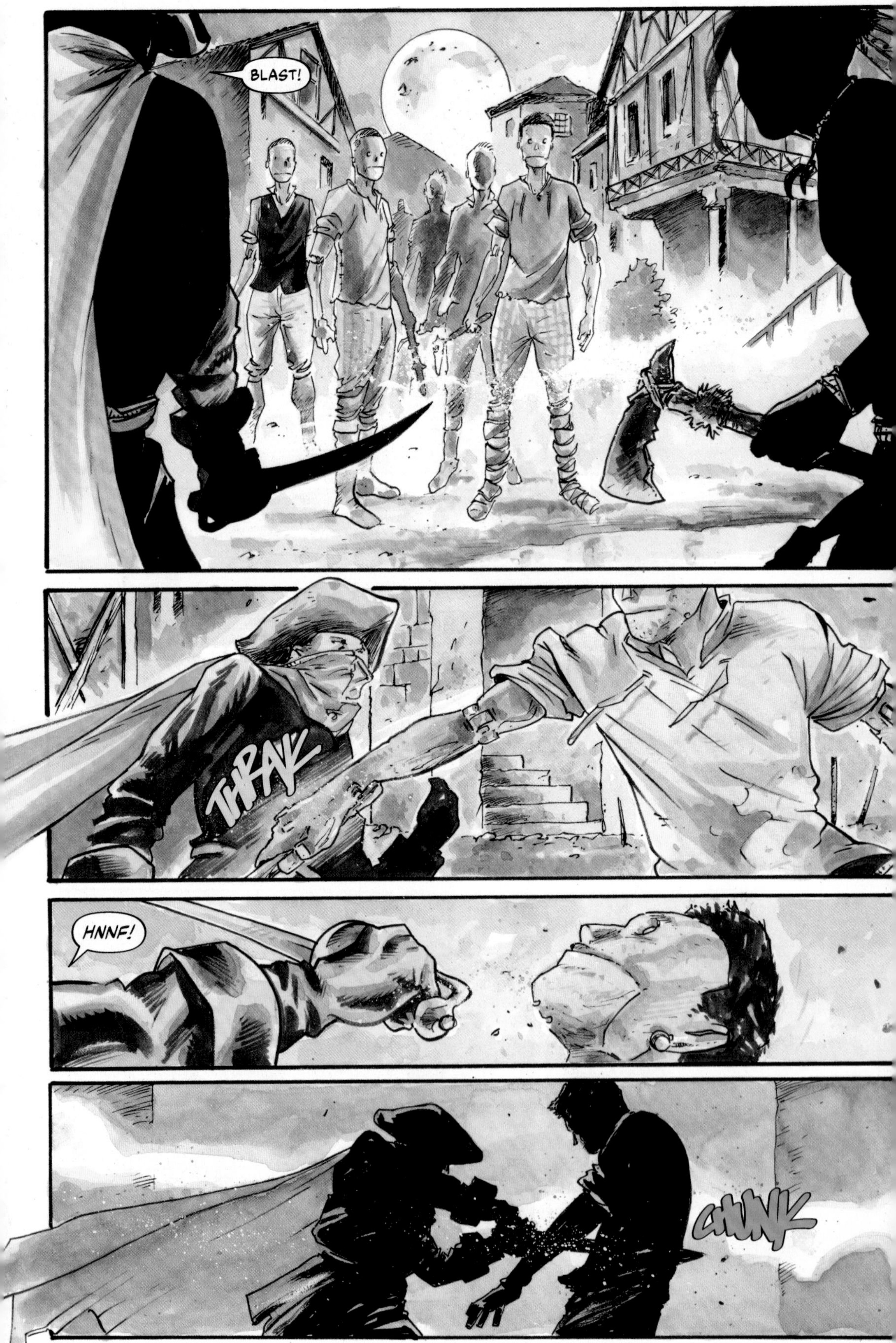
BLAST!
THRAK
HNNF!
CHUNK

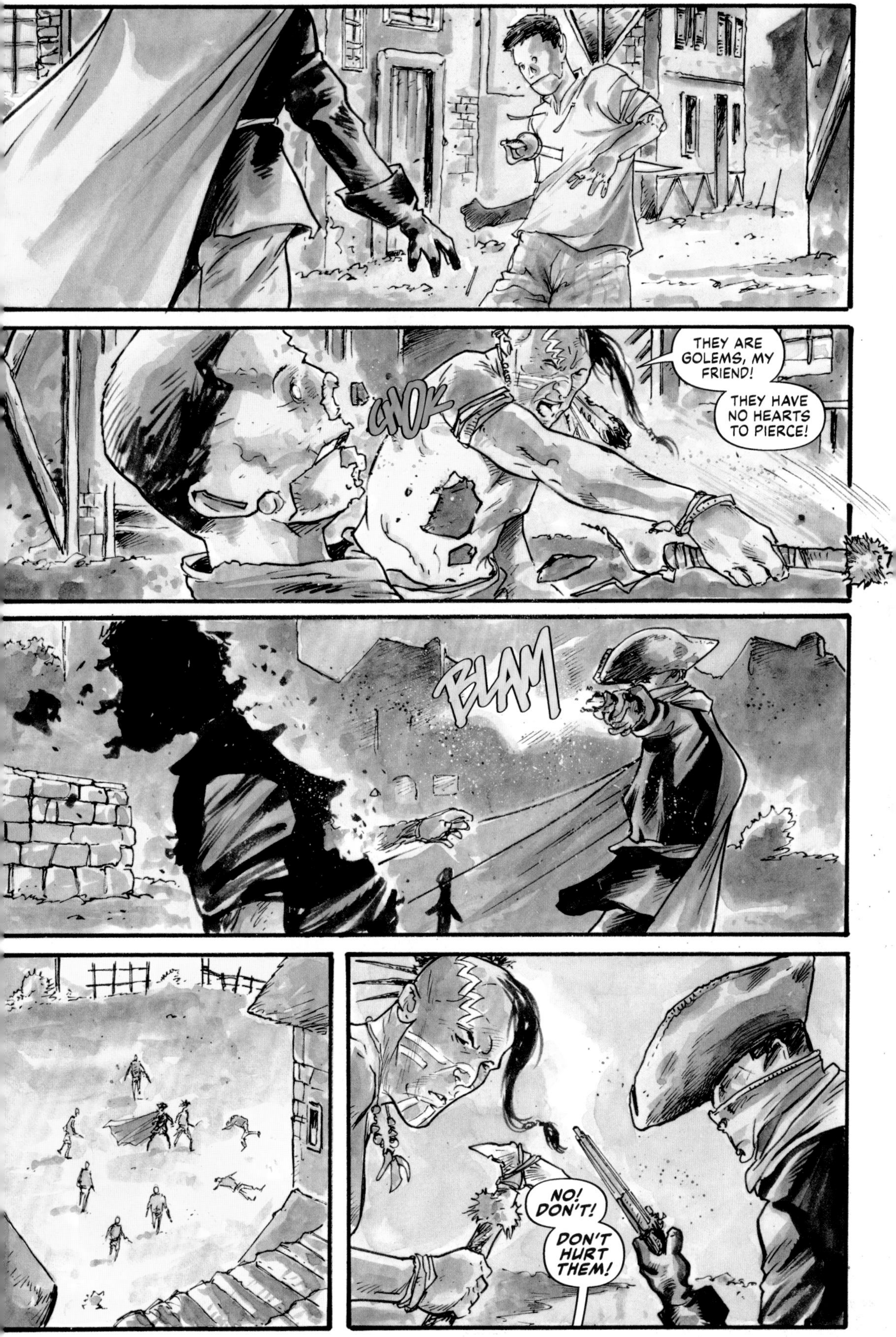
CHOK
THEY ARE GOLEMS, MY FRIEND!
THEY HAVE NO HEARTS TO PIERCE!
BLAM
NO! DON'T!
DON'T HURT THEM!

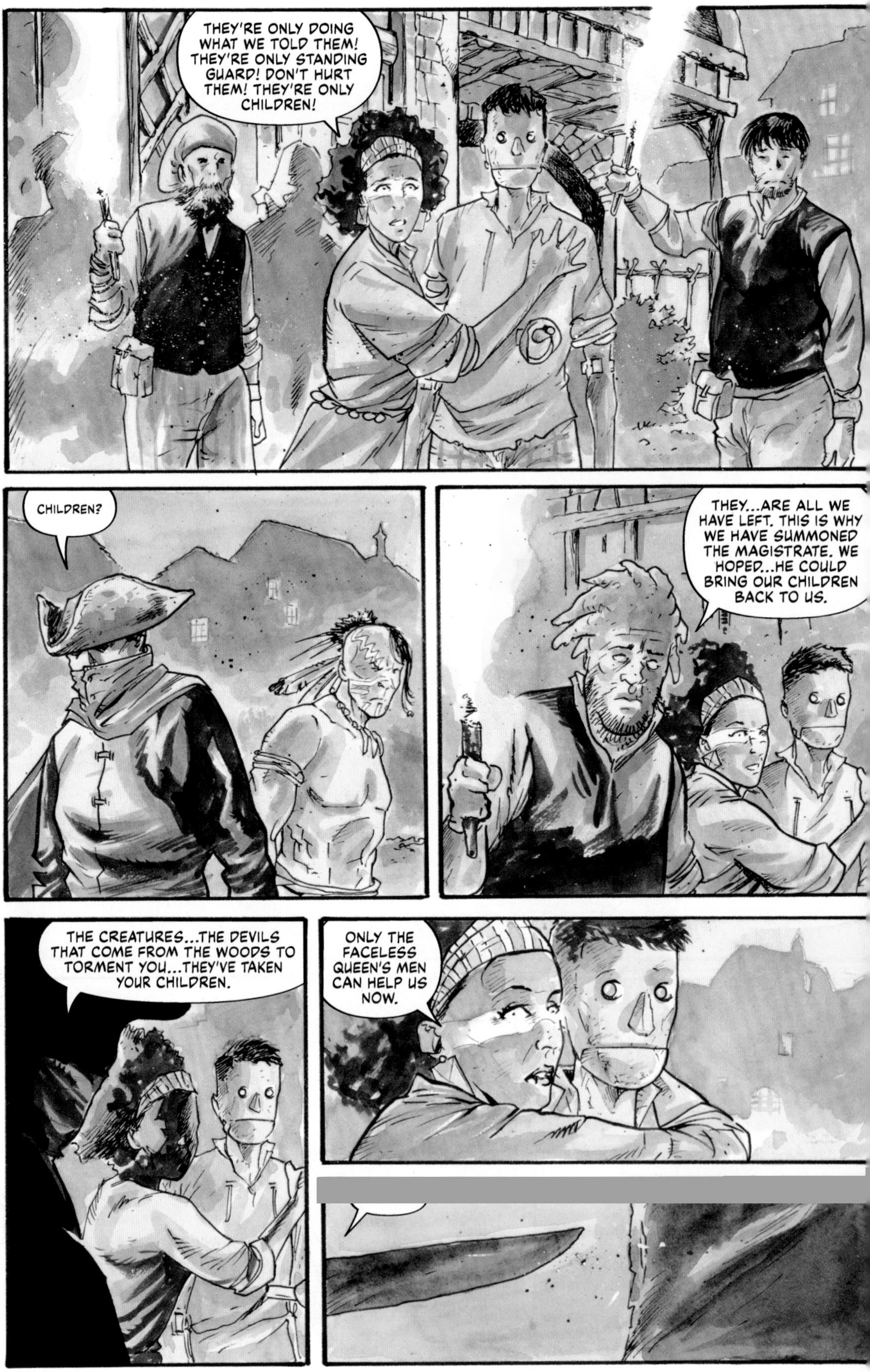
THEY'RE ONLY DOING WHAT WE TOLD THEM! THEY'RE ONLY STANDING GUARD! DON'T HURT THEM! THEY'RE ONLY CHILDREN!
CHILDREN?
THEY...ARE ALL WE HAVE LEFT. THIS IS WHY WE HAVE SUMMONED THE MAGISTRATE. WE HOPED...HE COULD BRING OUR CHILDREN BACK TO US.
THE CREATURES...THE DEVILS THAT COME FROM THE WOODS TO TORMENT YOU...THEY'VE TAKEN YOUR CHILDREN.
ONLY THE FACELESS QUEEN'S MEN CAN HELP US NOW.

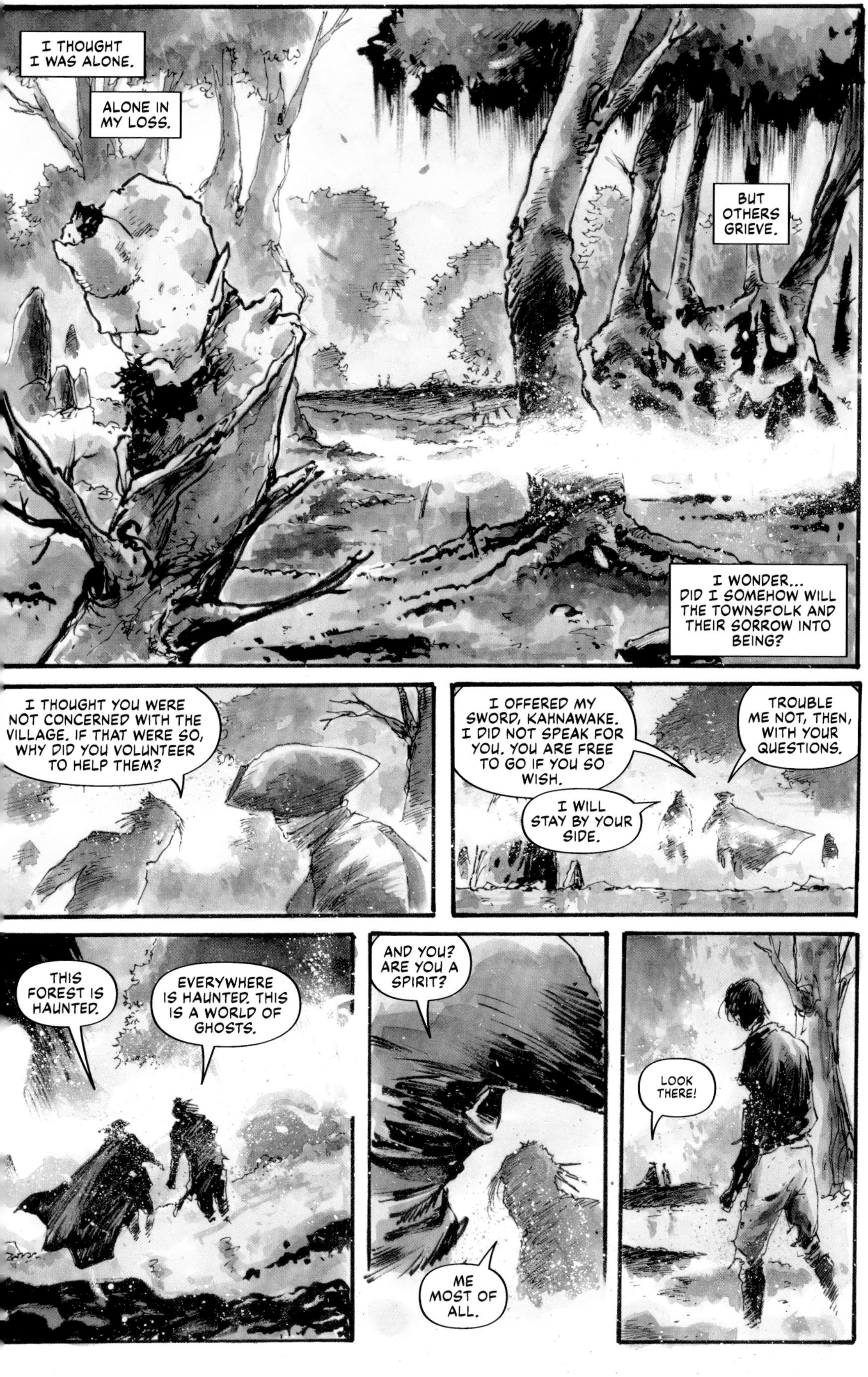
I THOUGHT I WAS ALONE.
ALONE IN MY LOSS.
BUT OTHERS GRIEVE.
I WONDER... DID I SOMEHOW WILL THE TOWNSFOLK AND THEIR SORROW INTO BEING?
I THOUGHT YOU WERE NOT CONCERNED WITH THE VILLAGE. IF THAT WERE SO, WHY DID YOU VOLUNTEER TO HELP THEM?
I OFFERED MY SWORD, KAHNAWAKE. I DID NOT SPEAK FOR YOU. YOU ARE FREE TO GO IF YOU SO WISH.
TROUBLE ME NOT, THEN, WITH YOUR QUESTIONS.
I WILL STAY BY YOUR SIDE.
THIS FOREST IS HAUNTED.
EVERYWHERE IS HAUNTED. THIS IS A WORLD OF GHOSTS.
AND YOU? ARE YOU A SPIRIT?
ME MOST OF ALL.
LOOK THERE!

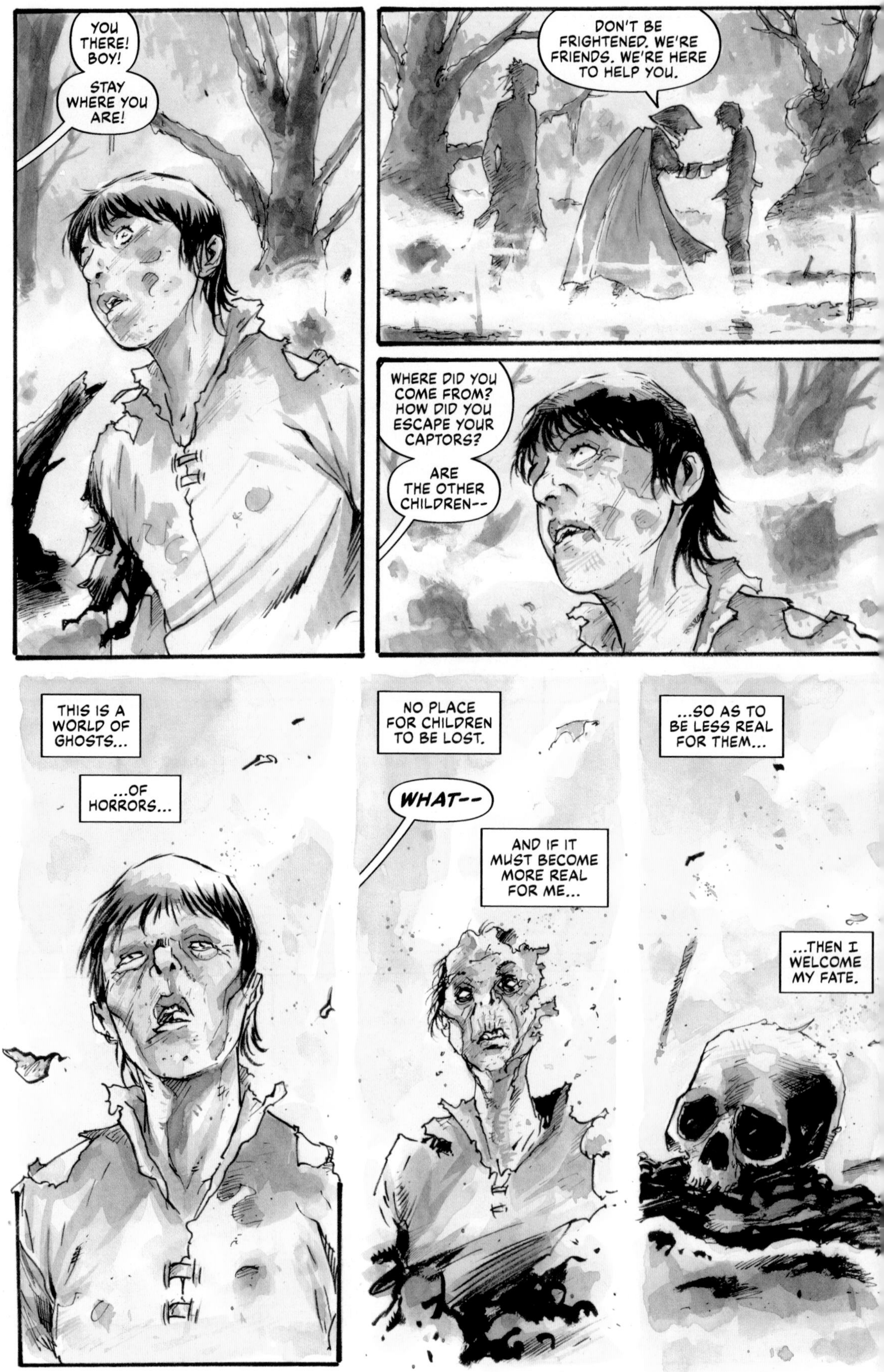
YOU THERE! BOY!
STAY WHERE YOU ARE!
DON'T BE FRIGHTENED. WE'RE FRIENDS. WE'RE HERE TO HELP YOU.
WHERE DID YOU COME FROM? HOW DID YOU ESCAPE YOUR CAPTORS?
ARE THE OTHER CHILDREN--
THIS IS A WORLD OF GHOSTS...
...OF HORRORS...
NO PLACE FOR CHILDREN TO BE LOST.
WHAT--
AND IF IT MUST BECOME MORE REAL FOR ME...
...SO AS TO BE LESS REAL FOR THEM...
...THEN I WELCOME MY FATE.

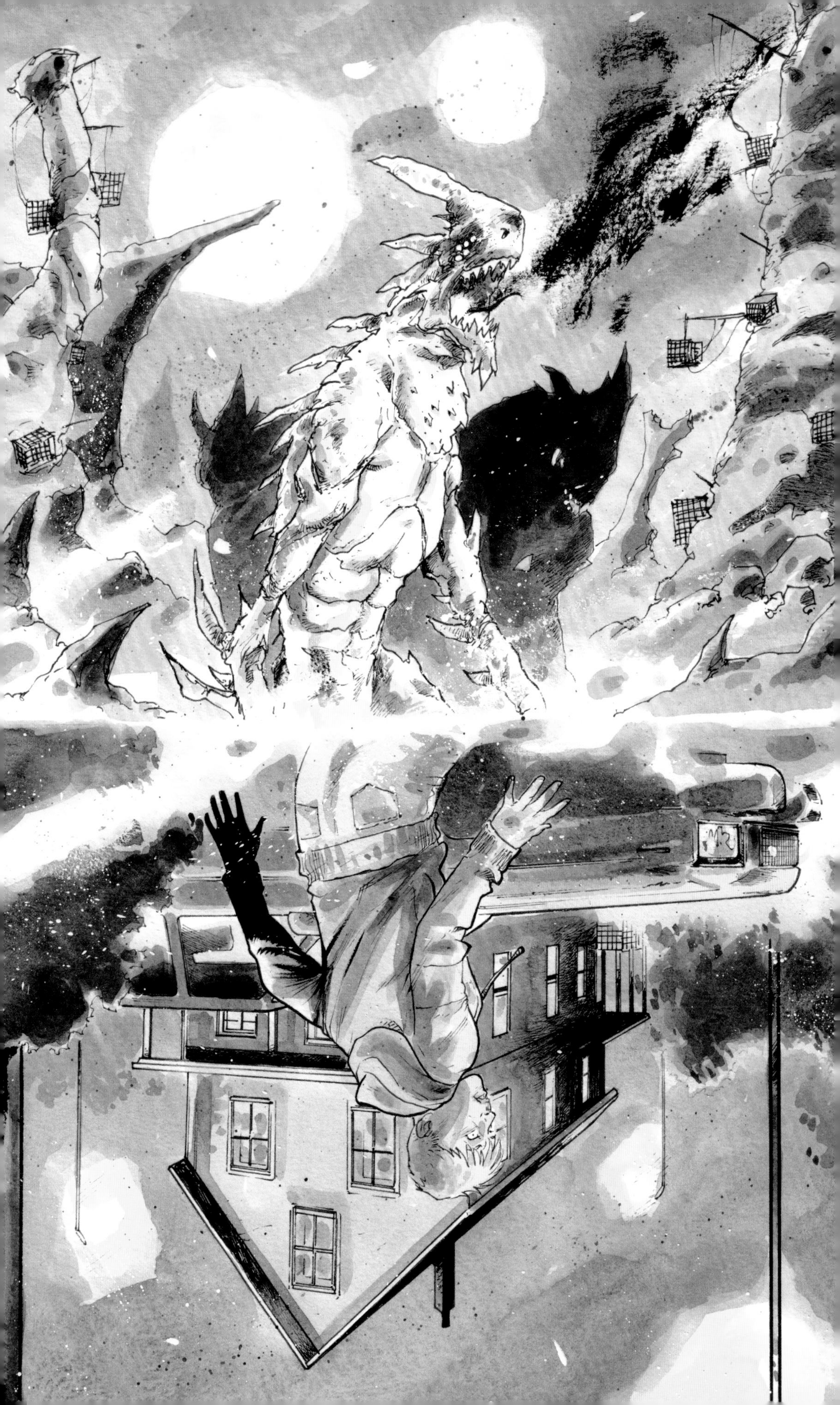

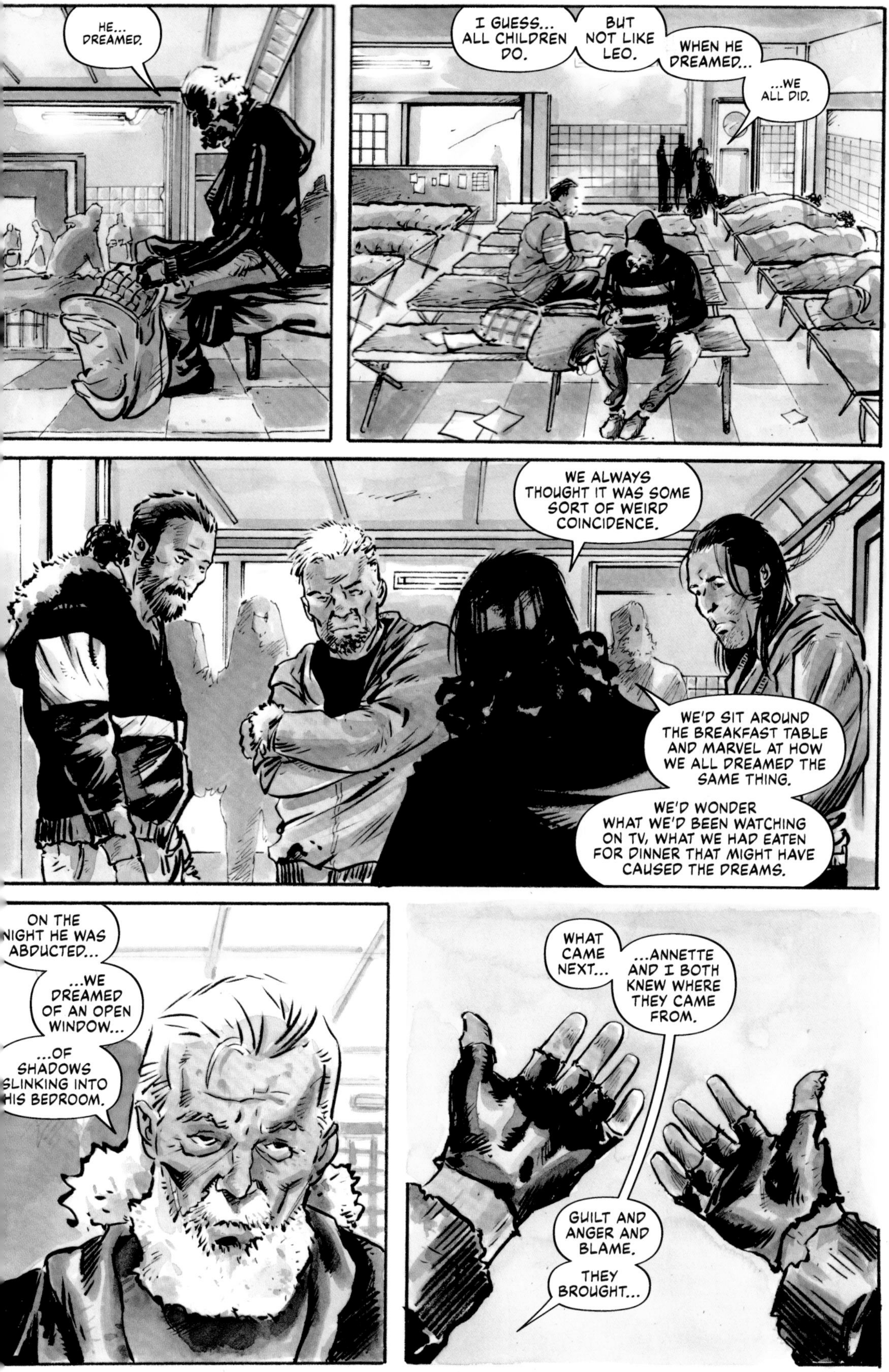

HE... DREAMED.
I GUESS... ALL CHILDREN DO.
BUT NOT LIKE LEO.
WHEN HE DREAMED...
...WE ALL DID.
WE ALWAYS THOUGHT IT WAS SOME SORT OF WEIRD COINCIDENCE.
WE'D SIT AROUND THE BREAKFAST TABLE AND MARVEL AT HOW WE ALL DREAMED THE SAME THING.
WE'D WONDER WHAT WE'D BEEN WATCHING ON TV, WHAT WE HAD EATEN FOR DINNER THAT MIGHT HAVE CAUSED THE DREAMS.
ON THE NIGHT HE WAS ABDUCTED...
...WE DREAMED OF AN OPEN WINDOW...
...OF SHADOWS SLINKING INTO HIS BEDROOM.
WHAT CAME NEXT...
...ANNETTE AND I BOTH KNEW WHERE THEY CAME FROM.
GUILT AND ANGER AND BLAME.
THEY BROUGHT...

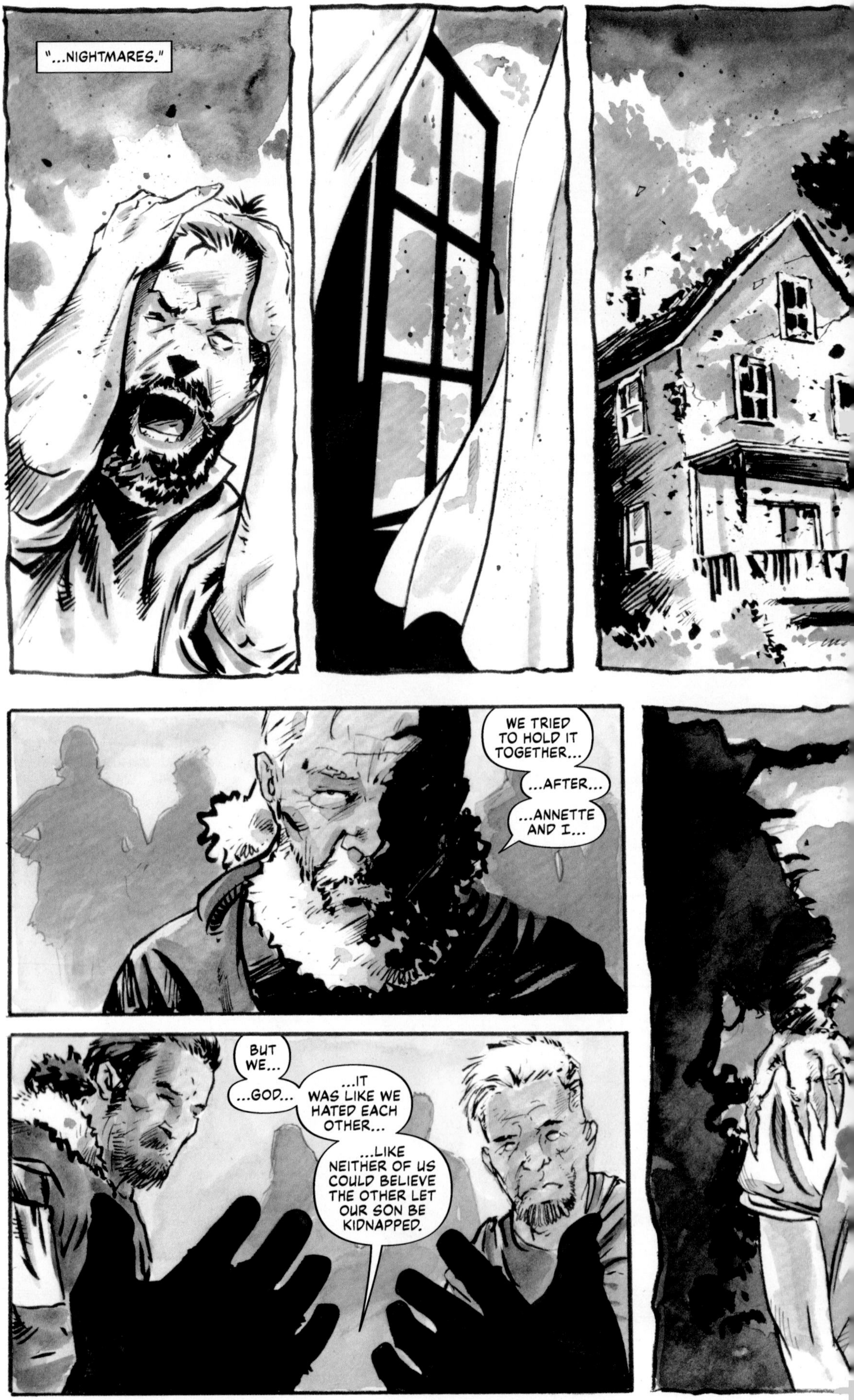
"...NIGHTMARES."
WE TRIED TO HOLD IT TOGETHER...
...AFTER...
...ANNETTE AND I...
BUT WE...
...GOD...
...IT WAS LIKE WE HATED EACH OTHER...
...LIKE NEITHER OF US COULD BELIEVE THE OTHER LET OUR SON BE KIDNAPPED.

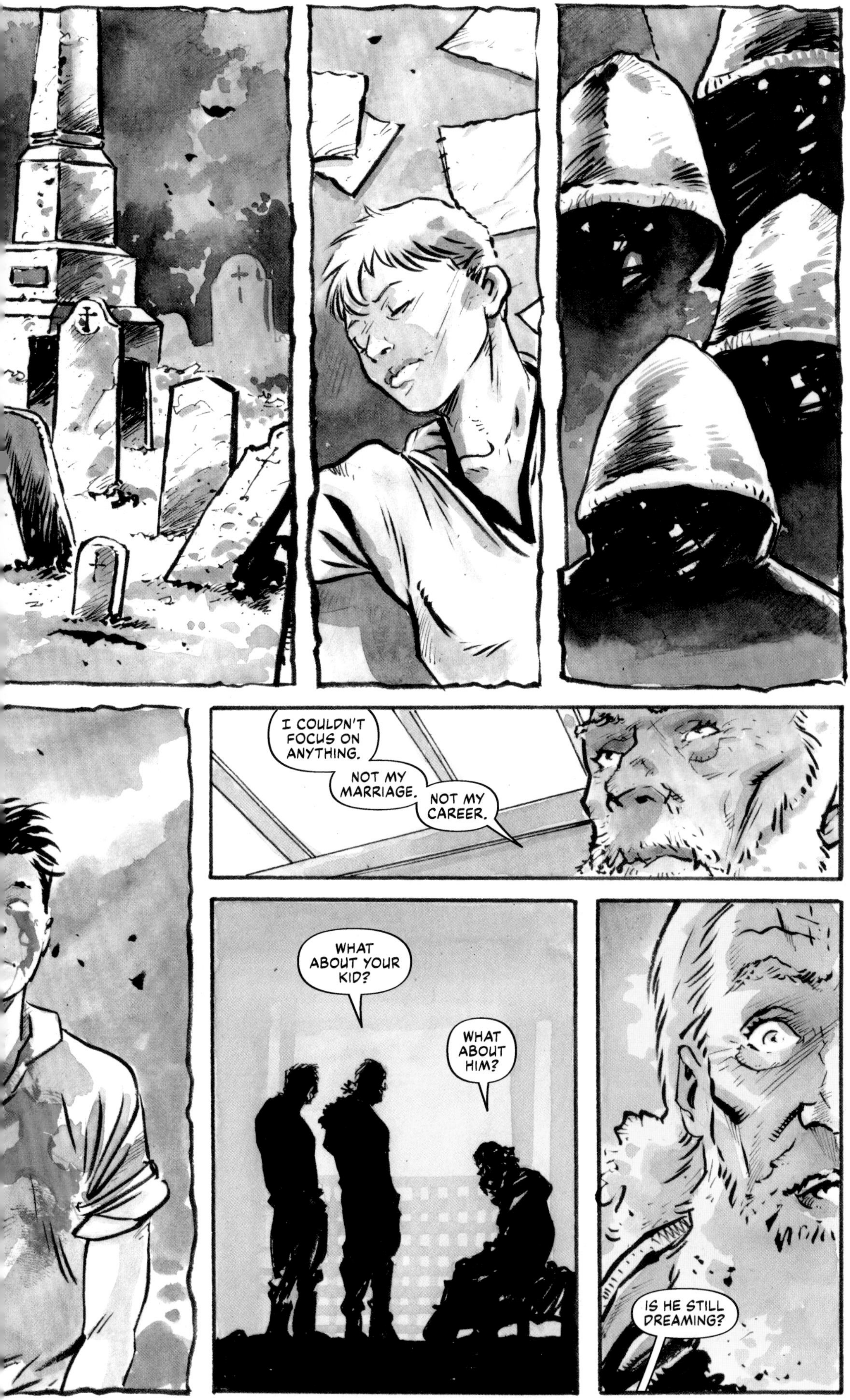
I COULDN'T FOCUS ON ANYTHING.
NOT MY MARRIAGE.
NOT MY CAREER.
WHAT ABOUT YOUR KID?
WHAT ABOUT HIM?
IS HE STILL DREAMING?

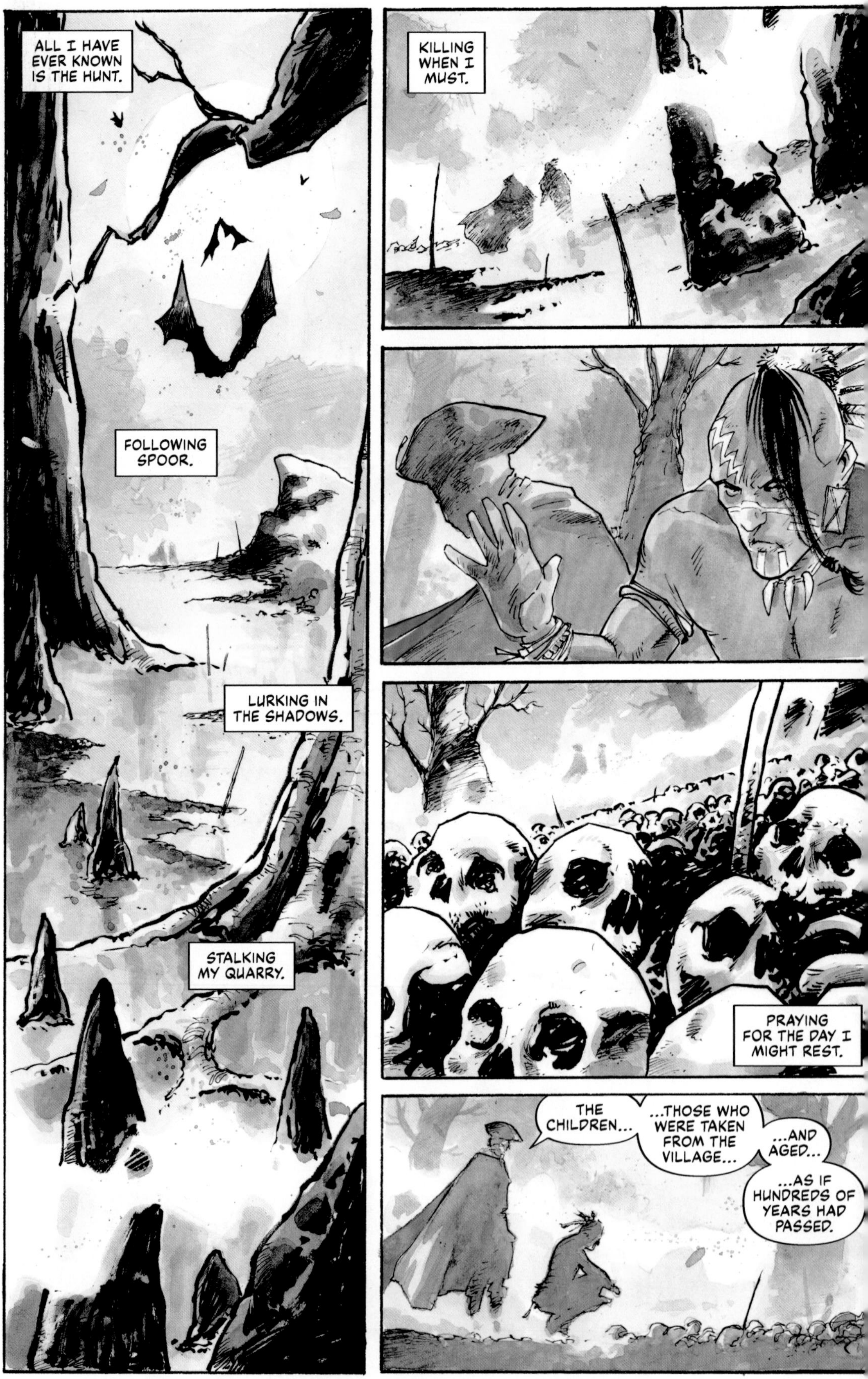

ALL I HAVE EVER KNOWN IS THE HUNT.
FOLLOWING SPOOR.
LURKING IN THE SHADOWS.
STALKING MY QUARRY.
KILLING WHEN I MUST.
PRAYING FOR THE DAY I MIGHT REST.
THE CHILDREN...
...THOSE WHO WERE TAKEN FROM THE VILLAGE...
...AND AGED...
...AS IF HUNDREDS OF YEARS HAD PASSED.

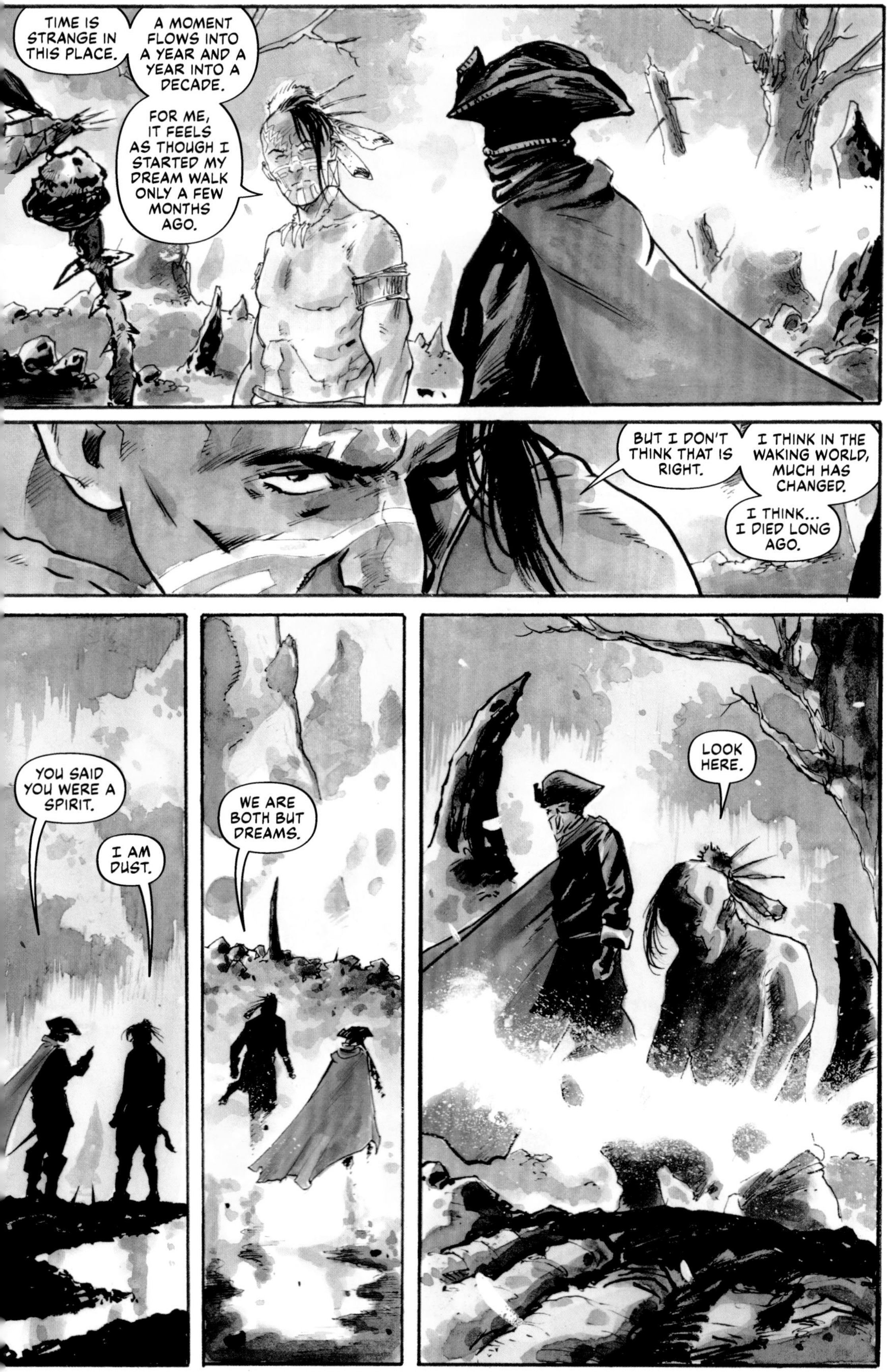
TIME IS STRANGE IN THIS PLACE.
A MOMENT FLOWS INTO A YEAR AND A YEAR INTO A DECADE.
FOR ME, IT FEELS AS THOUGH I STARTED MY DREAM WALK ONLY A FEW MONTHS AGO.
BUT I DON'T THINK THAT IS RIGHT.
I THINK IN THE WAKING WORLD, MUCH HAS CHANGED.
I THINK... I DIED LONG AGO.
YOU SAID YOU WERE A SPIRIT.
I AM DUST.
WE ARE BOTH BUT DREAMS.
LOOK HERE.

A WARREN OF PAIN AND SUFFERING.

CAGES GROWING FROM THE VERY WALLS.

FROM THE FOUNDATIONS.

A CITY BUILT ON ANGUISH.

THE CHILDREN! SOME OF THEM YET LIVE!

BUT LOOK!

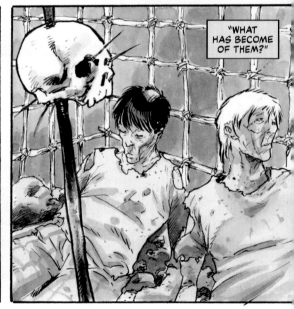

"WHAT HAS BECOME OF THEM?"

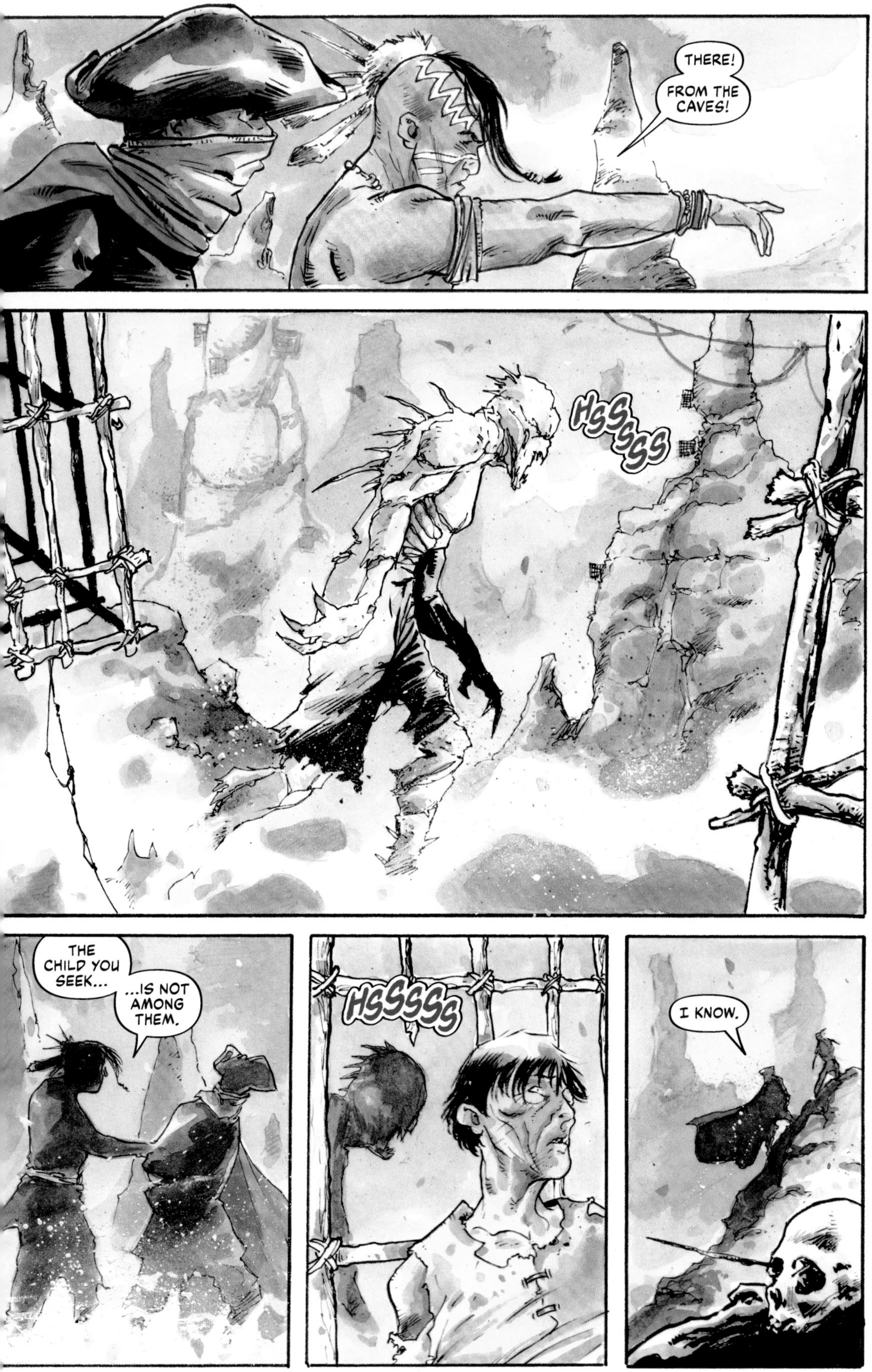
THERE!
FROM THE CAVES!
HSSSSS
THE CHILD YOU SEEK...
...IS NOT AMONG THEM.
HSSSSS
I KNOW.

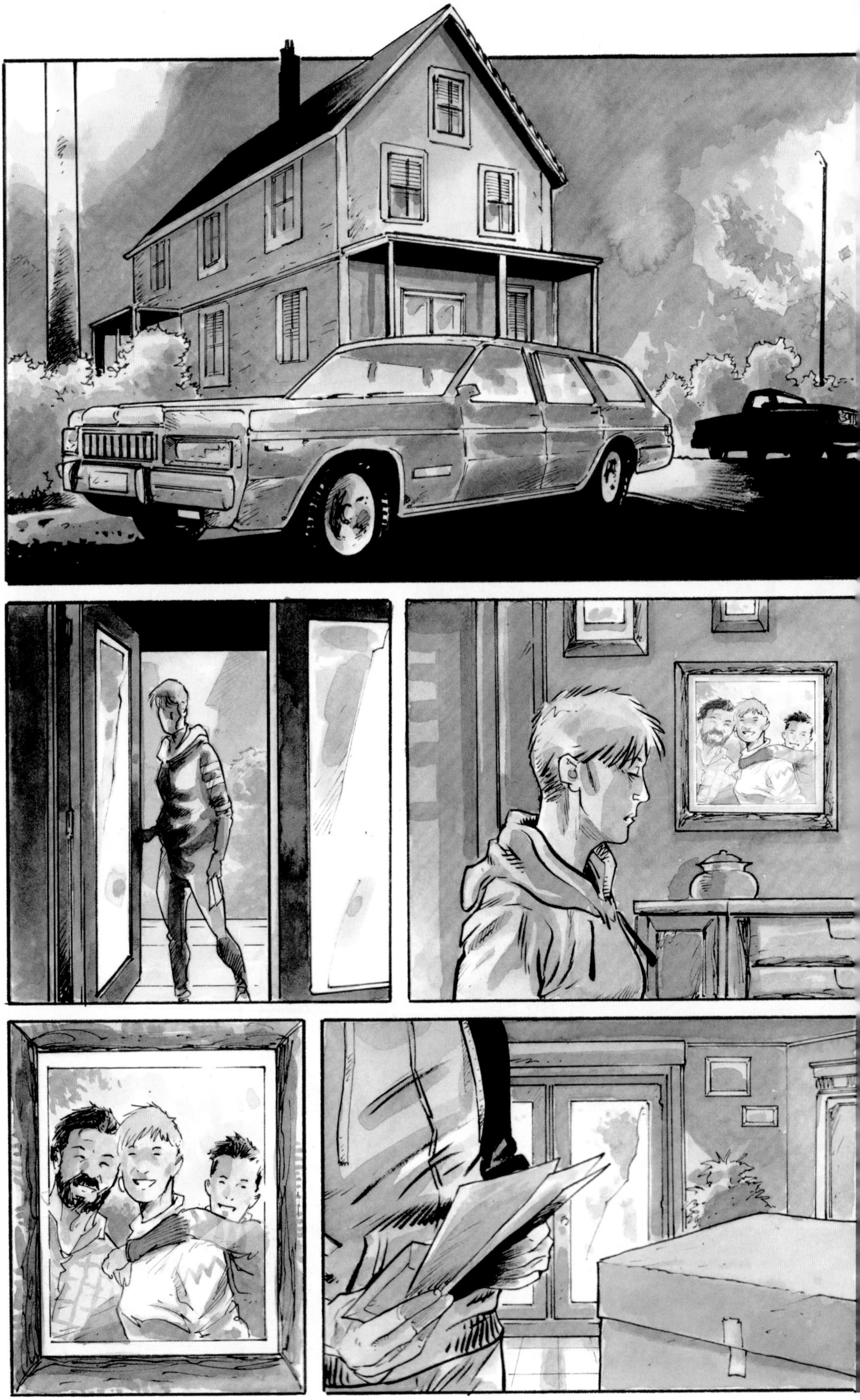

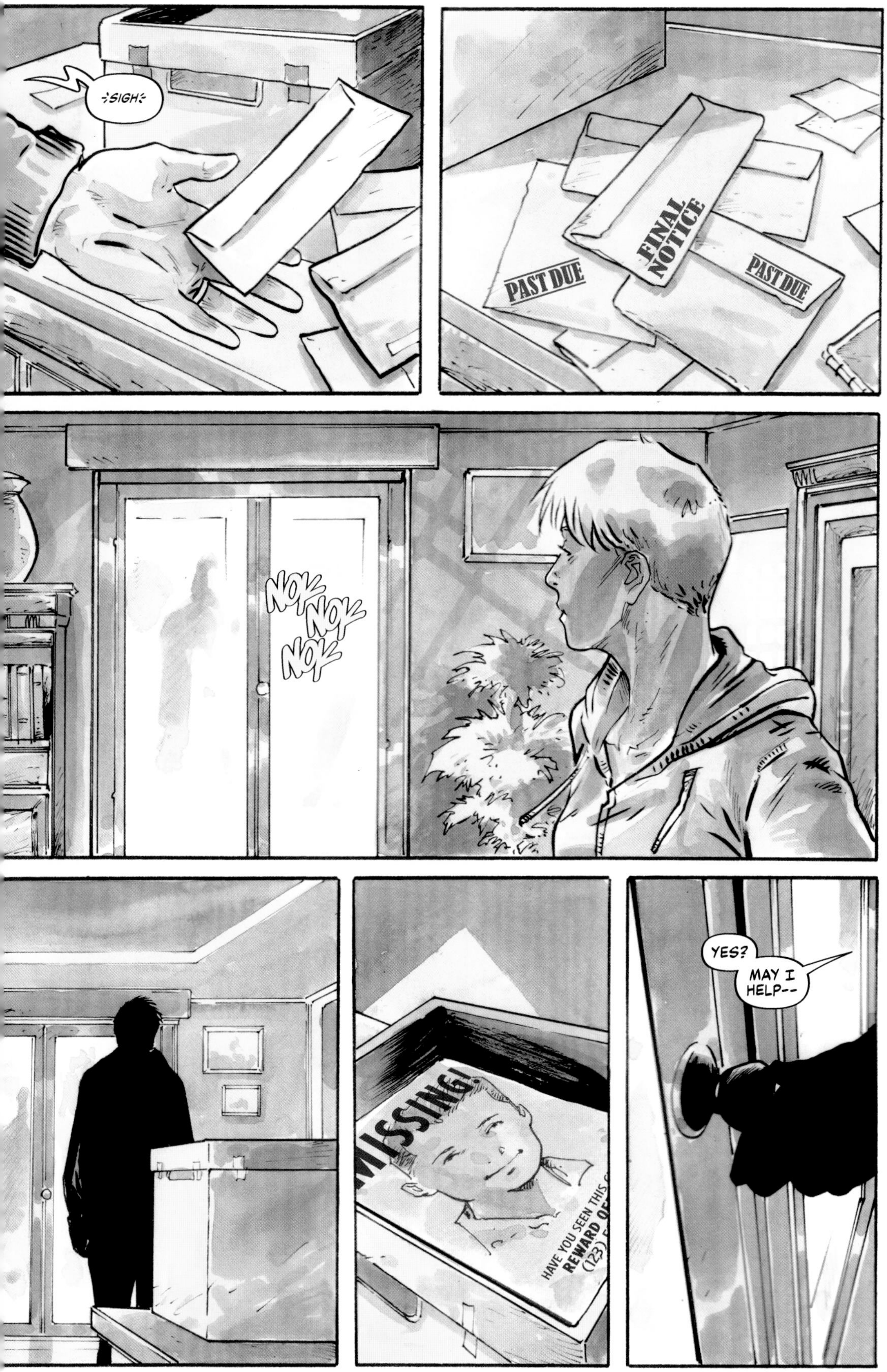
SIGH
FINAL NOTICE
PAST DUE
PAST DUE
NOK NOK NOK
MISSING!
HAVE YOU SEEN THIS
REWARD OF
(123)
YES?
MAY I HELP--

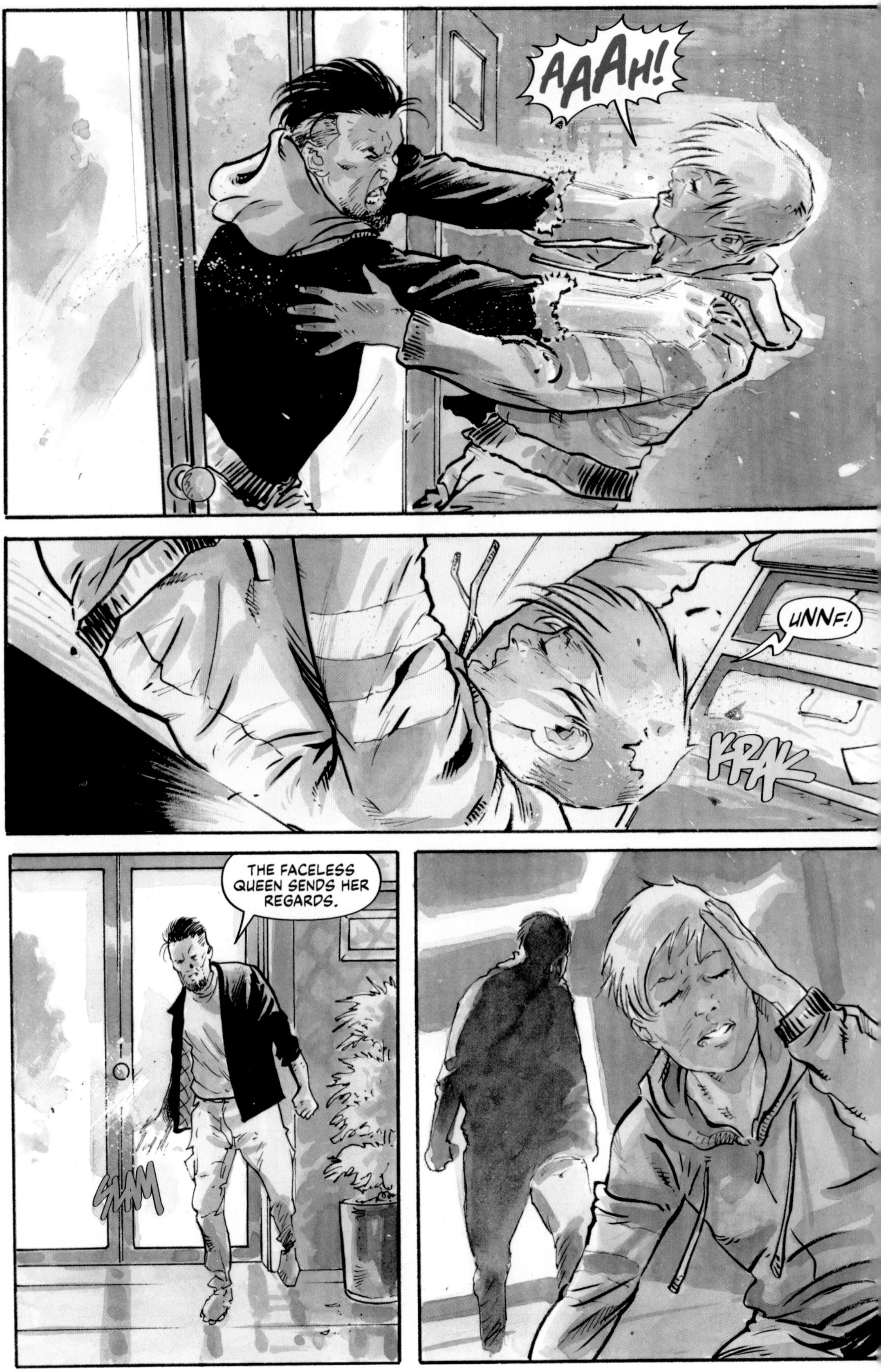
AAAH!
UNNF!
KRAK
THE FACELESS QUEEN SENDS HER REGARDS.
SLAM

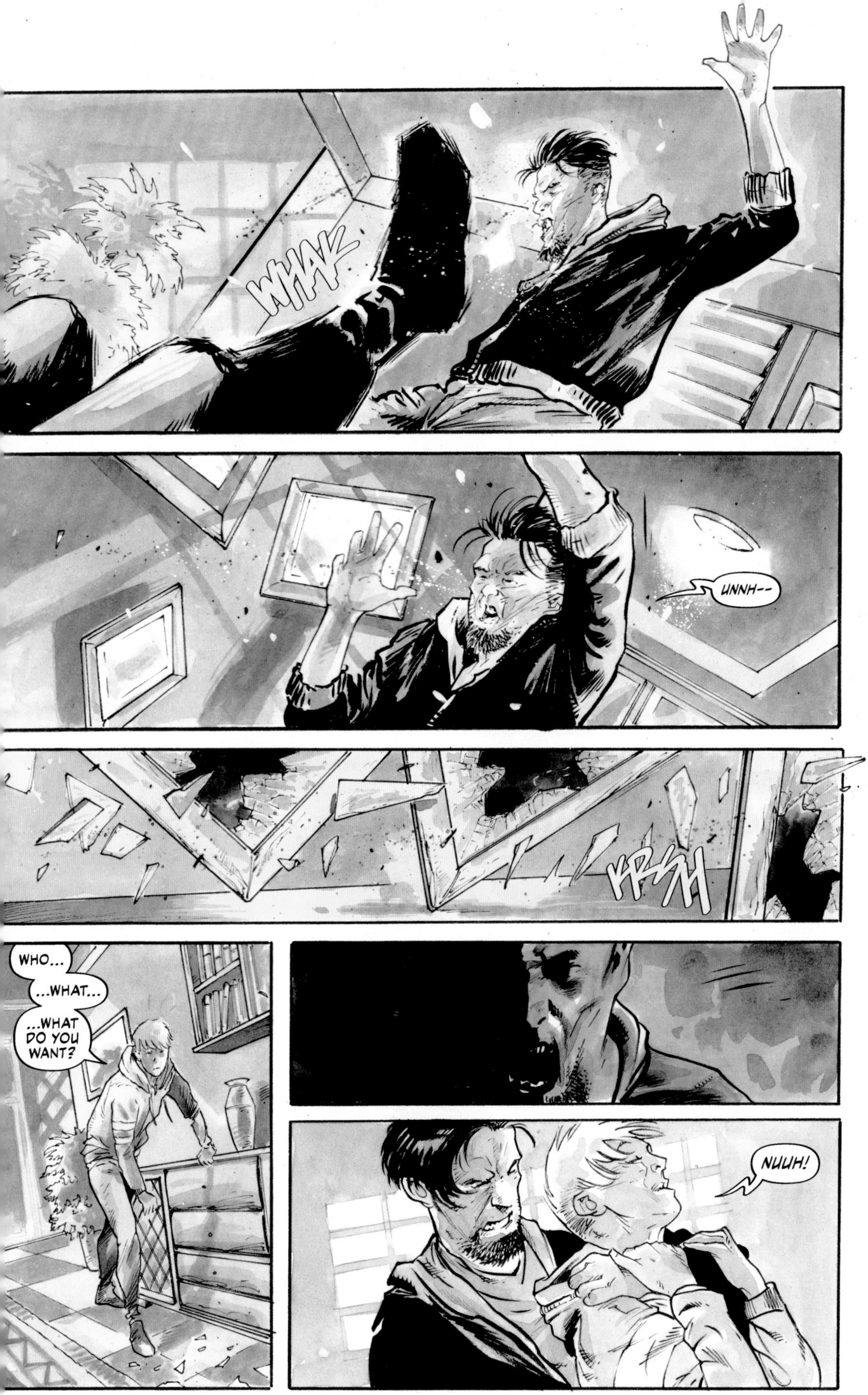
WHAK
UNNH--
KRSH
WHO...
...WHAT...
...WHAT DO YOU WANT?
NUUH!

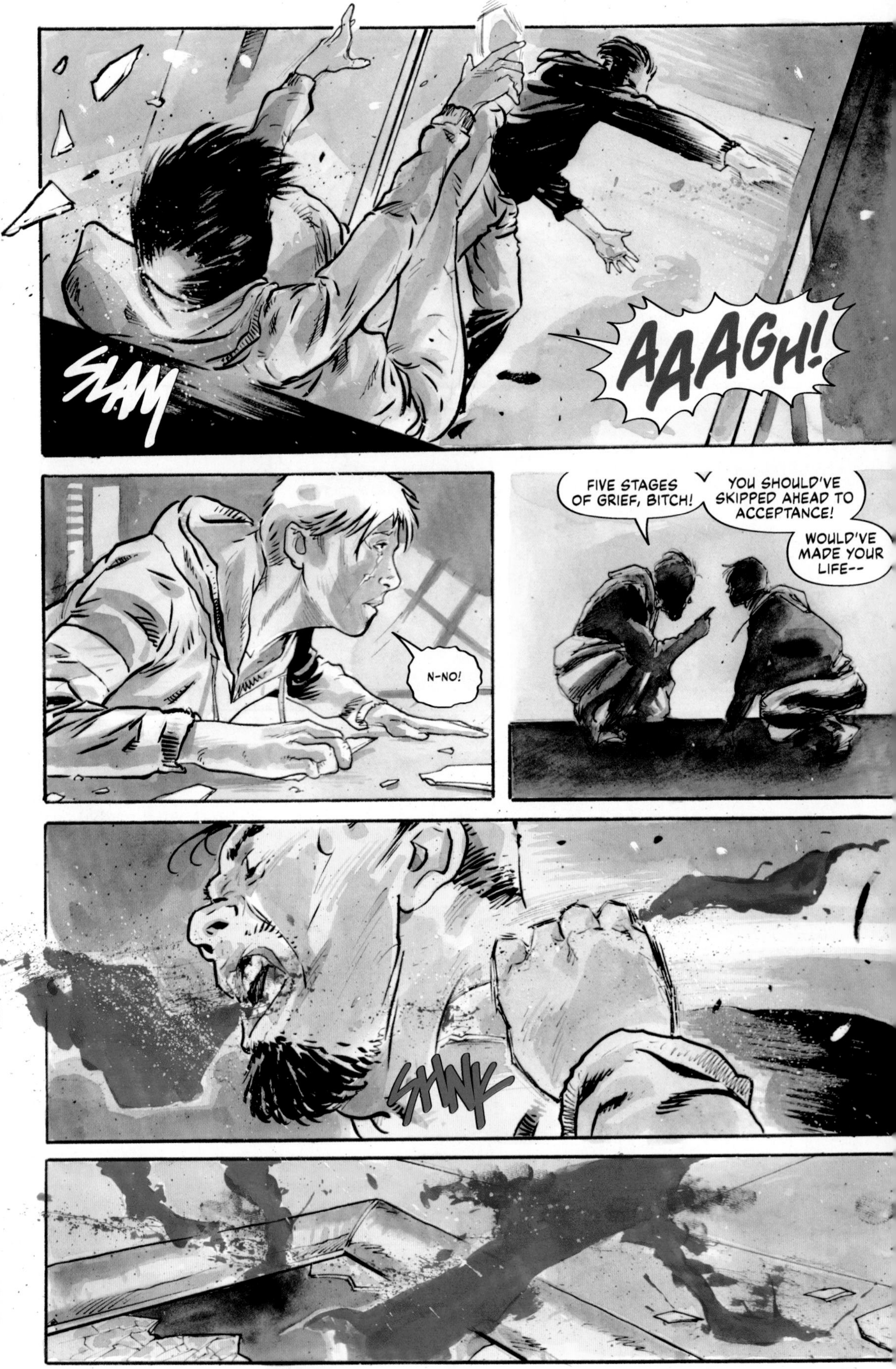
SLAM
AAAGH!
N-NO!
FIVE STAGES OF GRIEF, BITCH!
YOU SHOULD'VE SKIPPED AHEAD TO ACCEPTANCE!
WOULD'VE MADE YOUR LIFE--
SHNK

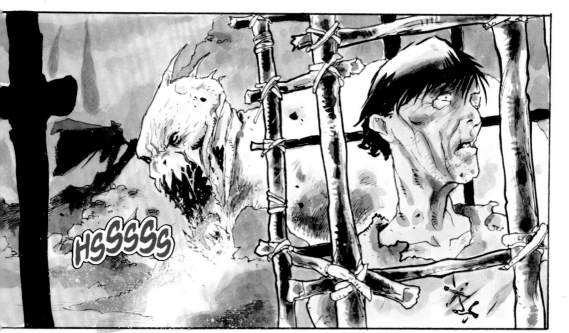

HSSSSS

SKSSSK

THIS CREATURE... WAS NOT ALONE.

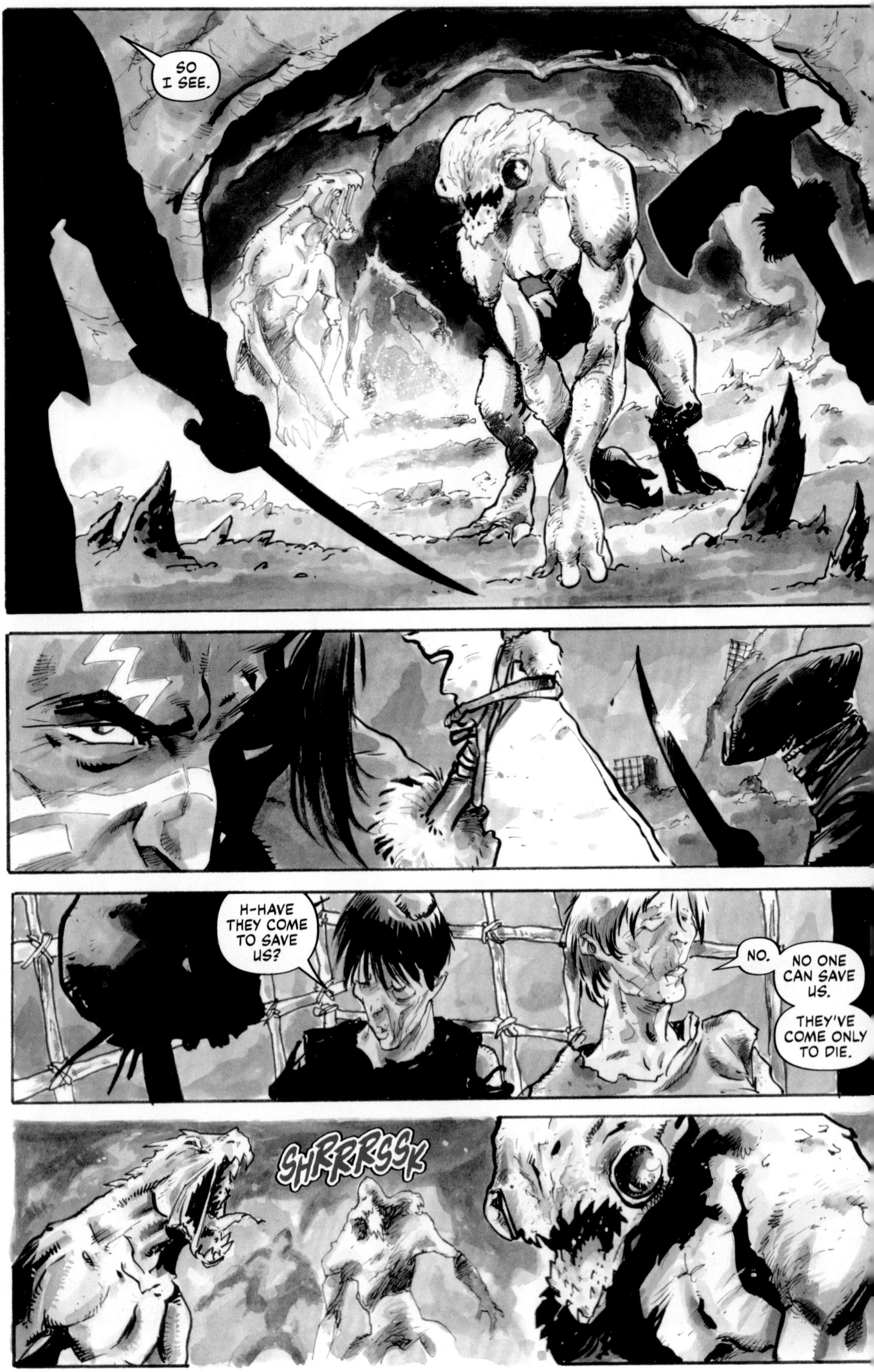
SO I SEE.
H-HAVE THEY COME TO SAVE US?
NO.
NO ONE CAN SAVE US.
THEY'VE COME ONLY TO DIE.
SHRRRSSK

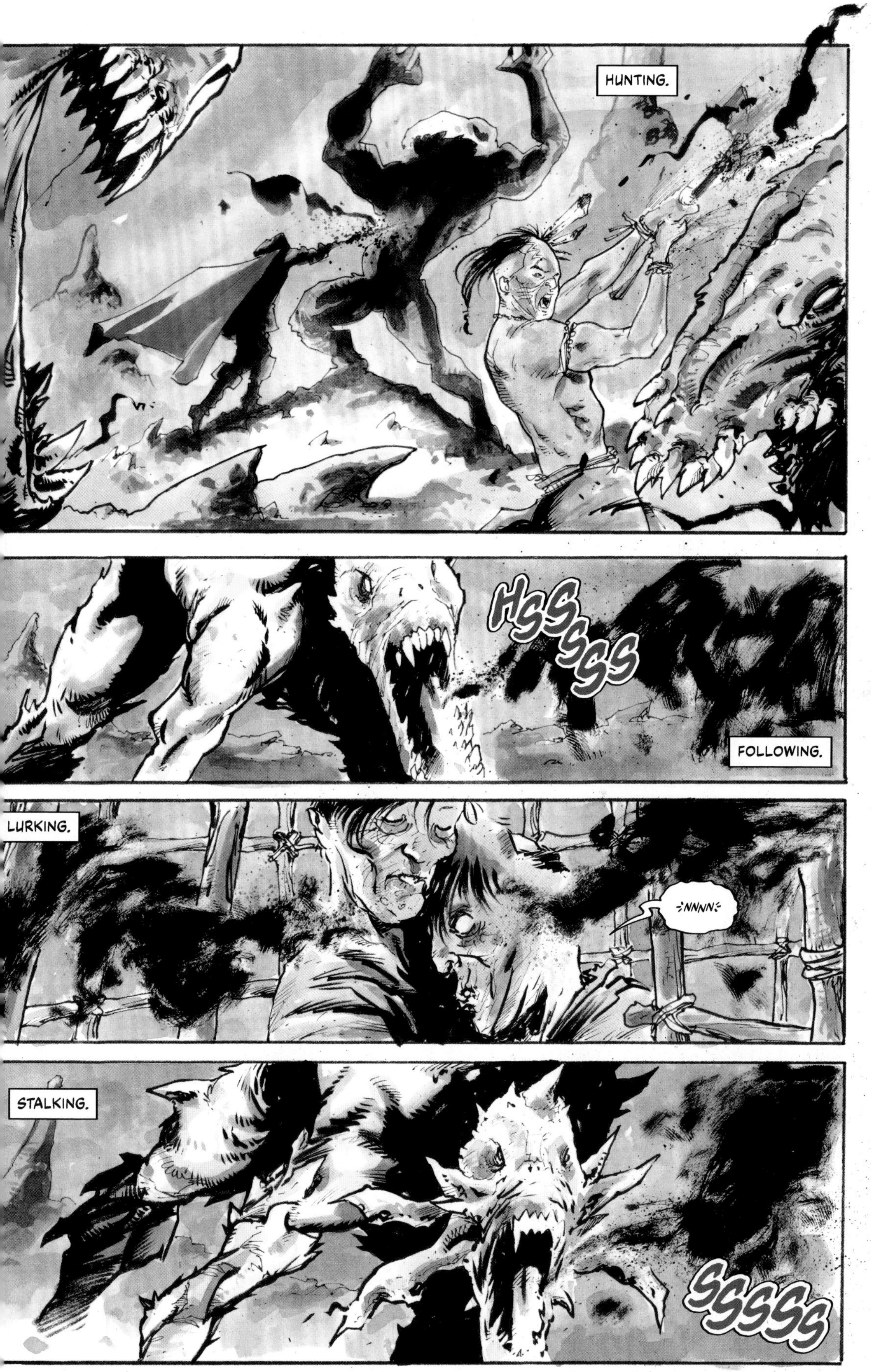
HUNTING.
HSSSSS
FOLLOWING.
LURKING.
NNNN
STALKING.
SSSSS

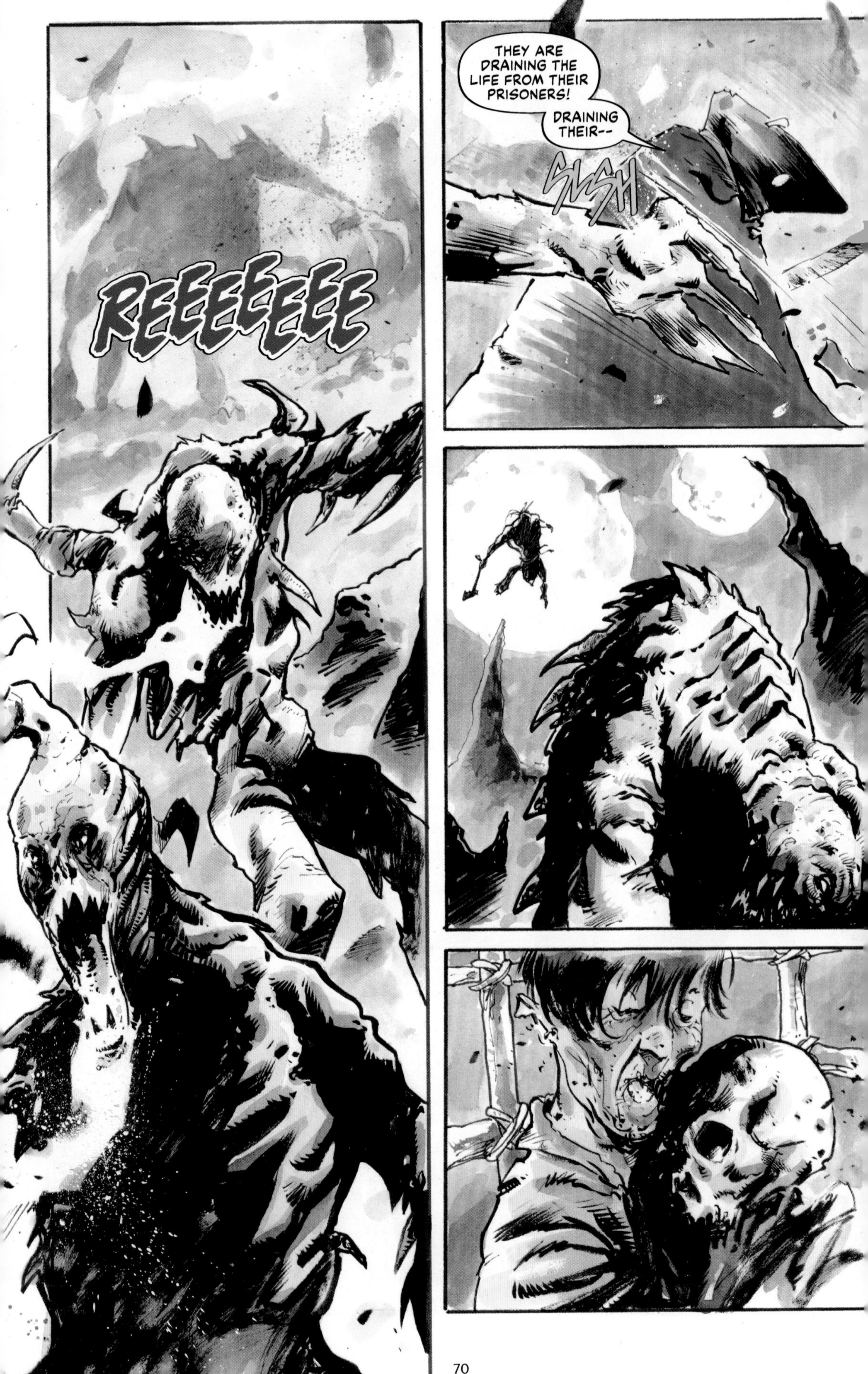
REEEEEEEE
THEY ARE DRAINING THE LIFE FROM THEIR PRISONERS!
DRAINING THEIR--
SLSH

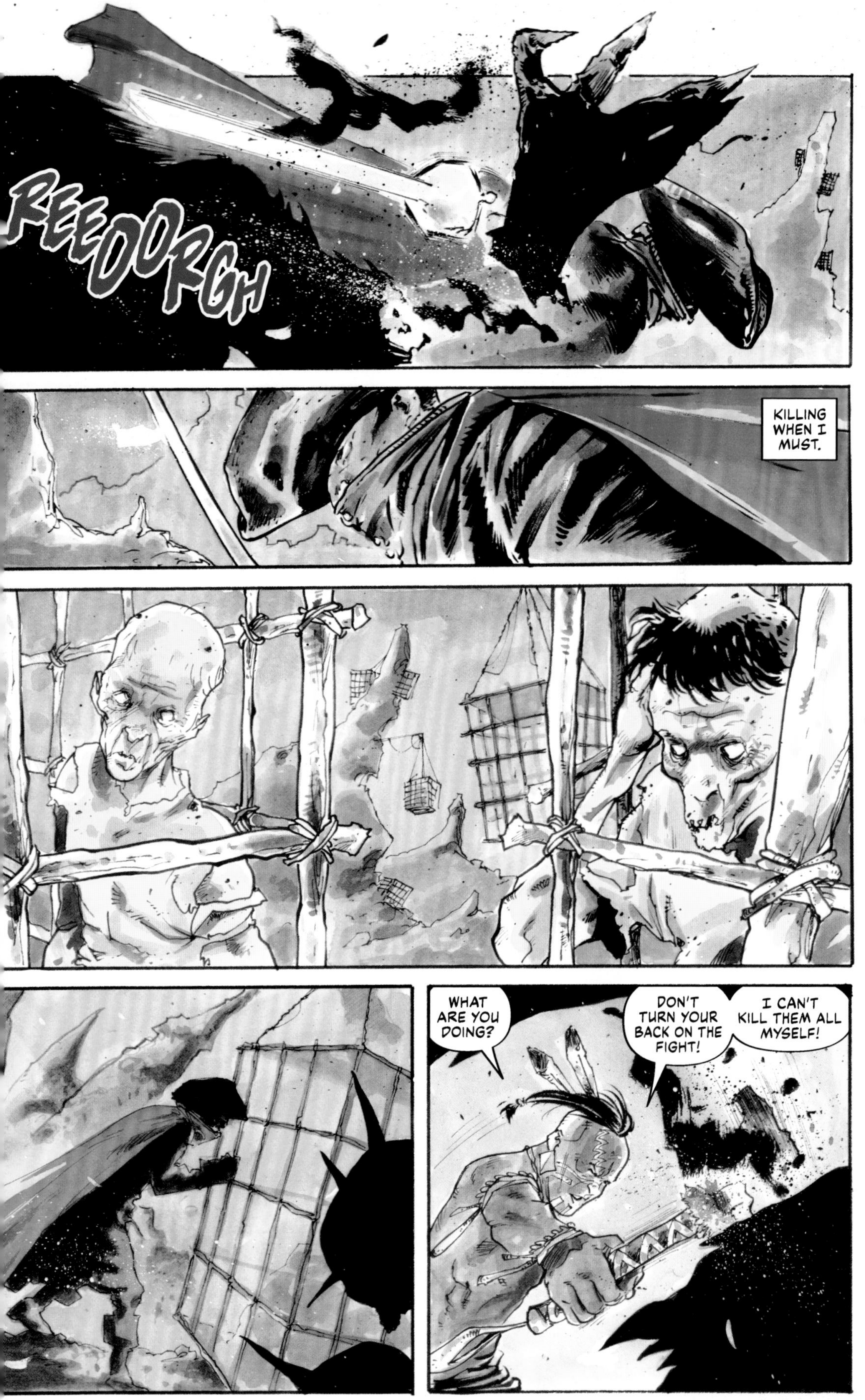
REEEOORGH
KILLING WHEN I MUST.
WHAT ARE YOU DOING?
DON'T TURN YOUR BACK ON THE FIGHT!
I CAN'T KILL THEM ALL MYSELF!

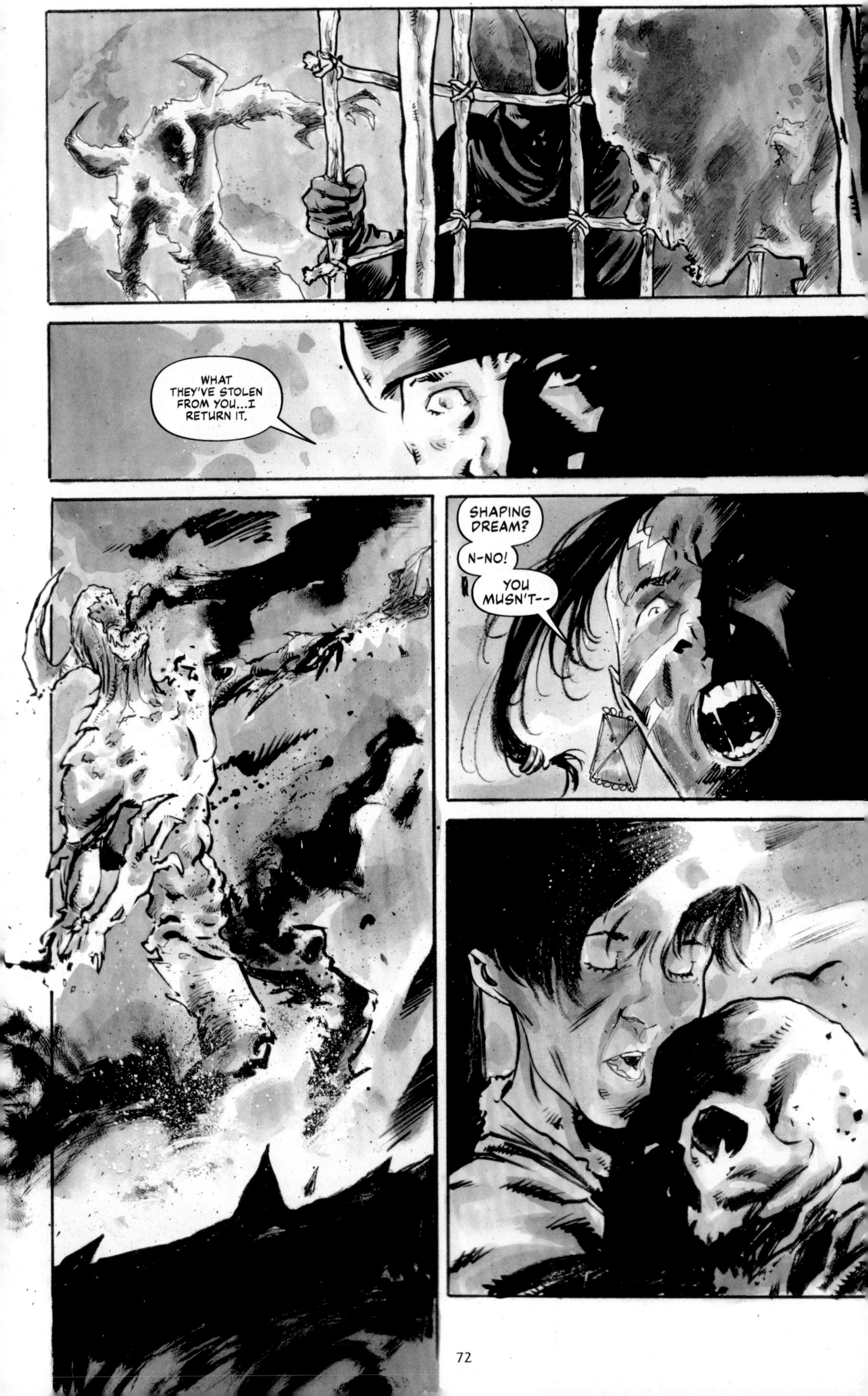
WHAT THEY'VE STOLEN FROM YOU...I RETURN IT.
SHAPING DREAM?
N-NO!
YOU MUSN'T--

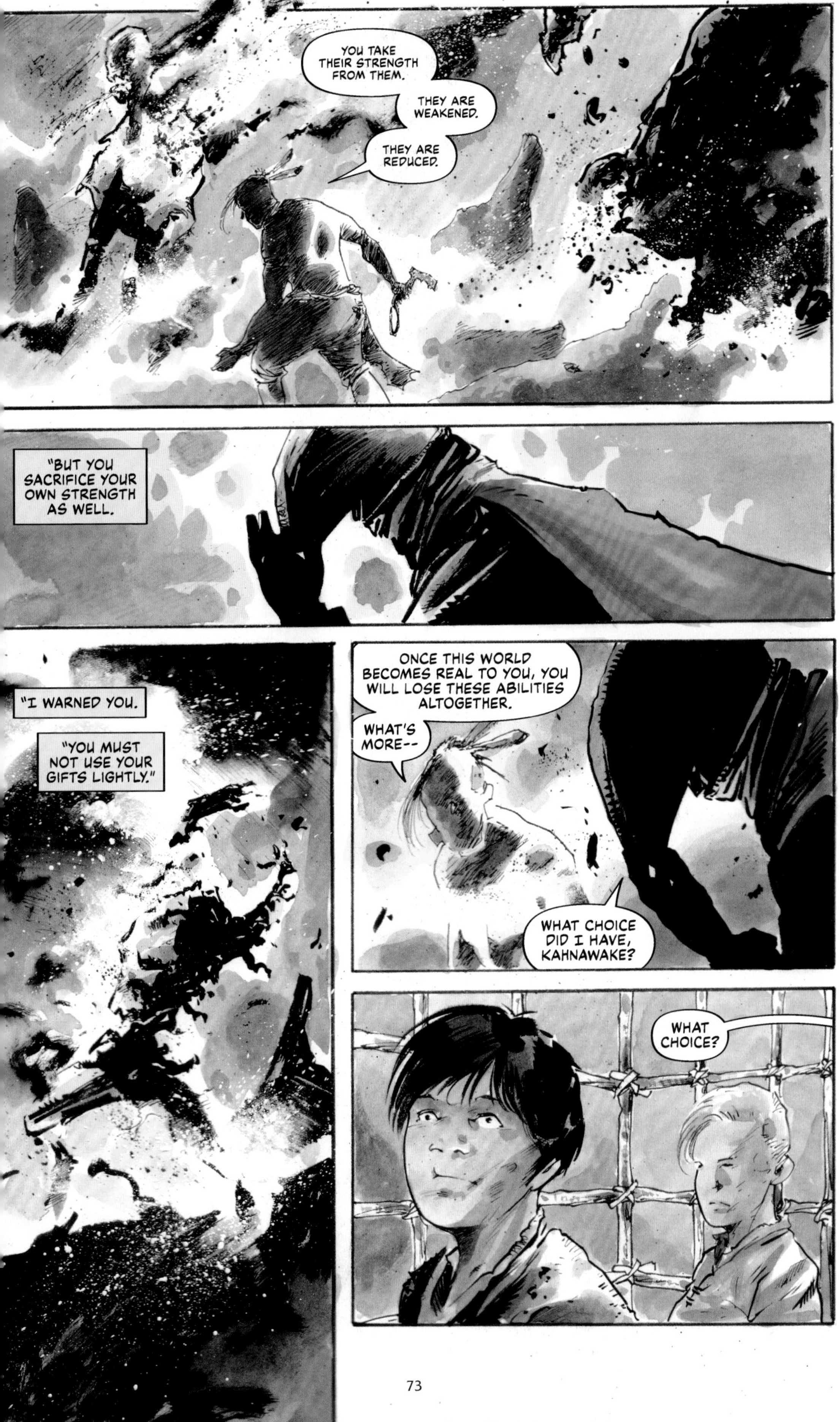
YOU TAKE THEIR STRENGTH FROM THEM.
THEY ARE WEAKENED.
THEY ARE REDUCED.
"BUT YOU SACRIFICE YOUR OWN STRENGTH AS WELL.
"I WARNED YOU.
"YOU MUST NOT USE YOUR GIFTS LIGHTLY."
ONCE THIS WORLD BECOMES REAL TO YOU, YOU WILL LOSE THESE ABILITIES ALTOGETHER.
WHAT'S MORE--
WHAT CHOICE DID I HAVE, KAHNAWAKE?
WHAT CHOICE?

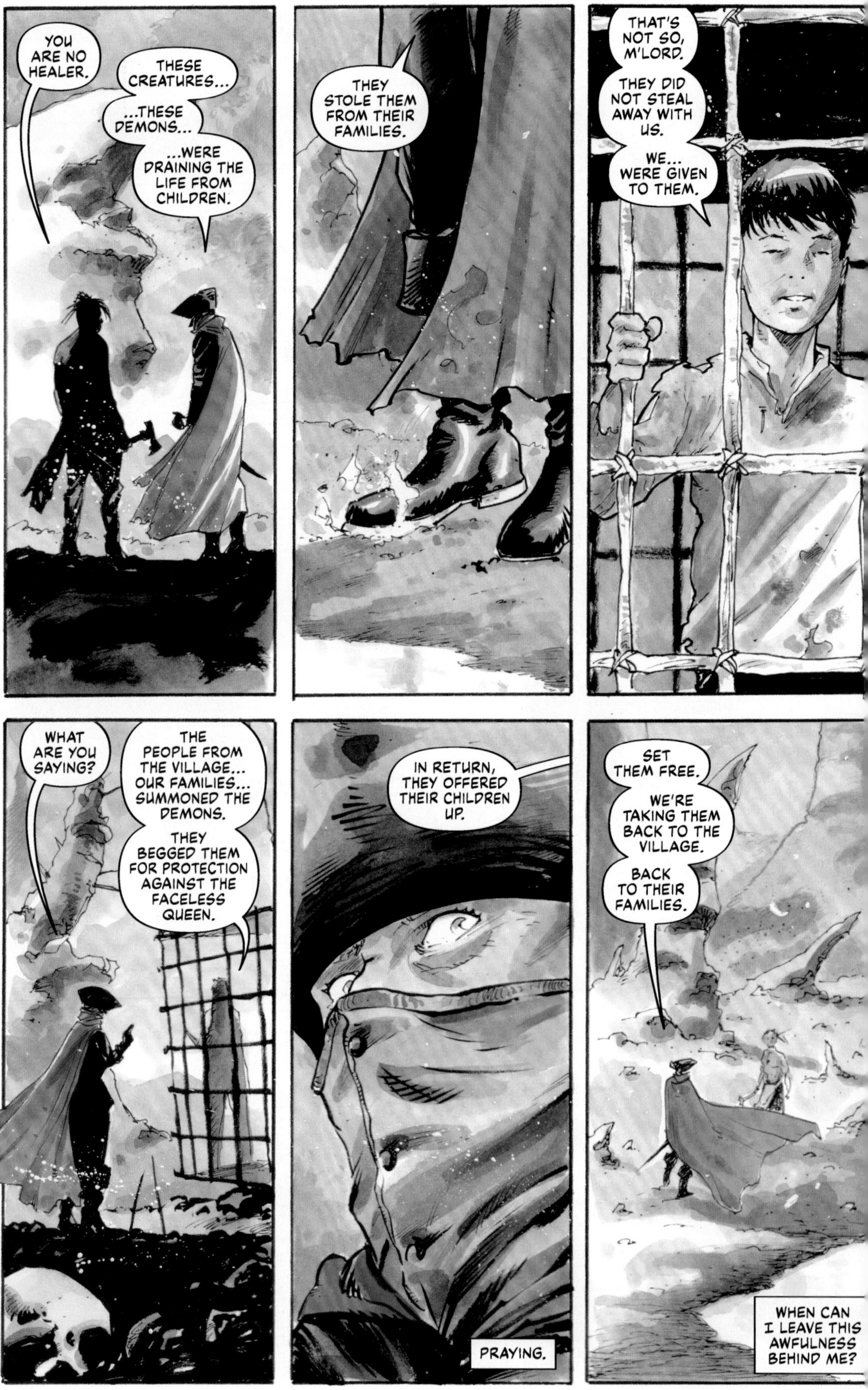
YOU ARE NO HEALER.
THESE CREATURES...
...THESE DEMONS...
...WERE DRAINING THE LIFE FROM CHILDREN.
THEY STOLE THEM FROM THEIR FAMILIES.
THAT'S NOT SO, M'LORD.
THEY DID NOT STEAL AWAY WITH US.
WE... WERE GIVEN TO THEM.
WHAT ARE YOU SAYING?
THE PEOPLE FROM THE VILLAGE... OUR FAMILIES... SUMMONED THE DEMONS.
THEY BEGGED THEM FOR PROTECTION AGAINST THE FACELESS QUEEN.
IN RETURN, THEY OFFERED THEIR CHILDREN UP.
PRAYING.
SET THEM FREE.
WE'RE TAKING THEM BACK TO THE VILLAGE.
BACK TO THEIR FAMILIES.
WHEN CAN I LEAVE THIS AWFULNESS BEHIND ME?

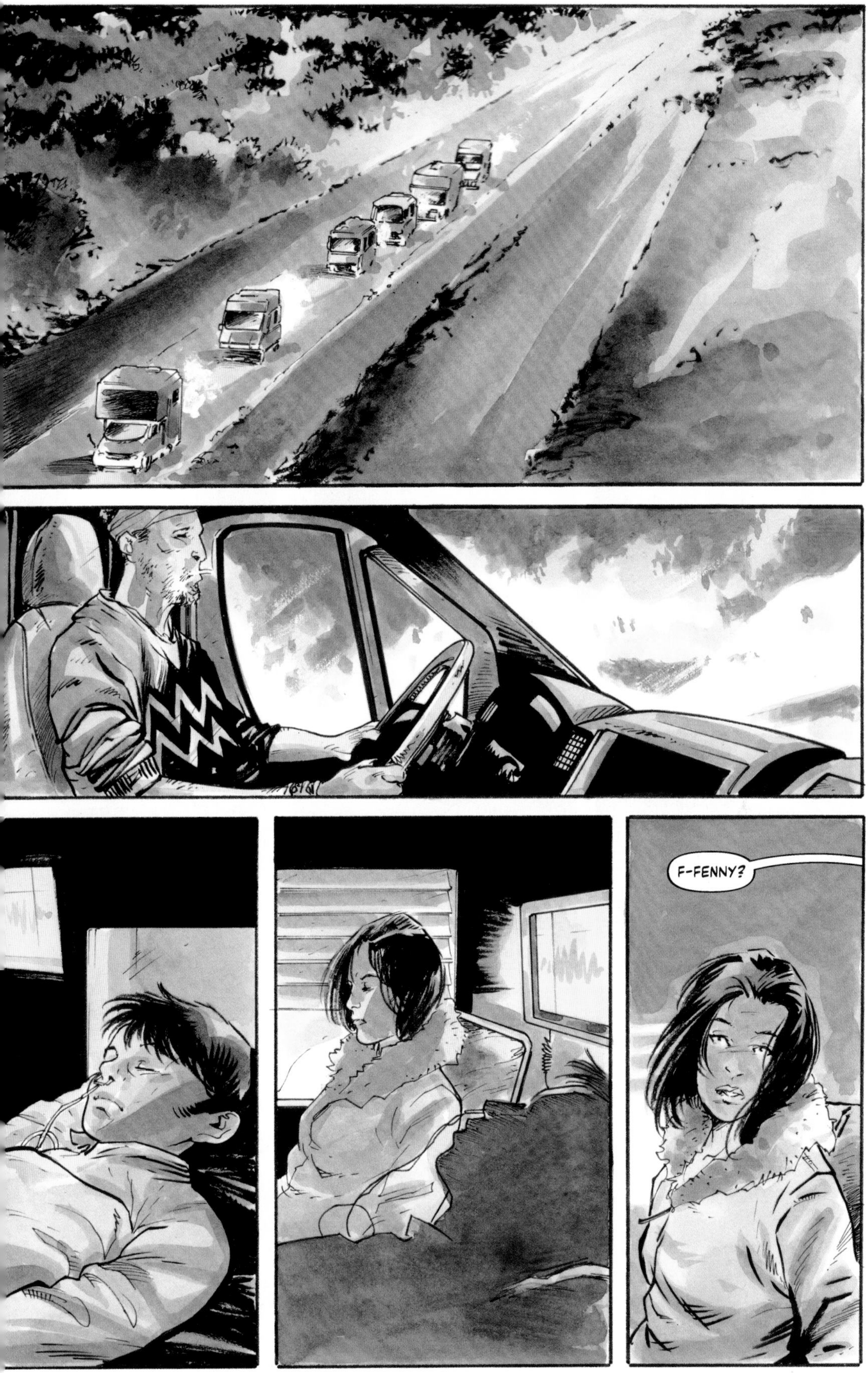
F-FENNY?

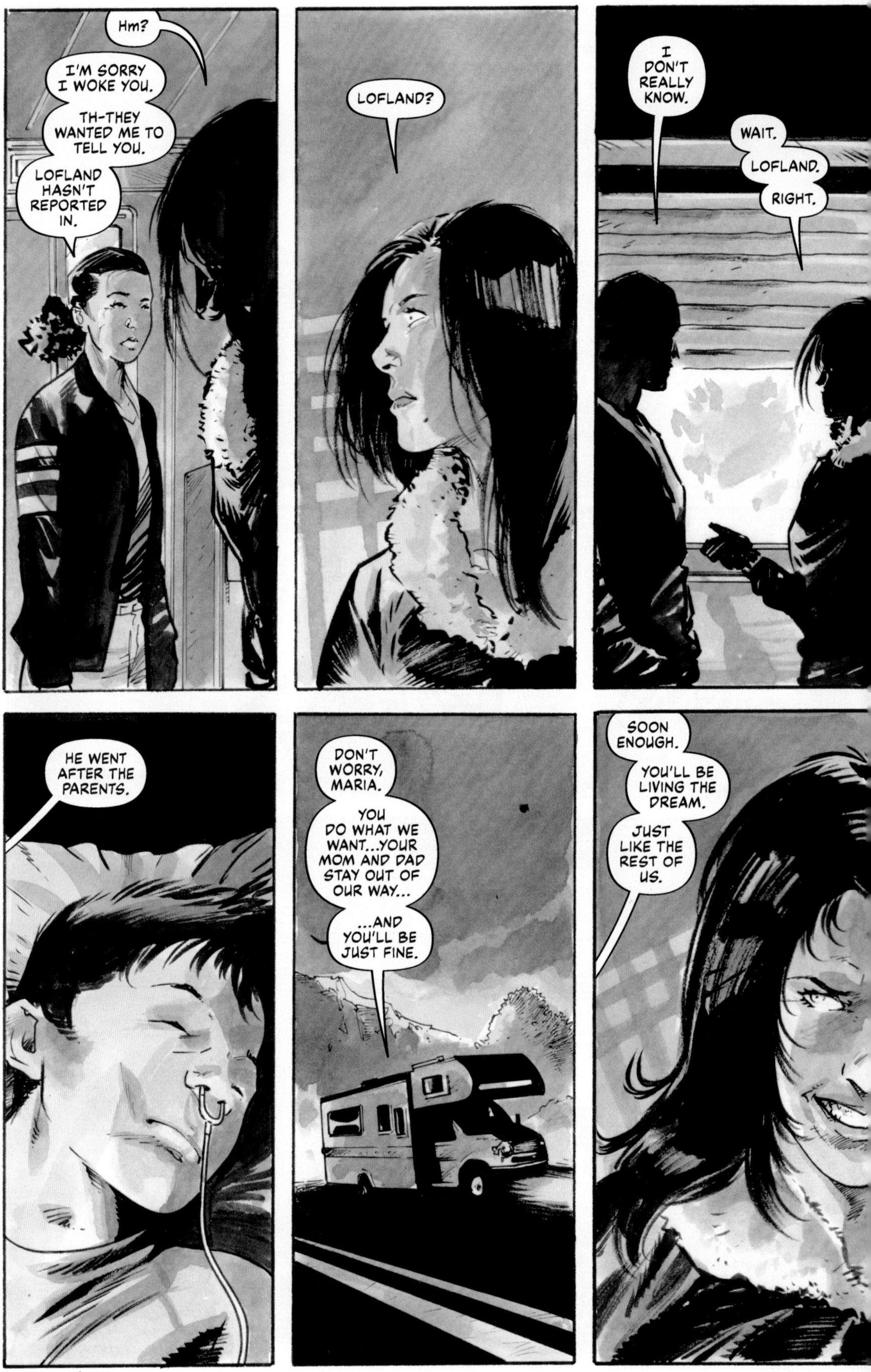
Hm?
I'M SORRY I WOKE YOU.
TH-THEY WANTED ME TO TELL YOU.
LOFLAND HASN'T REPORTED IN.
LOFLAND?
I DON'T REALLY KNOW.
WAIT.
LOFLAND.
RIGHT.
HE WENT AFTER THE PARENTS.
DON'T WORRY, MARIA.
YOU DO WHAT WE WANT...YOUR MOM AND DAD STAY OUT OF OUR WAY...
...AND YOU'LL BE JUST FINE.
SOON ENOUGH.
YOU'LL BE LIVING THE DREAM.
JUST LIKE THE REST OF US.

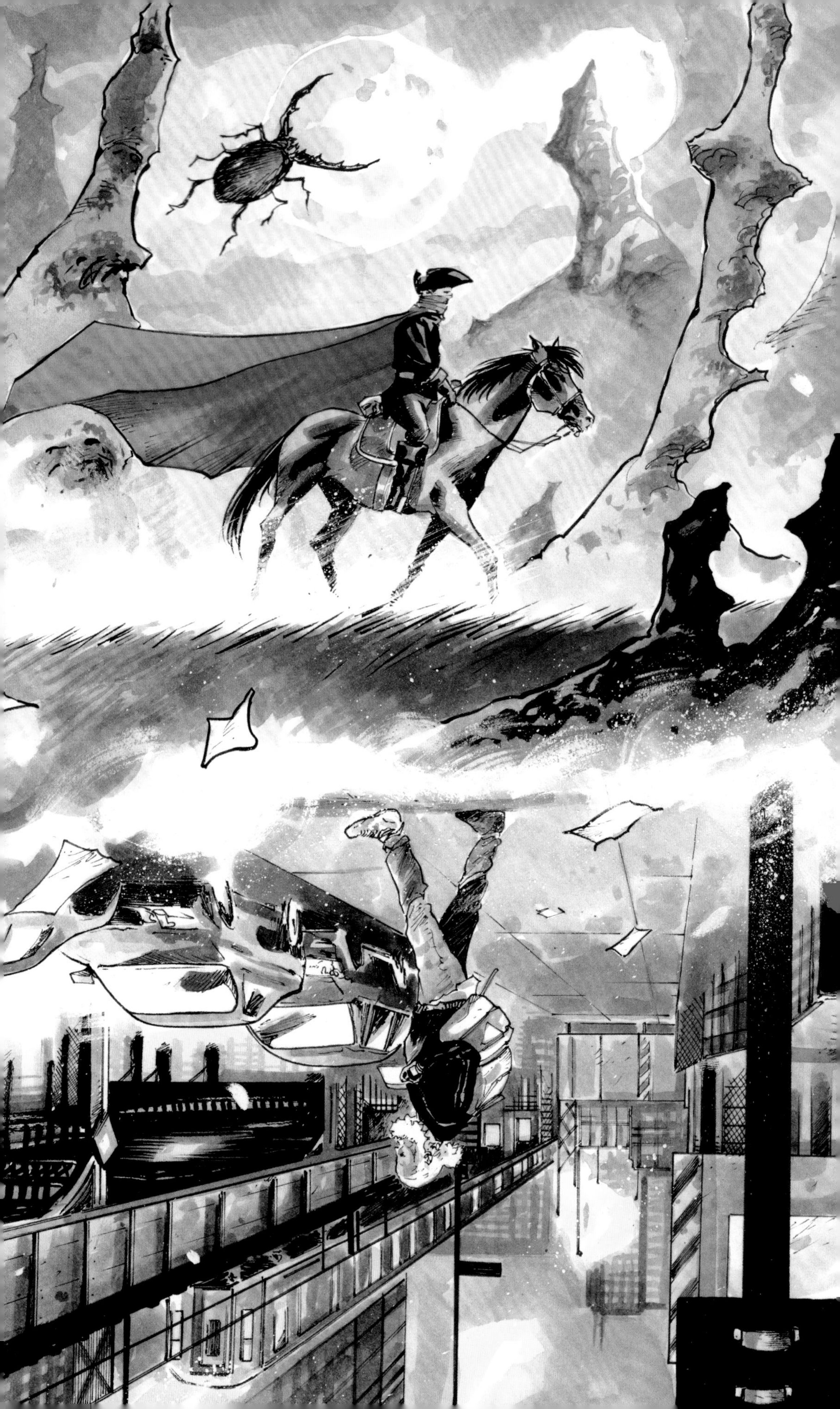

MISSING!

HAVE YOU SEEN THIS CHILD?
REWARD OFFERED
(123) 555-3455

SHR
PP

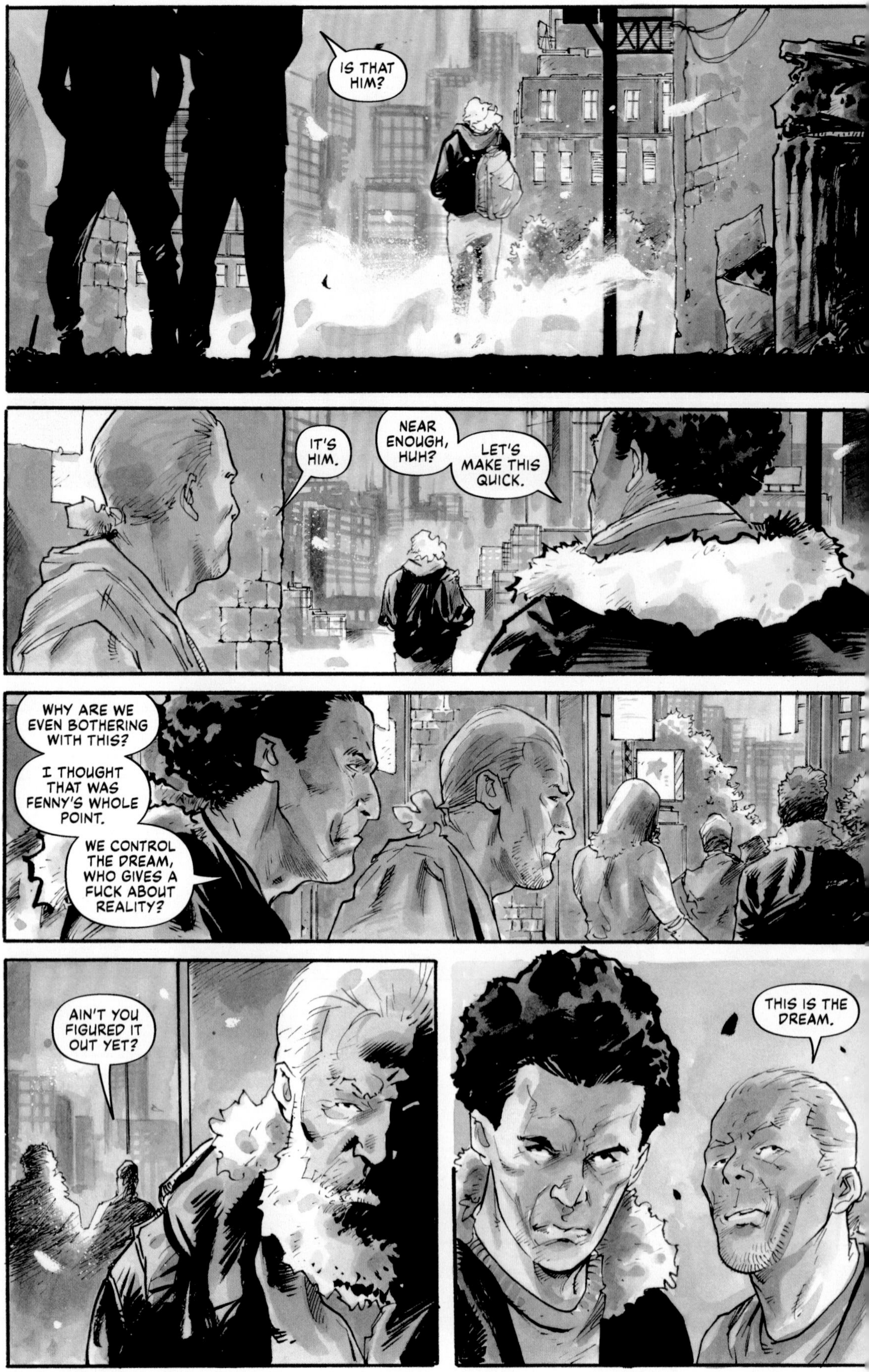
IS THAT HIM?
IT'S HIM.
NEAR ENOUGH, HUH?
LET'S MAKE THIS QUICK.
WHY ARE WE EVEN BOTHERING WITH THIS?
I THOUGHT THAT WAS FENNY'S WHOLE POINT.
WE CONTROL THE DREAM, WHO GIVES A FUCK ABOUT REALITY?
AIN'T YOU FIGURED IT OUT YET?
THIS IS THE DREAM.

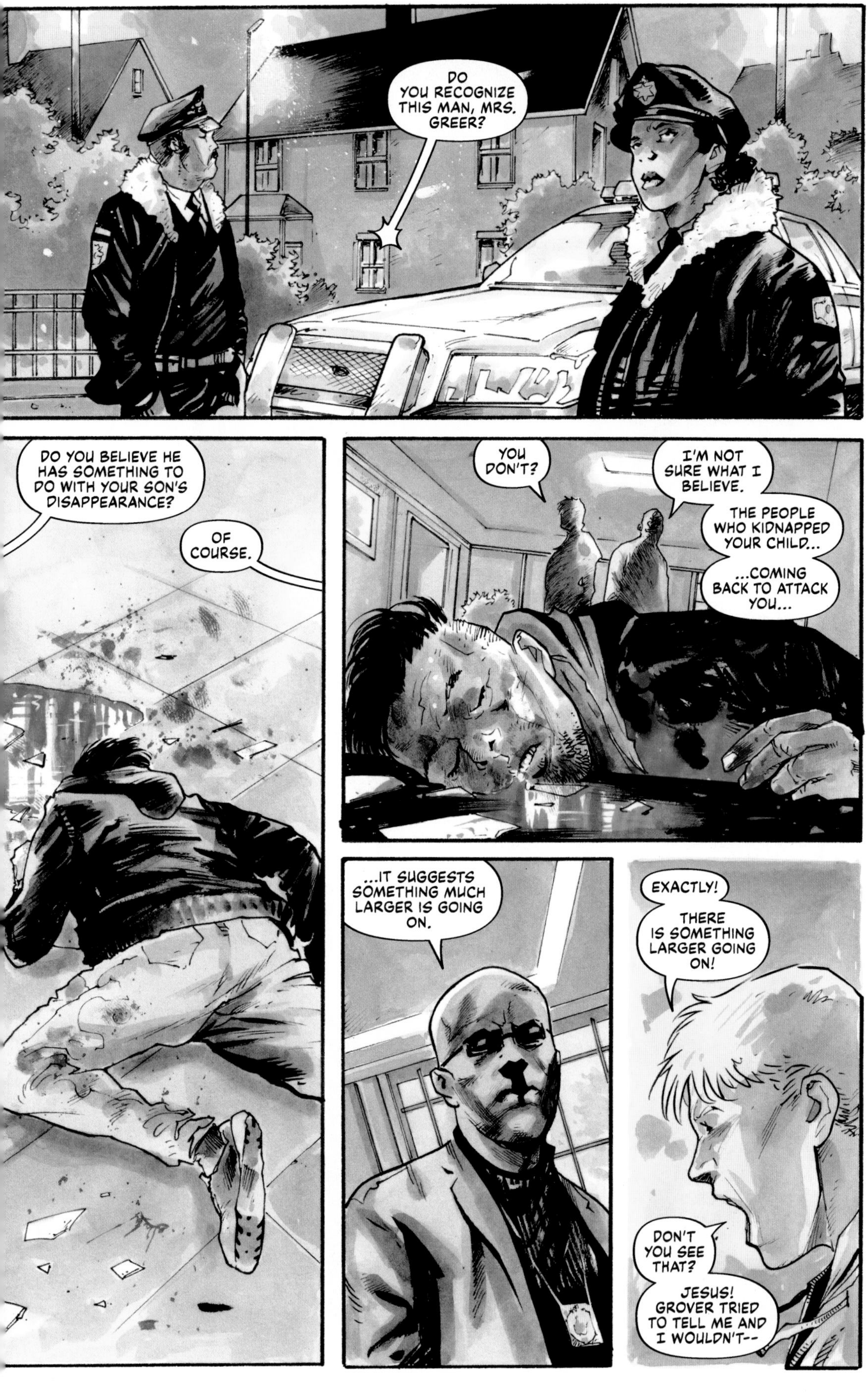
DO YOU RECOGNIZE THIS MAN, MRS. GREER?
DO YOU BELIEVE HE HAS SOMETHING TO DO WITH YOUR SON'S DISAPPEARANCE?
OF COURSE.
YOU DON'T?
I'M NOT SURE WHAT I BELIEVE.
THE PEOPLE WHO KIDNAPPED YOUR CHILD...
...COMING BACK TO ATTACK YOU...
...IT SUGGESTS SOMETHING MUCH LARGER IS GOING ON.
EXACTLY!
THERE IS SOMETHING LARGER GOING ON!
DON'T YOU SEE THAT?
JESUS! GROVER TRIED TO TELL ME AND I WOULDN'T--

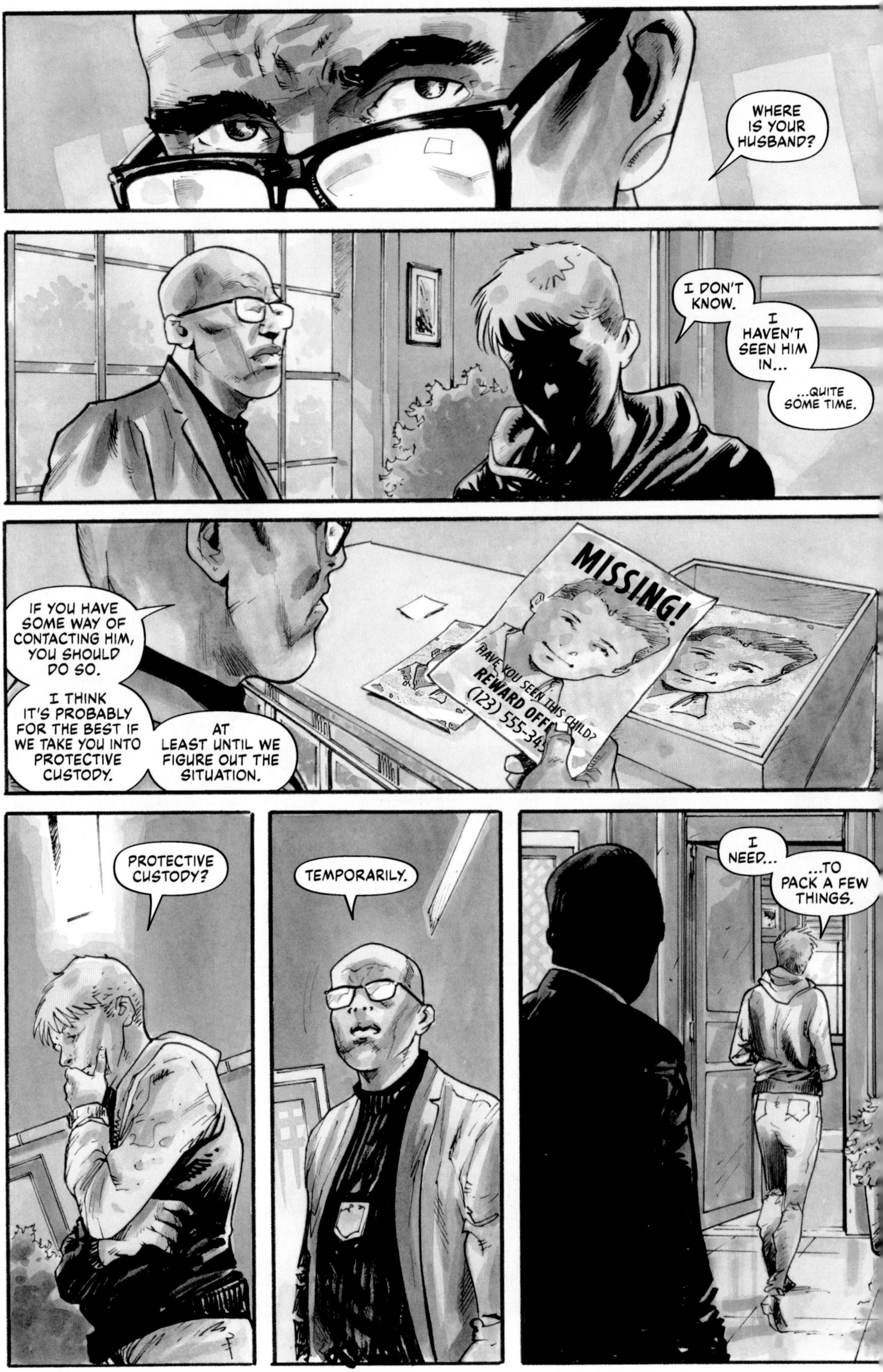
WHERE IS YOUR HUSBAND?
I DON'T KNOW.
I HAVEN'T SEEN HIM IN...
...QUITE SOME TIME.
MISSING!
HAVE YOU SEEN THIS CHILD?
IF YOU HAVE SOME WAY OF CONTACTING HIM, YOU SHOULD DO SO.
I THINK IT'S PROBABLY FOR THE BEST IF WE TAKE YOU INTO PROTECTIVE CUSTODY.
AT LEAST UNTIL WE FIGURE OUT THE SITUATION.
PROTECTIVE CUSTODY?
TEMPORARILY.
I NEED...
...TO PACK A FEW THINGS.

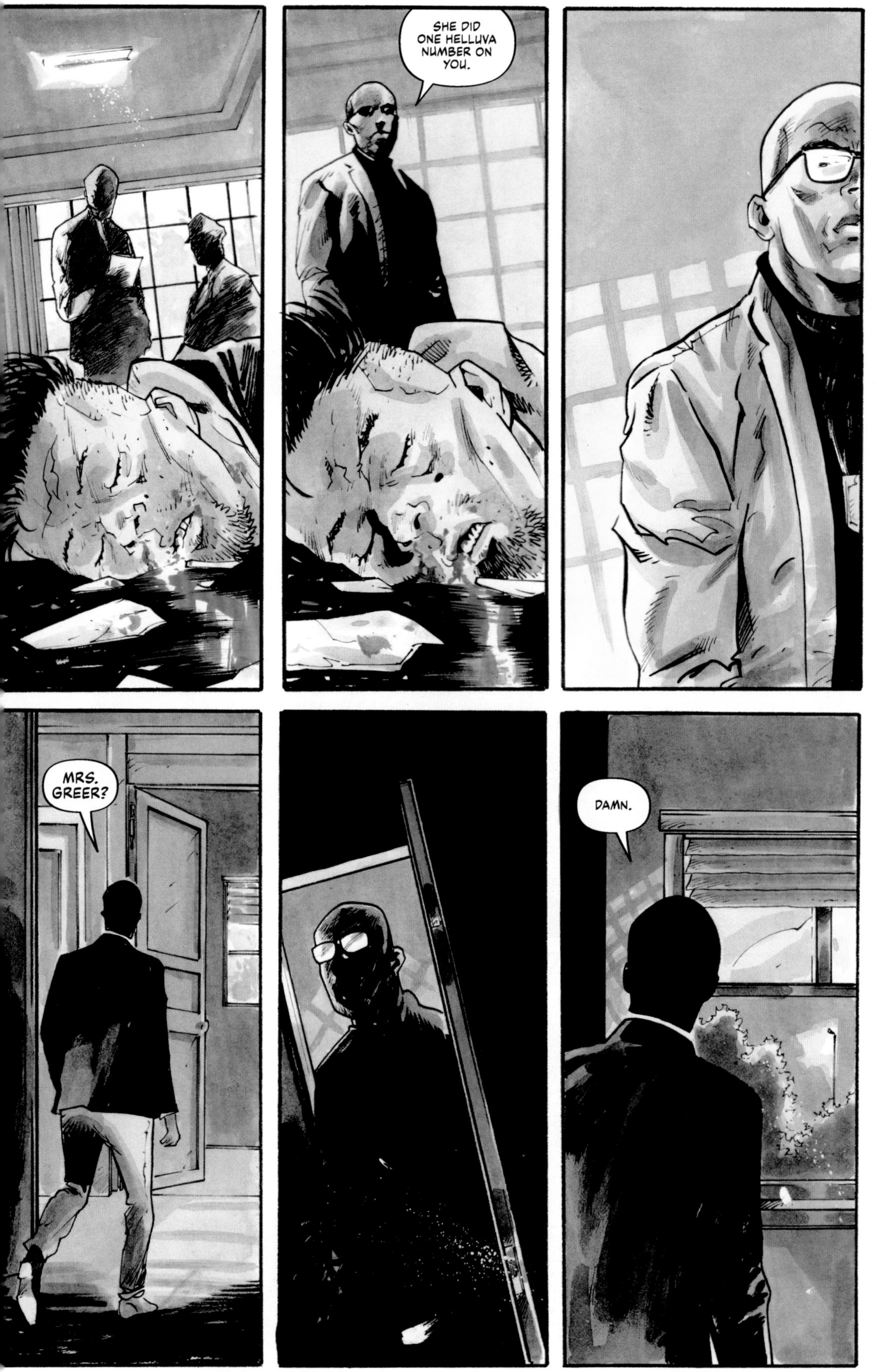
SHE DID ONE HELLUVA NUMBER ON YOU.
MRS. GREER?
DAMN.

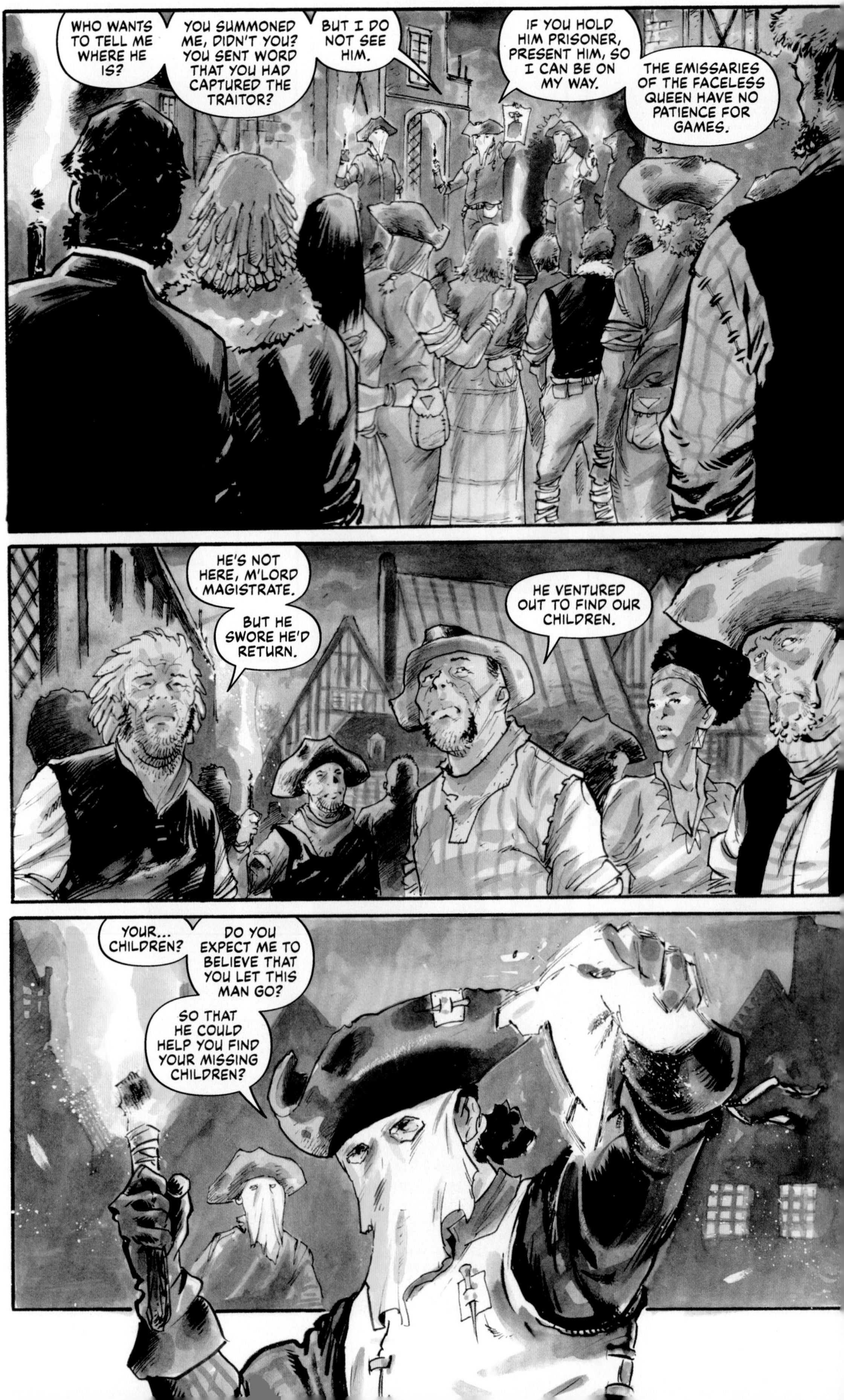
WHO WANTS TO TELL ME WHERE HE IS?
YOU SUMMONED ME, DIDN'T YOU? YOU SENT WORD THAT YOU HAD CAPTURED THE TRAITOR?
BUT I DO NOT SEE HIM.
IF YOU HOLD HIM PRISONER, PRESENT HIM, SO I CAN BE ON MY WAY.
THE EMISSARIES OF THE FACELESS QUEEN HAVE NO PATIENCE FOR GAMES.
HE'S NOT HERE, M'LORD MAGISTRATE.
BUT HE SWORE HE'D RETURN.
HE VENTURED OUT TO FIND OUR CHILDREN.
YOUR... CHILDREN?
DO YOU EXPECT ME TO BELIEVE THAT YOU LET THIS MAN GO?
SO THAT HE COULD HELP YOU FIND YOUR MISSING CHILDREN?

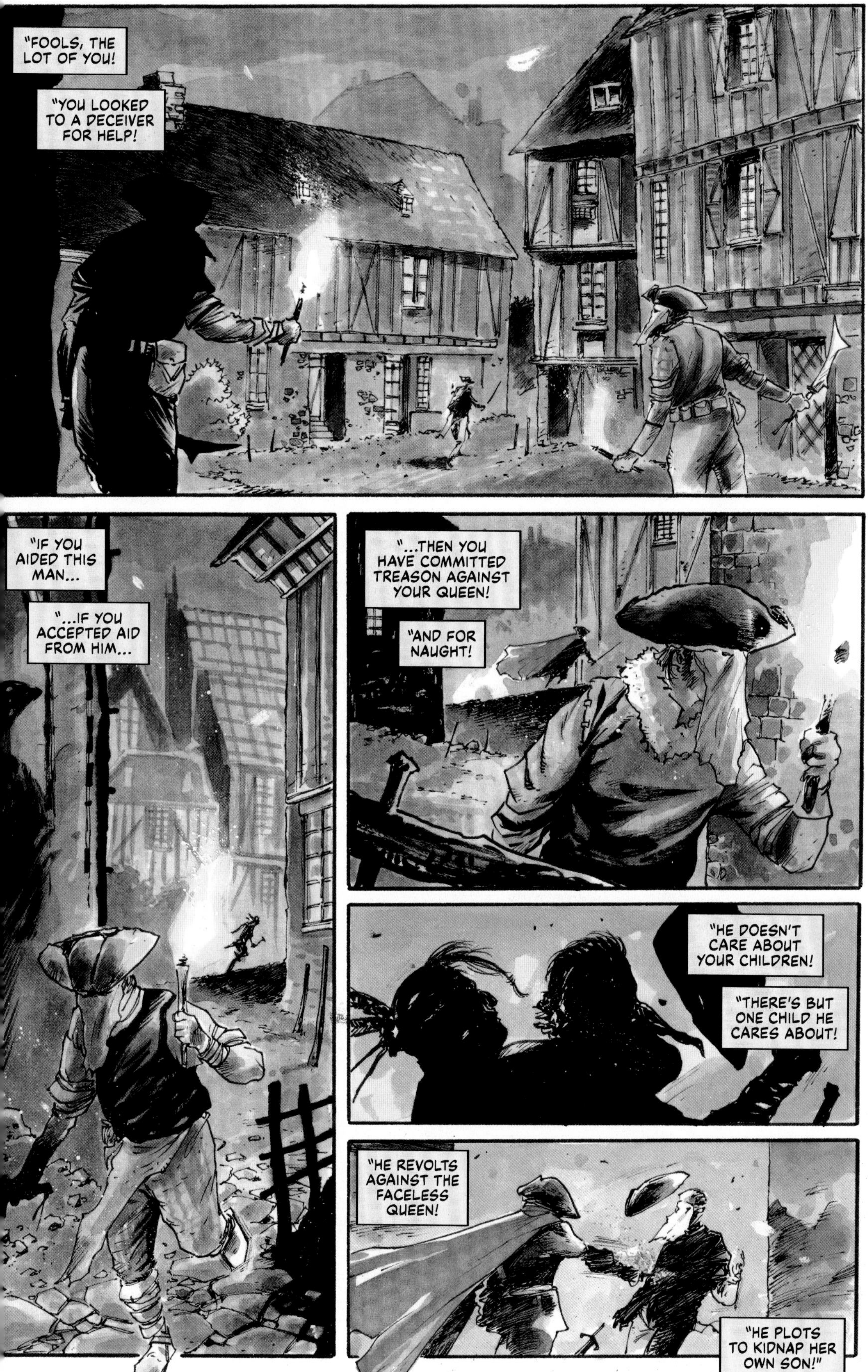

"FOOLS, THE LOT OF YOU!
"YOU LOOKED TO A DECEIVER FOR HELP!
"IF YOU AIDED THIS MAN...
"...IF YOU ACCEPTED AID FROM HIM...
"...THEN YOU HAVE COMMITTED TREASON AGAINST YOUR QUEEN!
"AND FOR NAUGHT!
"HE DOESN'T CARE ABOUT YOUR CHILDREN!
"THERE'S BUT ONE CHILD HE CARES ABOUT!
"HE REVOLTS AGAINST THE FACELESS QUEEN!
"HE PLOTS TO KIDNAP HER OWN SON!"

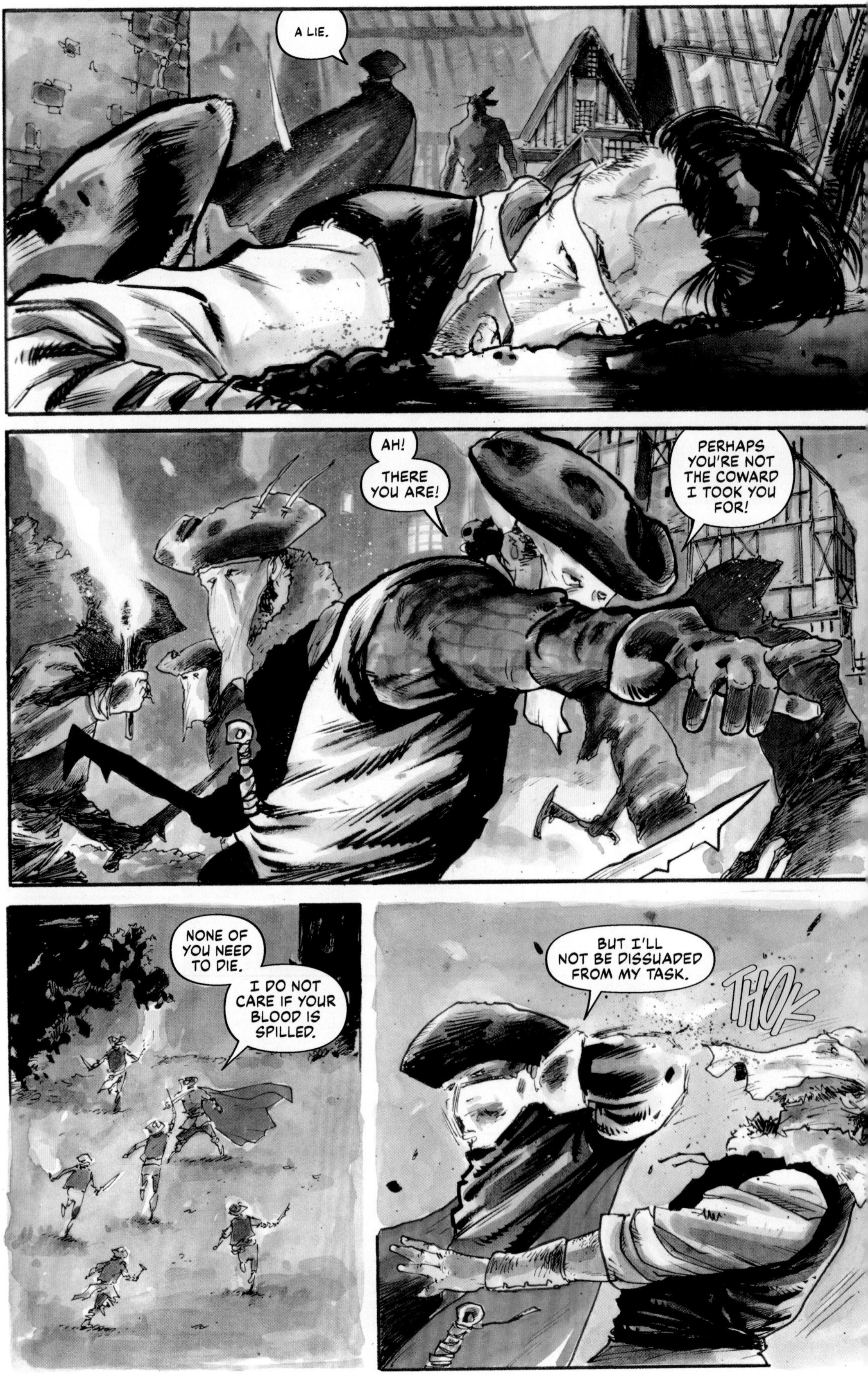
A LIE.
AH!
THERE YOU ARE!
PERHAPS YOU'RE NOT THE COWARD I TOOK YOU FOR!
NONE OF YOU NEED TO DIE.
I DO NOT CARE IF YOUR BLOOD IS SPILLED.
BUT I'LL NOT BE DISSUADED FROM MY TASK.
THOK

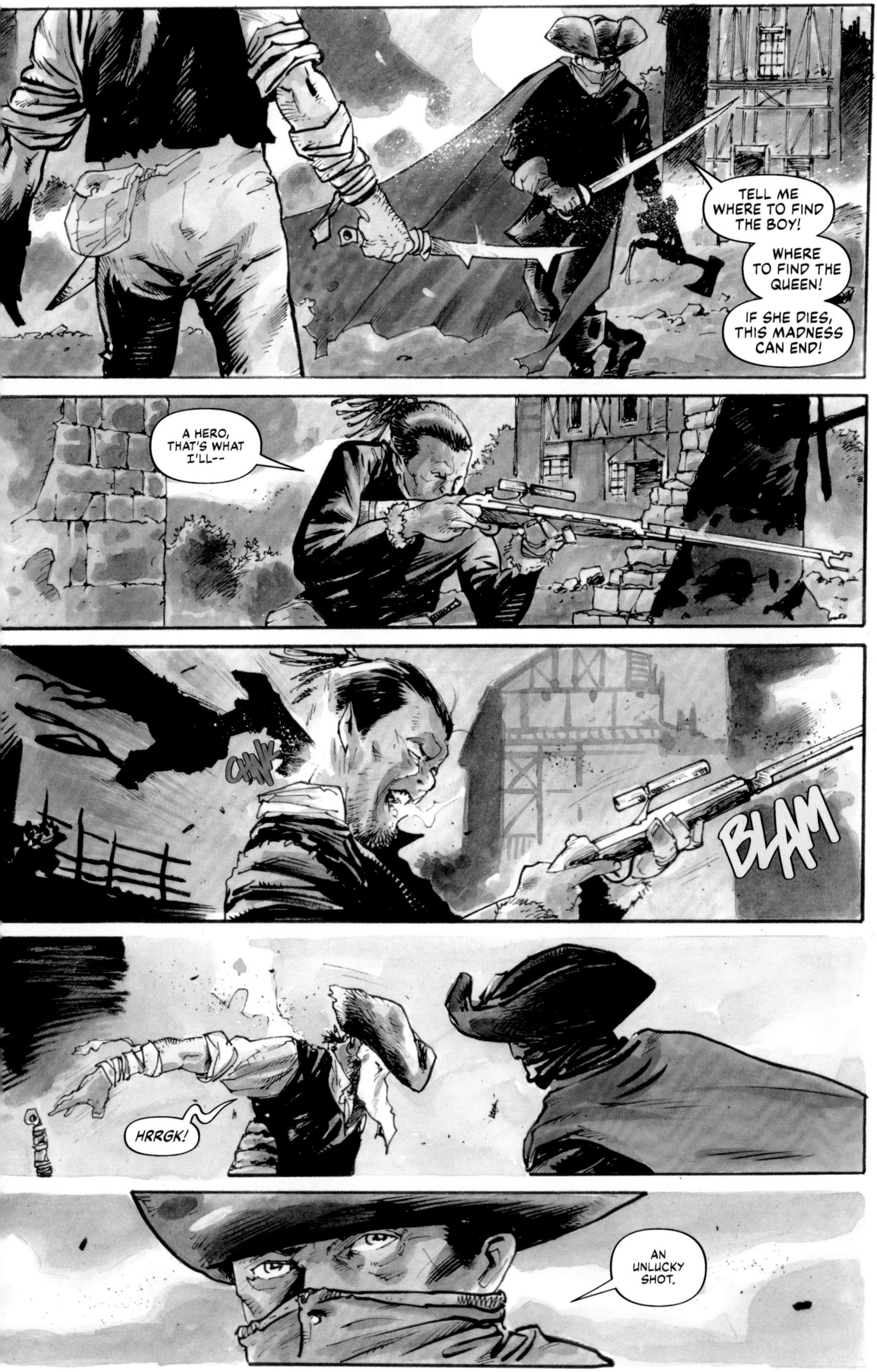
TELL ME WHERE TO FIND THE BOY!
WHERE TO FIND THE QUEEN!
IF SHE DIES, THIS MADNESS CAN END!
A HERO, THAT'S WHAT I'LL--
CHNK
BLAM
HRRGK!
AN UNLUCKY SHOT.

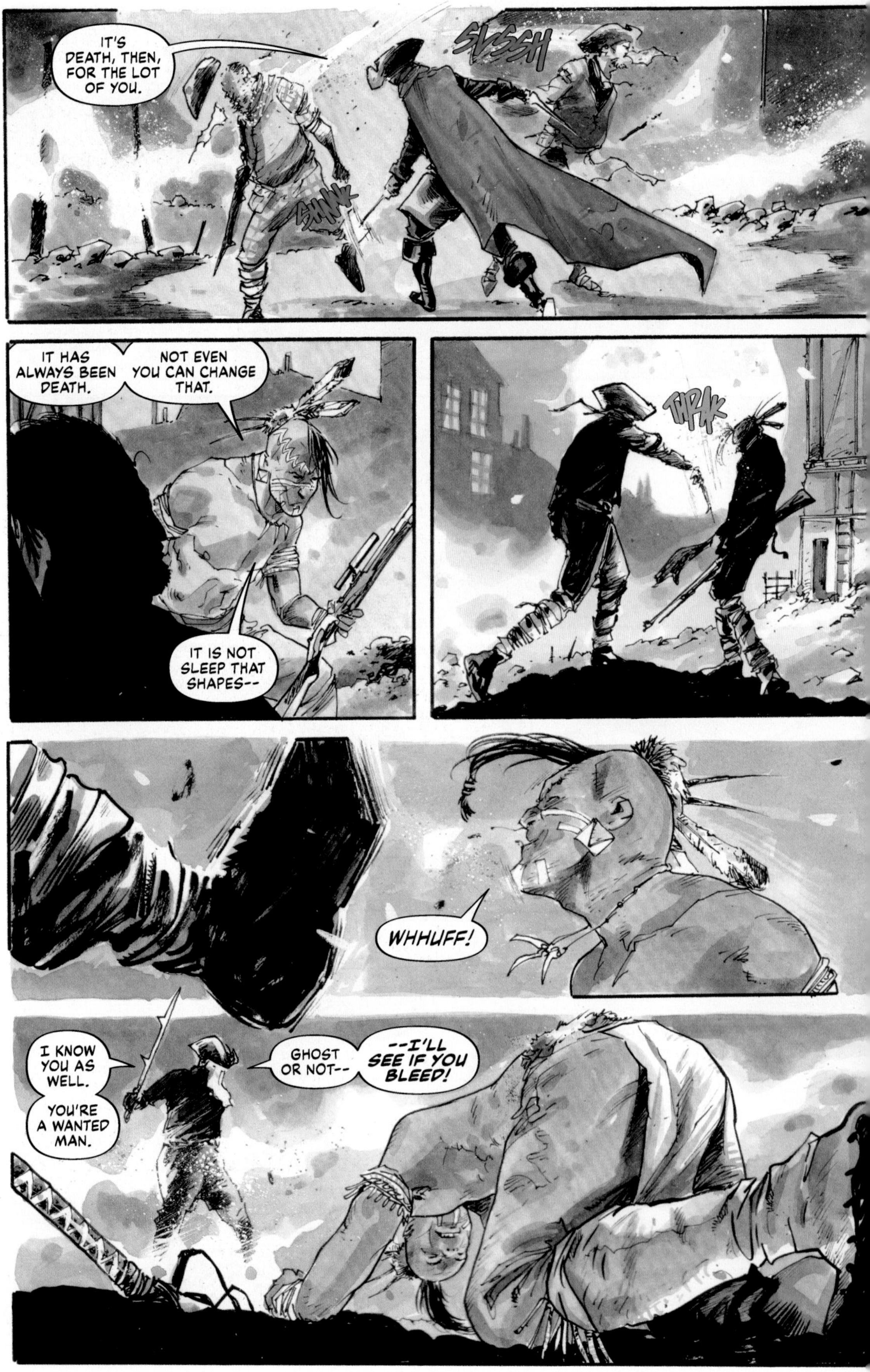
IT'S DEATH, THEN, FOR THE LOT OF YOU.
SVSSH
SHNK
IT HAS ALWAYS BEEN DEATH.
NOT EVEN YOU CAN CHANGE THAT.
IT IS NOT SLEEP THAT SHAPES--
THRAK
WHHUFF!
I KNOW YOU AS WELL.
YOU'RE A WANTED MAN.
GHOST OR NOT--
--I'LL SEE IF YOU BLEED!

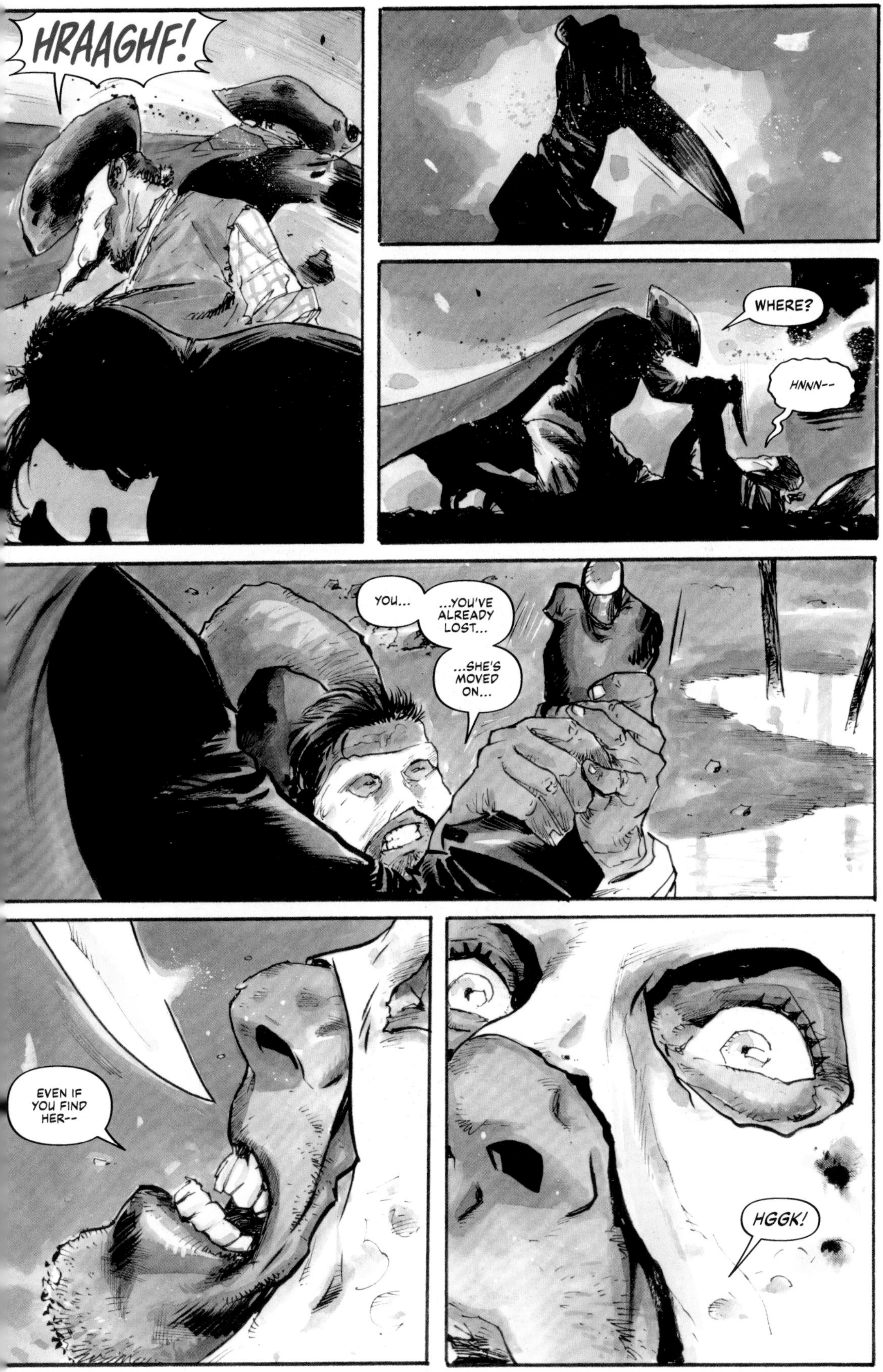

HRAAGHF!
WHERE?
HNNN--
YOU...
...YOU'VE ALREADY LOST...
...SHE'S MOVED ON...
EVEN IF YOU FIND HER--
HGGK!

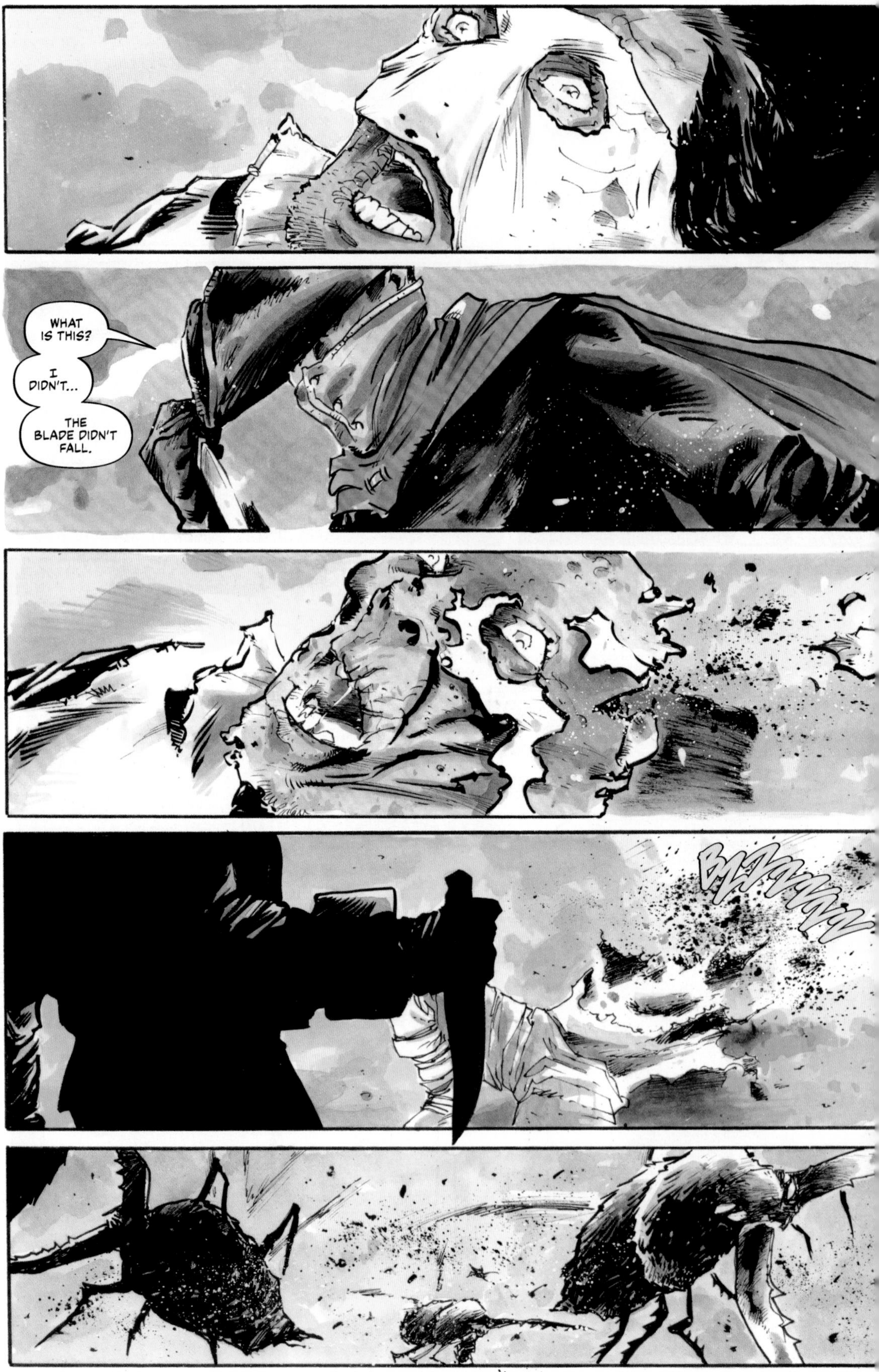

WHAT IS THIS?
I DIDN'T...
THE BLADE DIDN'T FALL.
BZZVVVVVV

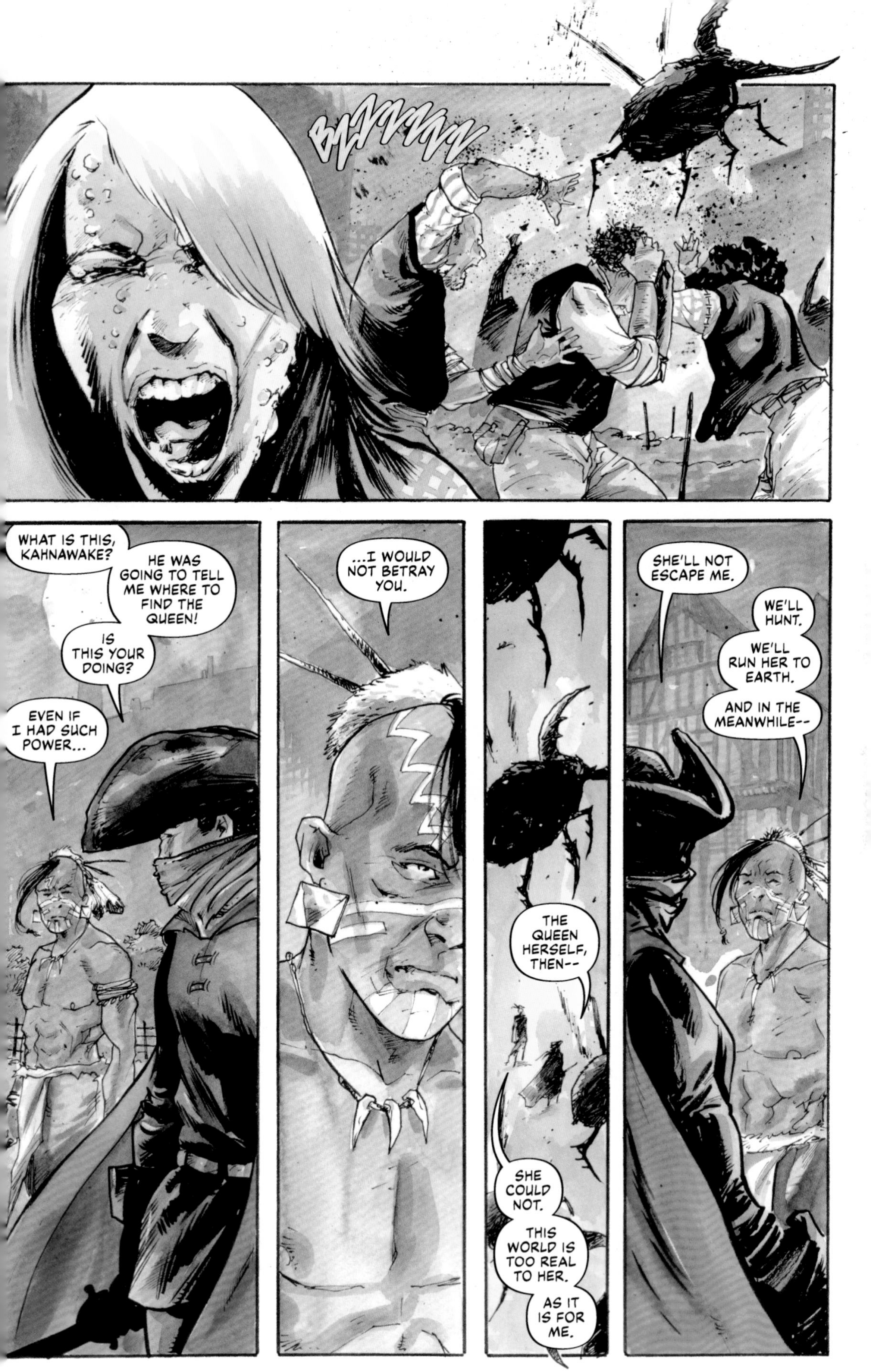
BZZZZZZZ
WHAT IS THIS, KAHNAWAKE?
HE WAS GOING TO TELL ME WHERE TO FIND THE QUEEN!
IS THIS YOUR DOING?
EVEN IF I HAD SUCH POWER...
...I WOULD NOT BETRAY YOU.
THE QUEEN HERSELF, THEN--
SHE COULD NOT.
THIS WORLD IS TOO REAL TO HER.
AS IT IS FOR ME.
SHE'LL NOT ESCAPE ME.
WE'LL HUNT.
WE'LL RUN HER TO EARTH.
AND IN THE MEANWHILE--

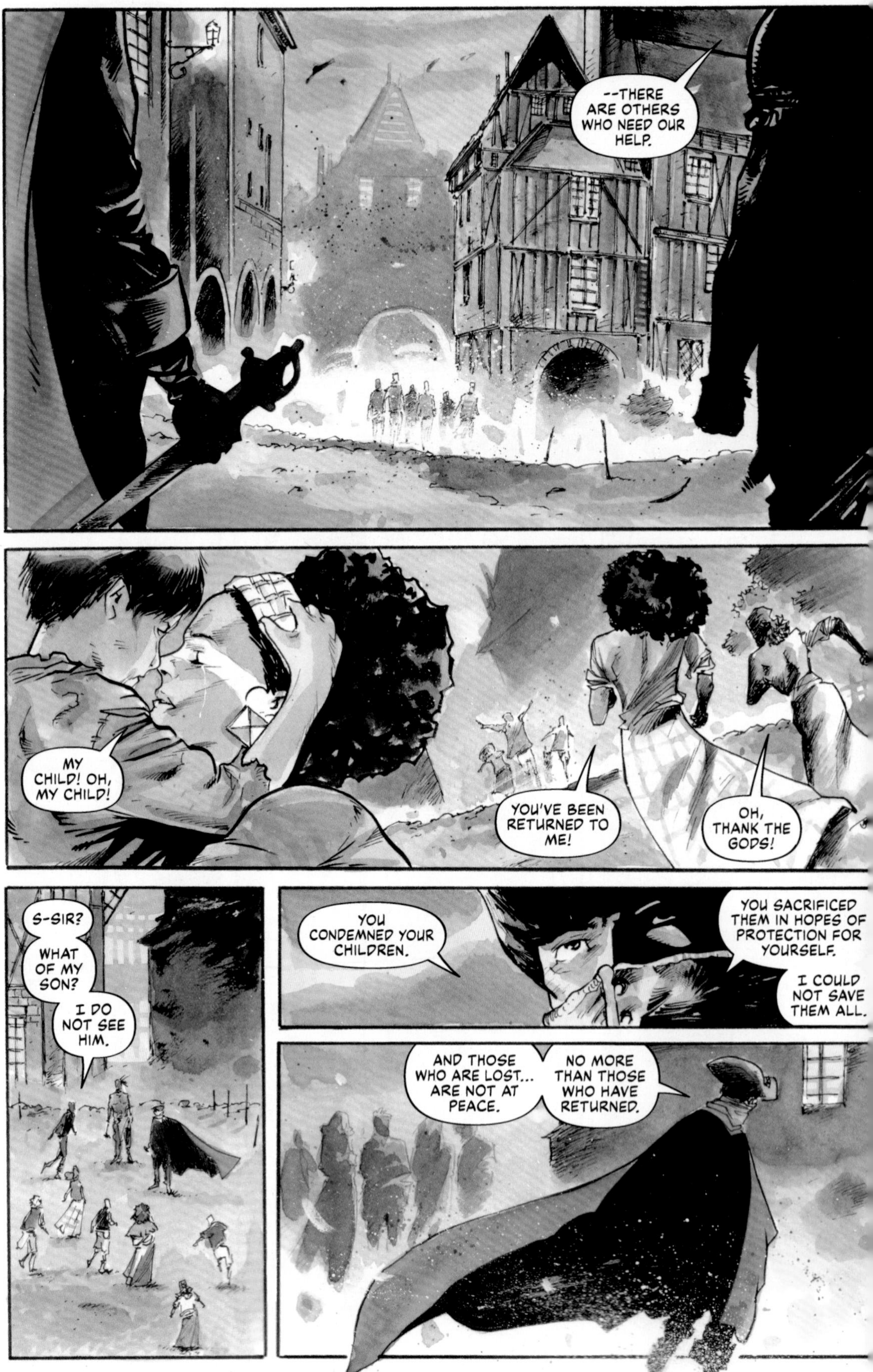
--THERE ARE OTHERS WHO NEED OUR HELP.
MY CHILD! OH, MY CHILD!
YOU'VE BEEN RETURNED TO ME!
OH, THANK THE GODS!
S-SIR?
WHAT OF MY SON?
I DO NOT SEE HIM.
YOU CONDEMNED YOUR CHILDREN.
YOU SACRIFICED THEM IN HOPES OF PROTECTION FOR YOURSELF.
I COULD NOT SAVE THEM ALL.
AND THOSE WHO ARE LOST... ARE NOT AT PEACE.
NO MORE THAN THOSE WHO HAVE RETURNED.

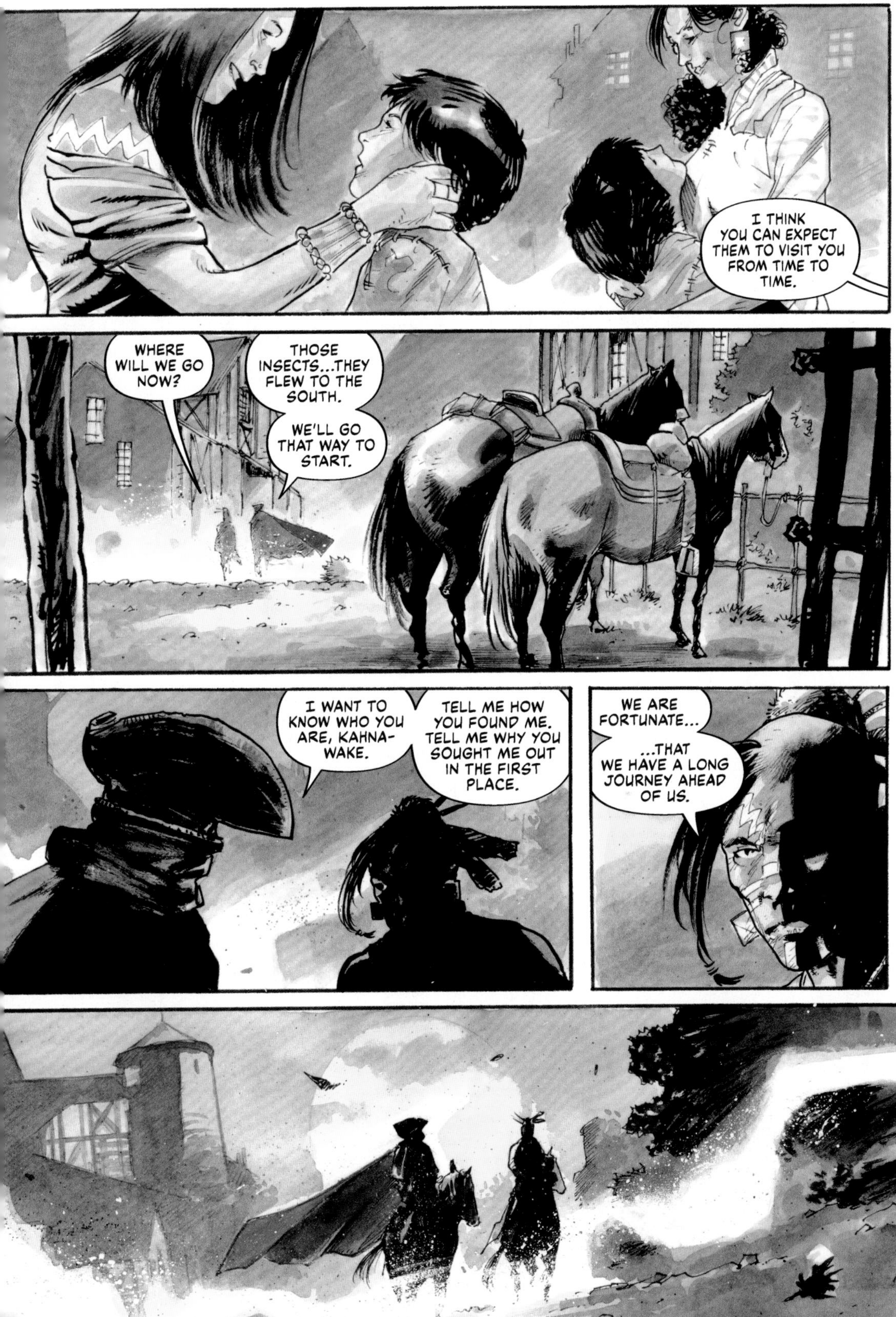
I THINK YOU CAN EXPECT THEM TO VISIT YOU FROM TIME TO TIME.
WHERE WILL WE GO NOW?
THOSE INSECTS...THEY FLEW TO THE SOUTH.
WE'LL GO THAT WAY TO START.
I WANT TO KNOW WHO YOU ARE, KAHNA-WAKE.
TELL ME HOW YOU FOUND ME. TELL ME WHY YOU SOUGHT ME OUT IN THE FIRST PLACE.
WE ARE FORTUNATE...
...THAT WE HAVE A LONG JOURNEY AHEAD OF US.

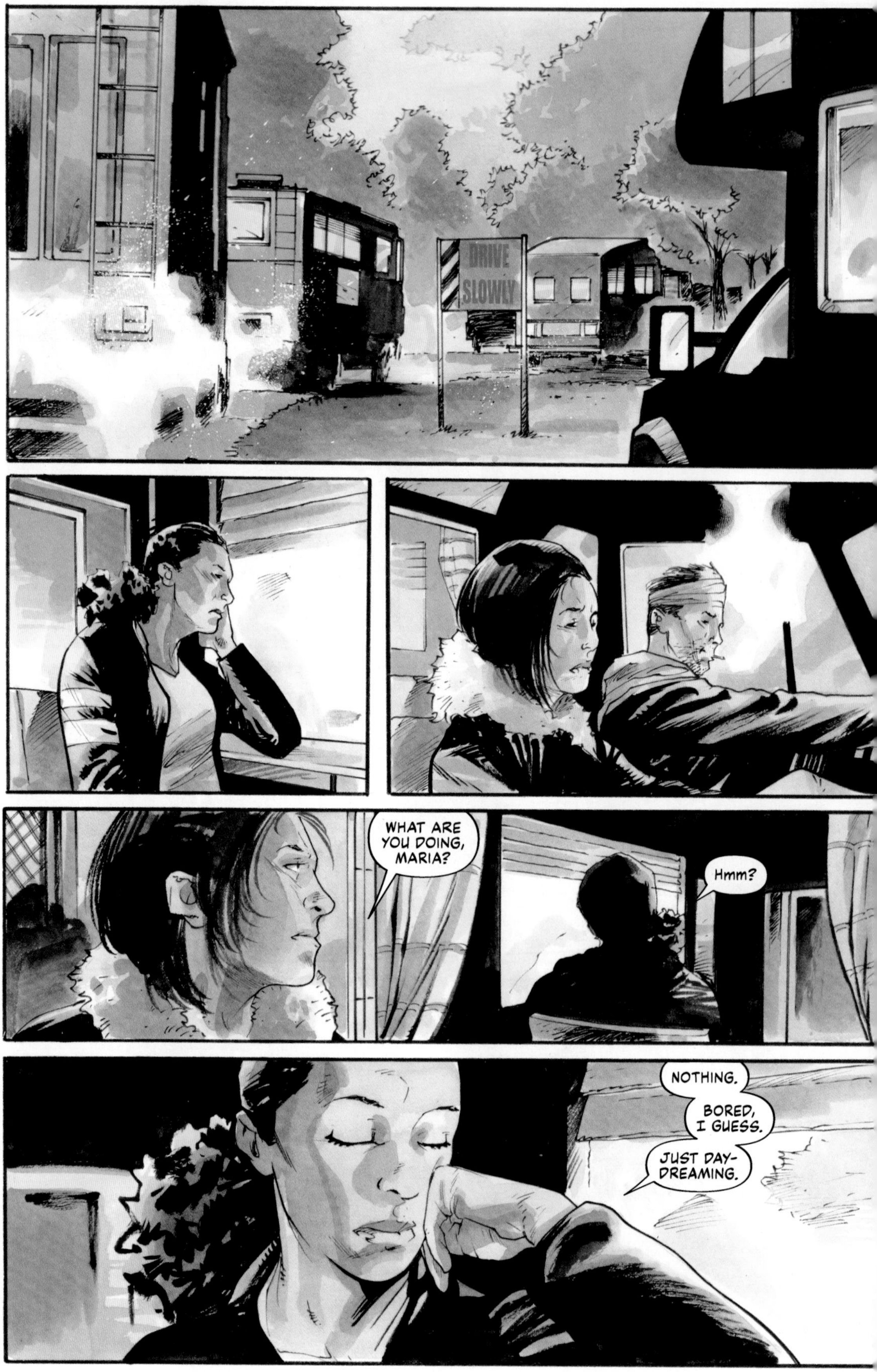
DRIVE SLOWLY
WHAT ARE YOU DOING, MARIA?
Hmm?
NOTHING.
BORED, I GUESS.
JUST DAY-DREAMING.

"DAY-DREAMING," SHE SAYS.

Heh.

YOU BUTTON THAT UP, GET ME?

YOUR DREAMS--DAY OR NIGHT--BELONG TO US NOW.

AND YOU FOCUS ON THE REAL WORLD UNLESS I TELL YOU OTHERWISE.

YOU GET ME?

YES, FENNY.

I GET YOU.

I...

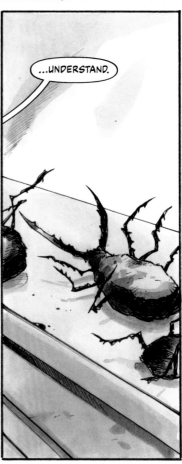

...UNDERSTAND.

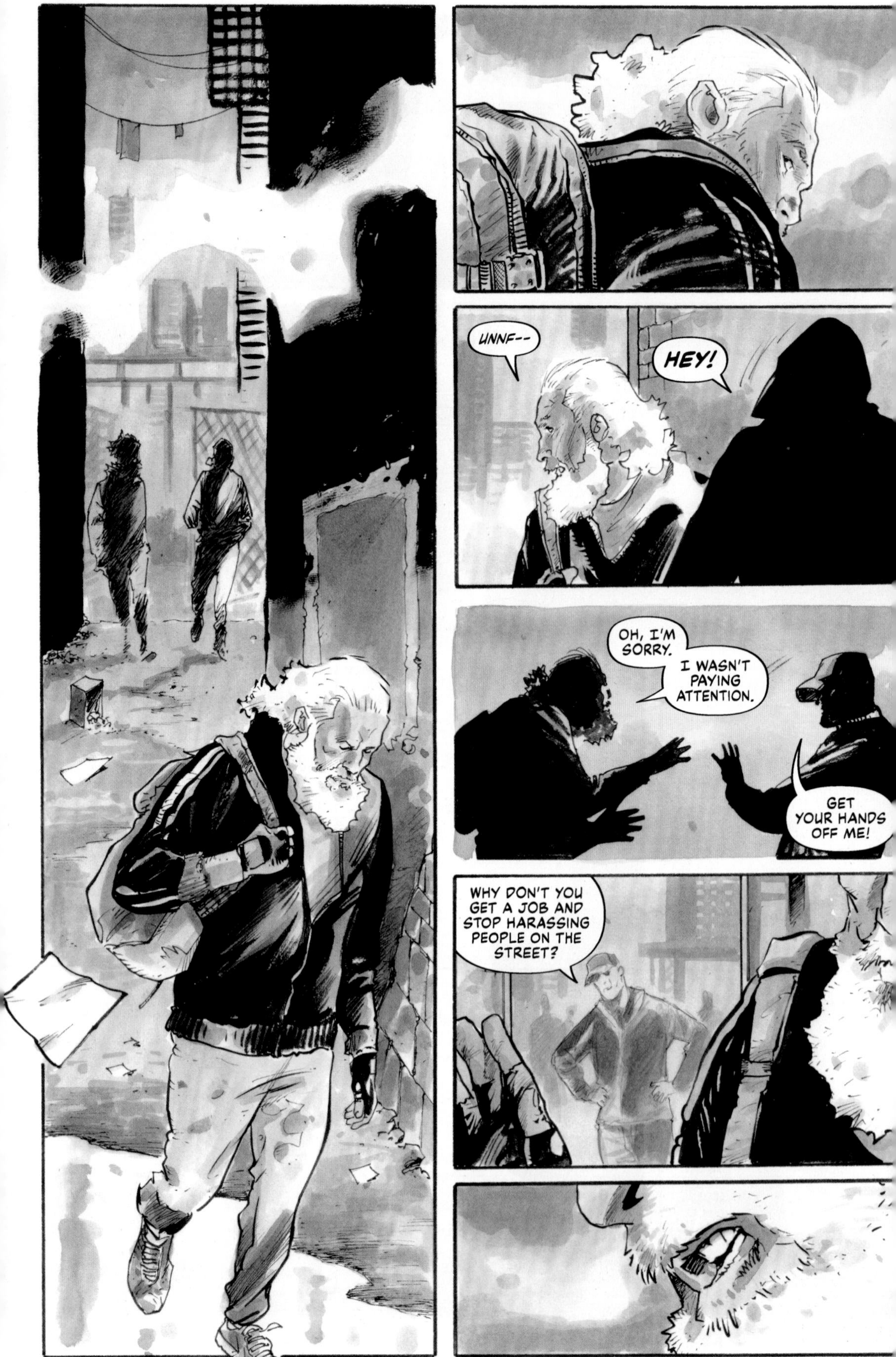
UNNF--
HEY!
OH, I'M SORRY.
I WASN'T PAYING ATTENTION.
GET YOUR HANDS OFF ME!
WHY DON'T YOU GET A JOB AND STOP HARASSING PEOPLE ON THE STREET?

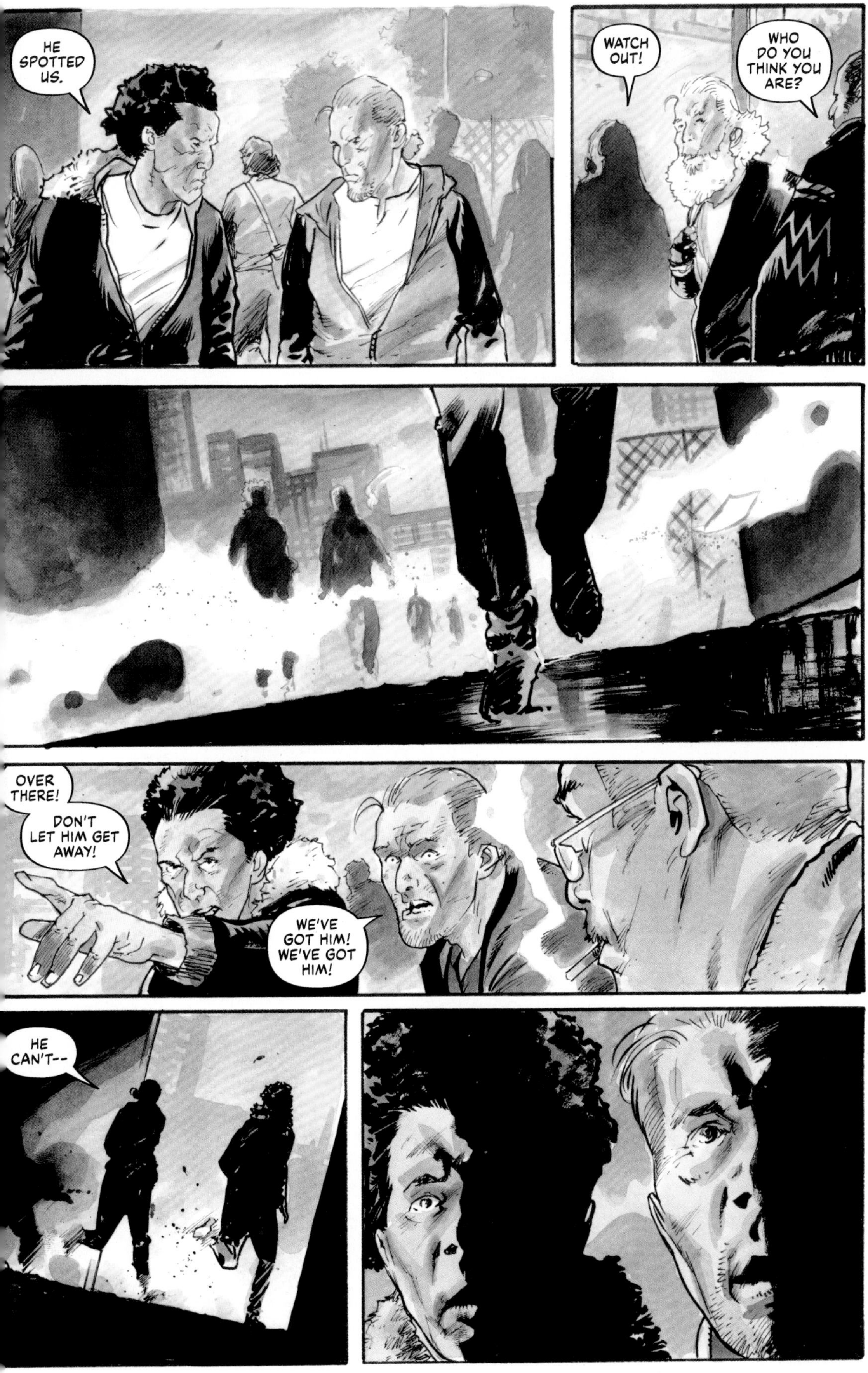
HE SPOTTED US.
WATCH OUT!
WHO DO YOU THINK YOU ARE?
OVER THERE!
DON'T LET HIM GET AWAY!
WE'VE GOT HIM! WE'VE GOT HIM!
HE CAN'T--

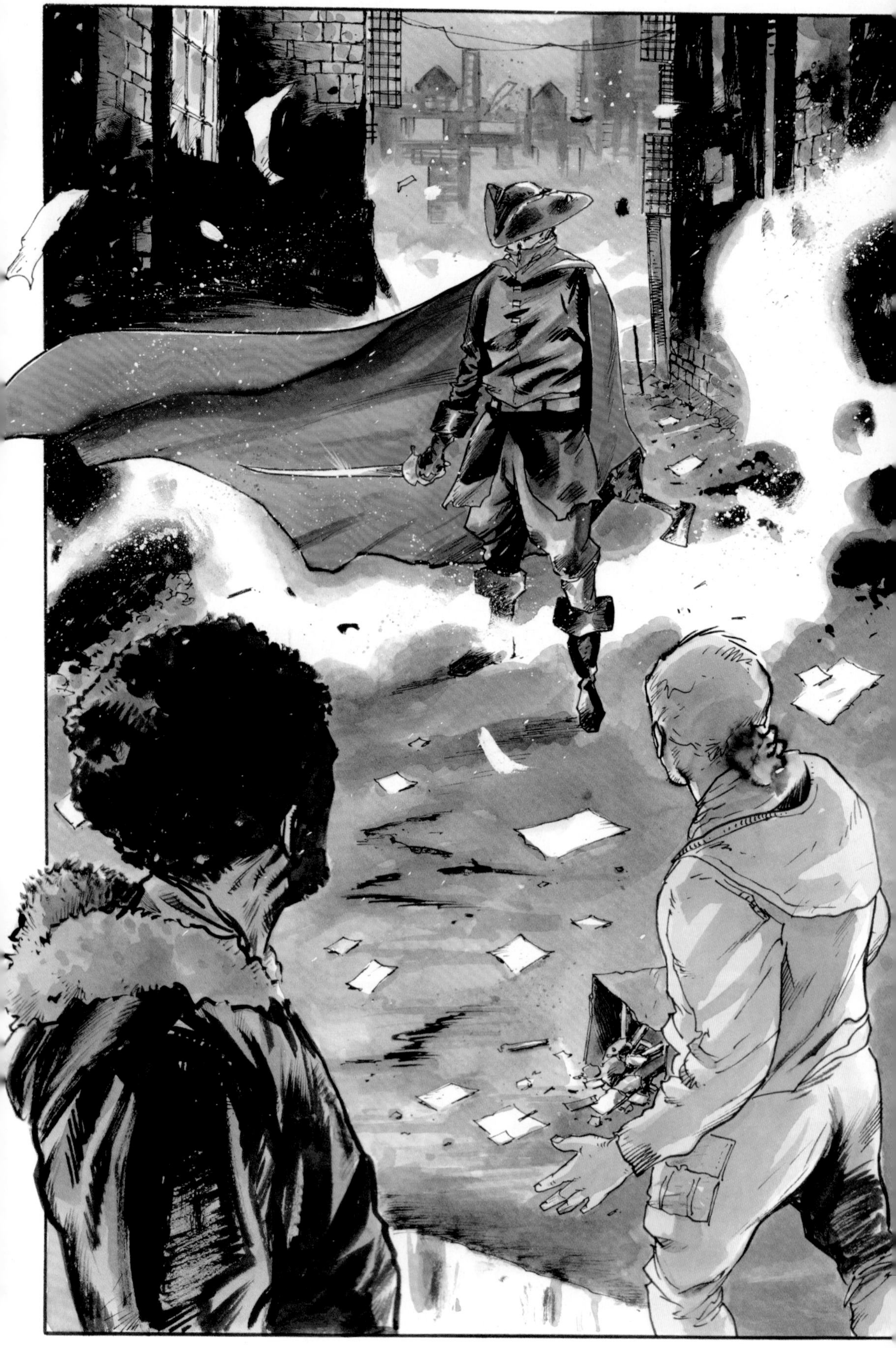

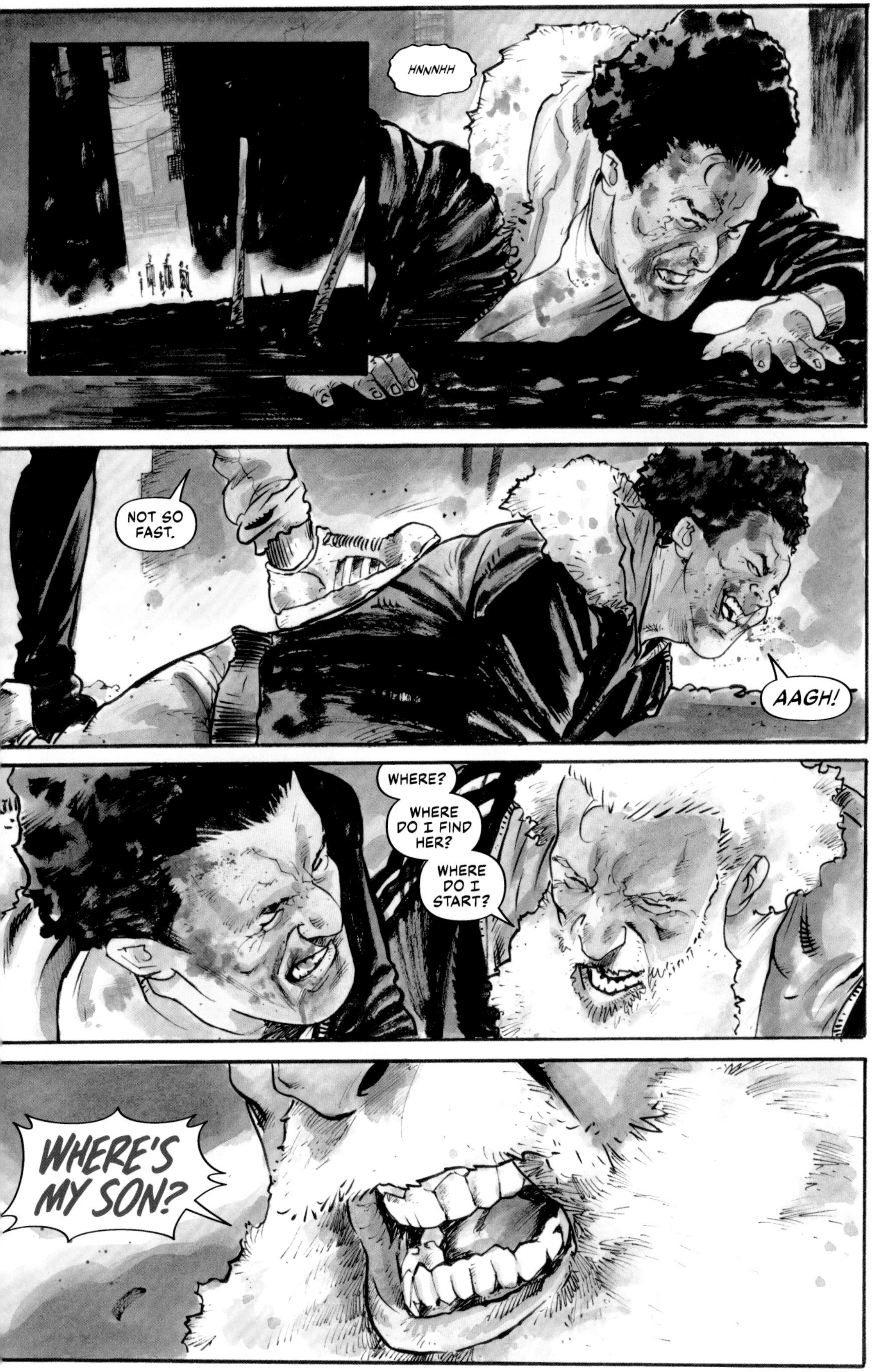
HNNNHH
NOT SO FAST.
AAGH!
WHERE?
WHERE DO I FIND HER?
WHERE DO I START?
WHERE'S MY SON?

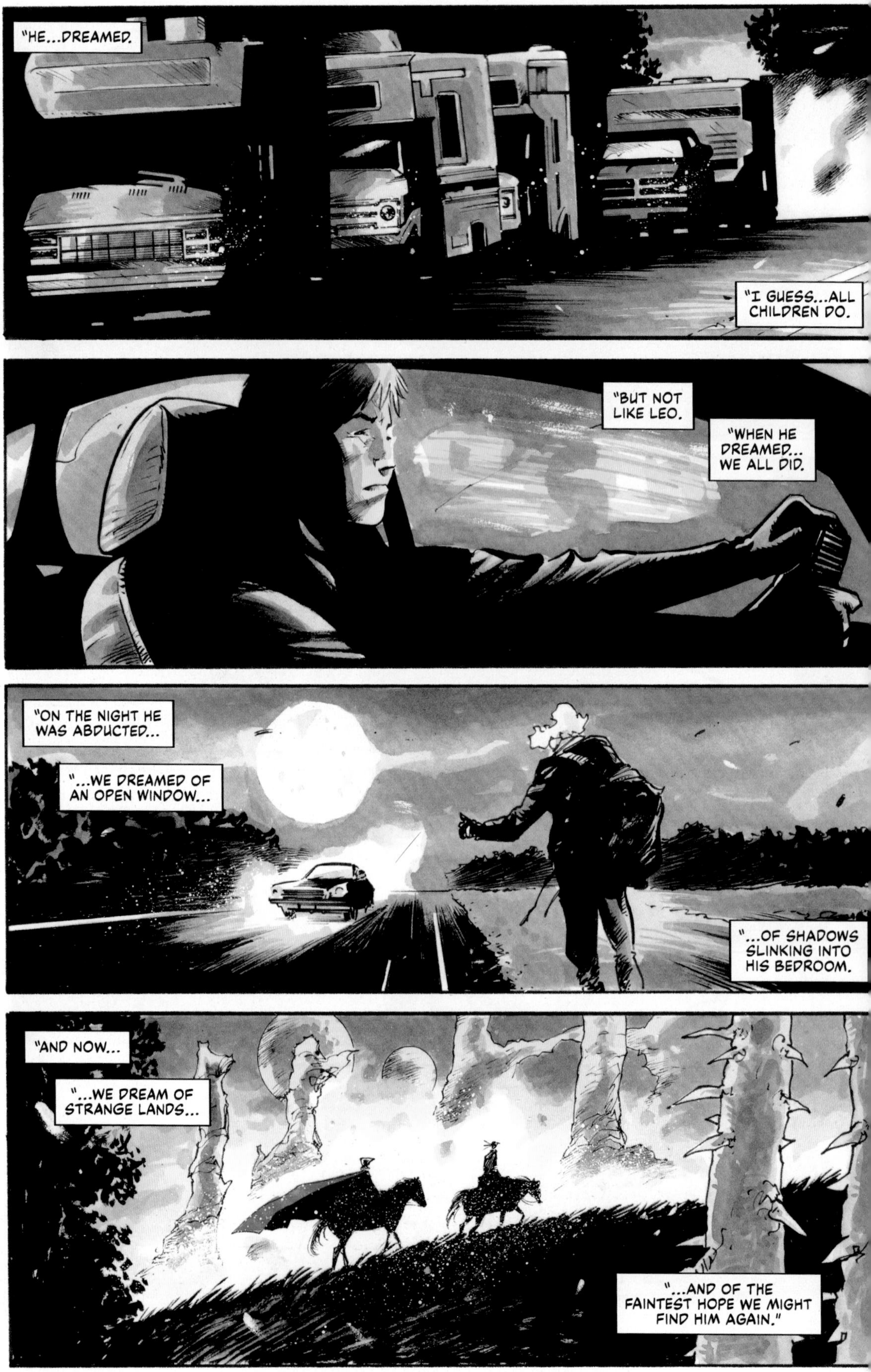
"HE...DREAMED.
"I GUESS...ALL CHILDREN DO.
"BUT NOT LIKE LEO.
"WHEN HE DREAMED... WE ALL DID.
"ON THE NIGHT HE WAS ABDUCTED...
"...WE DREAMED OF AN OPEN WINDOW...
"...OF SHADOWS SLINKING INTO HIS BEDROOM.
"AND NOW...
"...WE DREAM OF STRANGE LANDS...
"...AND OF THE FAINTEST HOPE WE MIGHT FIND HIM AGAIN."

Parasomnia #1 CVR B by **RAFAEL ALBUQUERQUE**

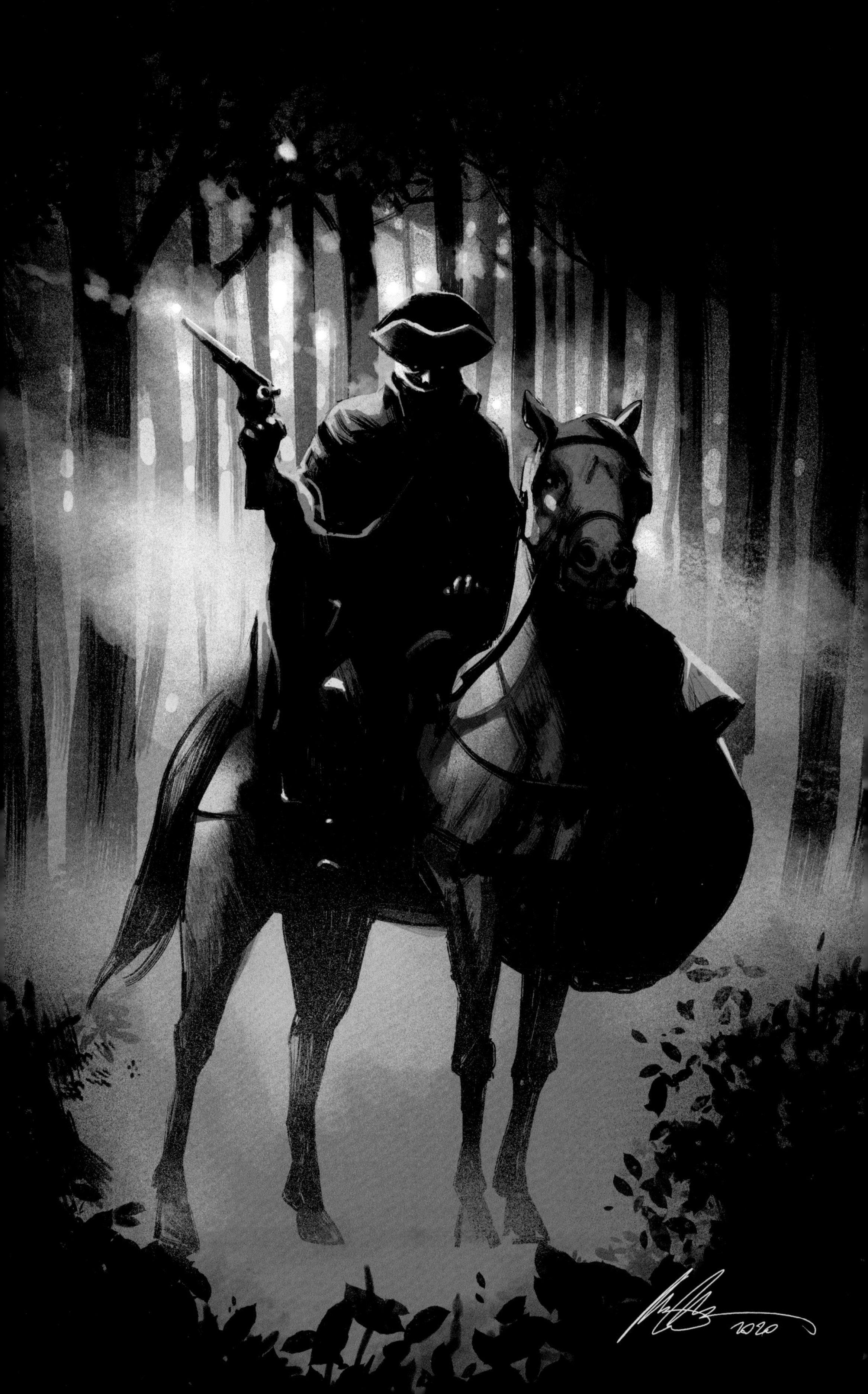

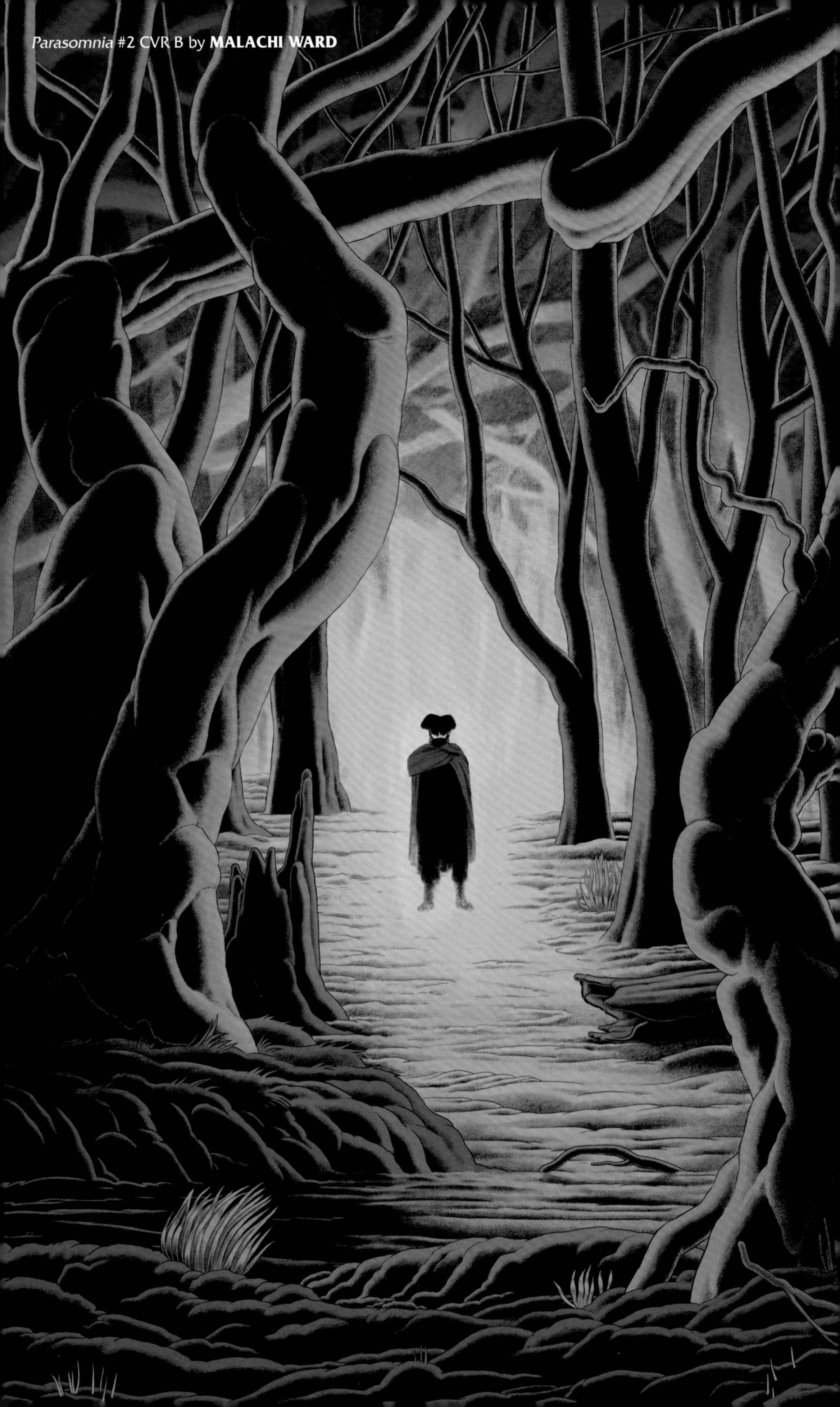

Parasomnia #2 CVR B by **MALACHI WARD**

Parasomnia #3 CVR B by
PATRIC REYNOLDS WITH LEE LOUGHRIDGE

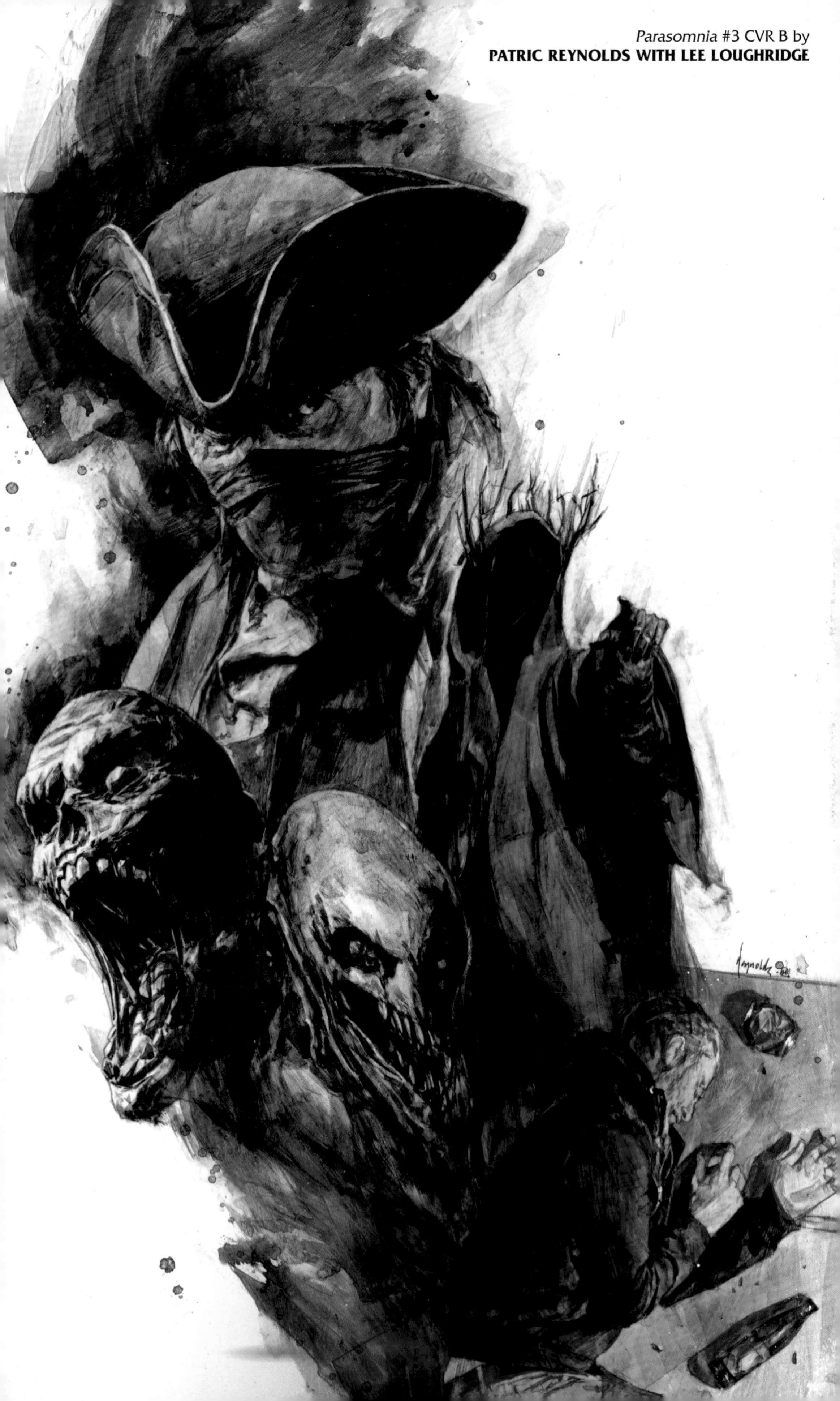

Parasomnia #4 CVR B by **TYLER CROOK**

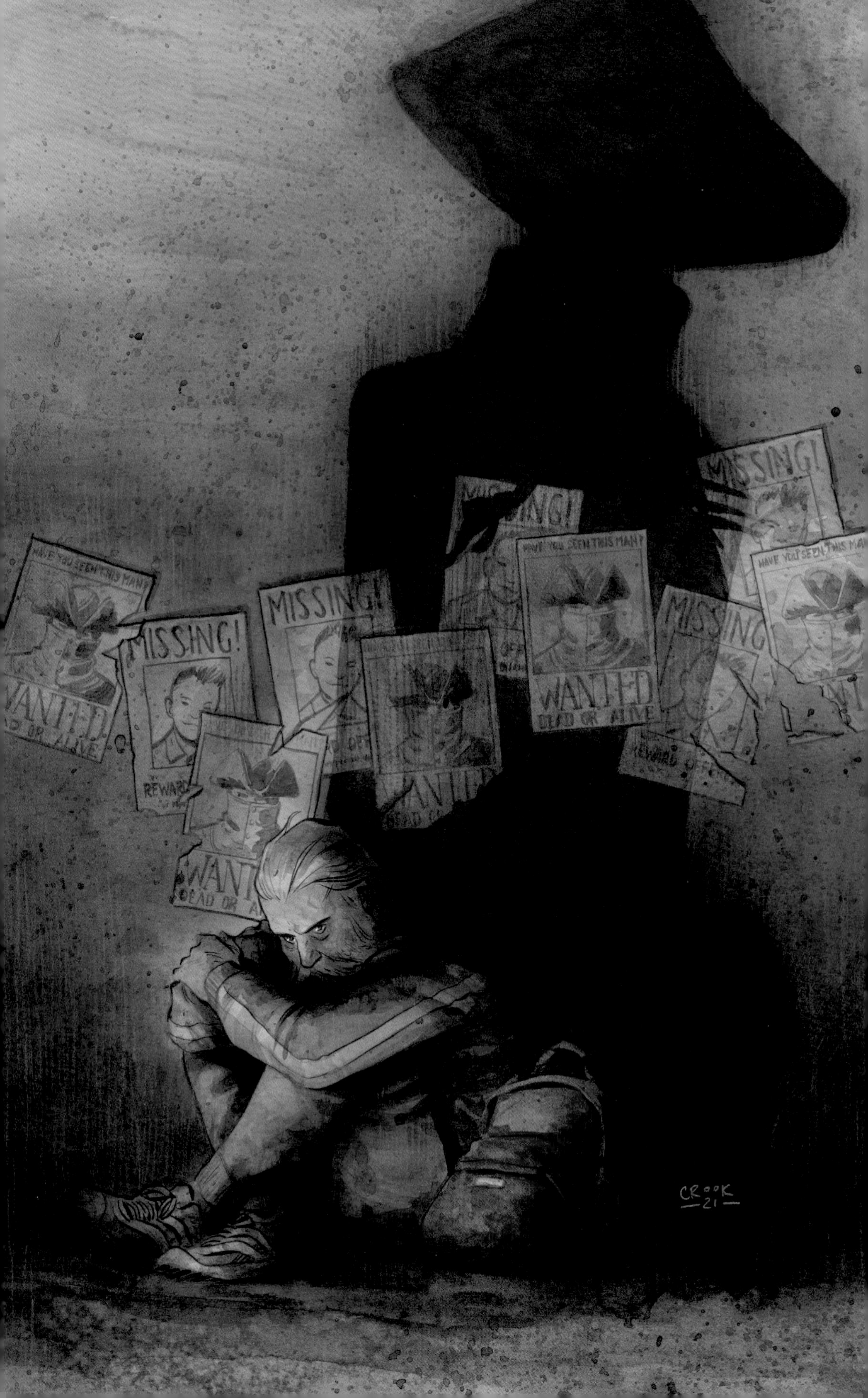
MISSING!
HAVE YOU SEEN THIS MAN?
WANTED
DEAD OR ALIVE
REWARD
CROOK 21

PARASOMNIA™

BUNN • MUTTI • BOWLAND

SKETCHBOOK

NOTES BY ANDREA MUTTI

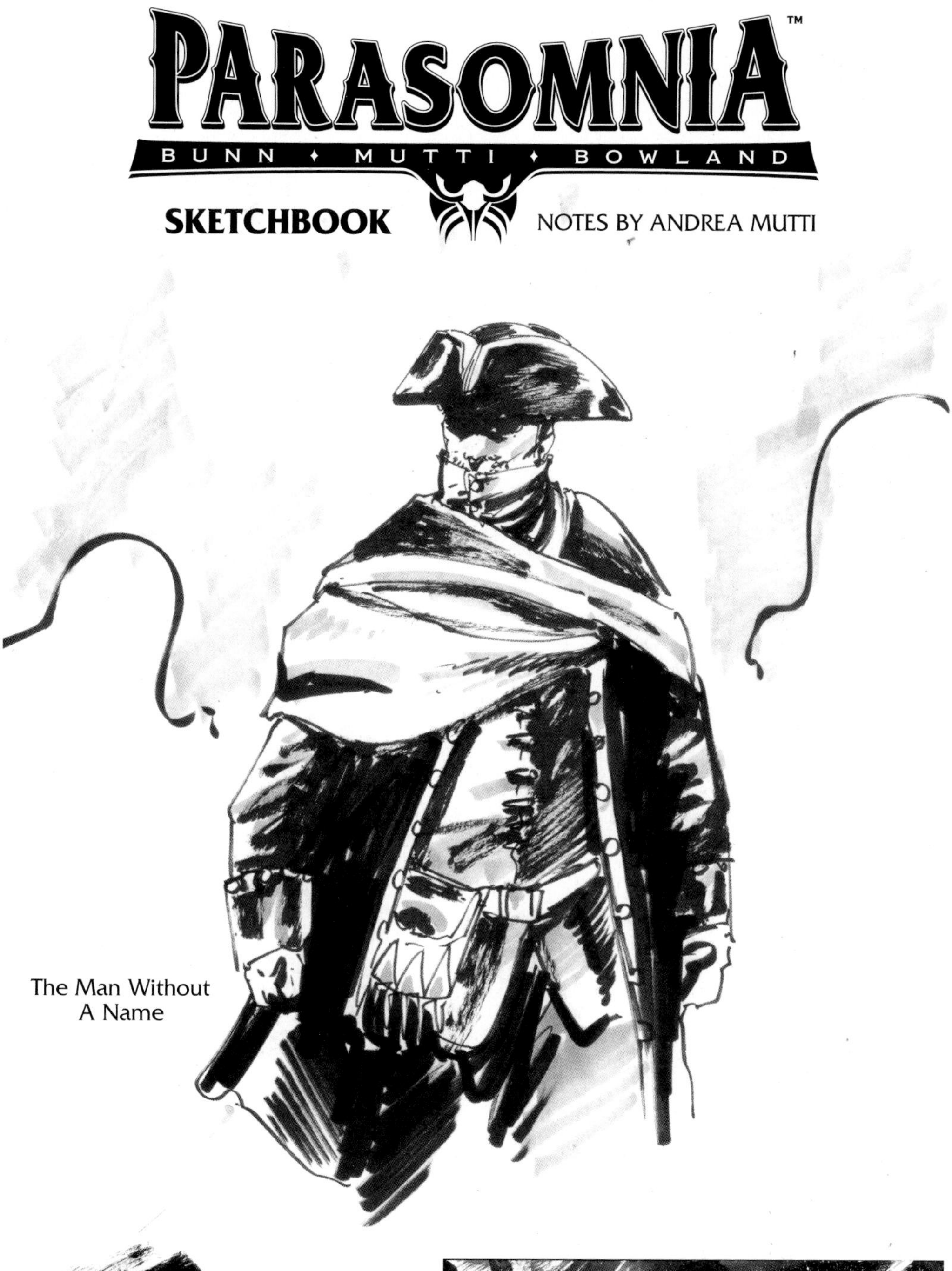

The Man Without
A Name

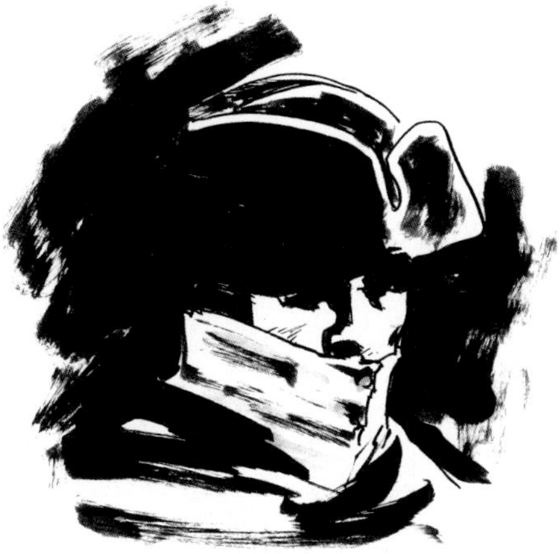

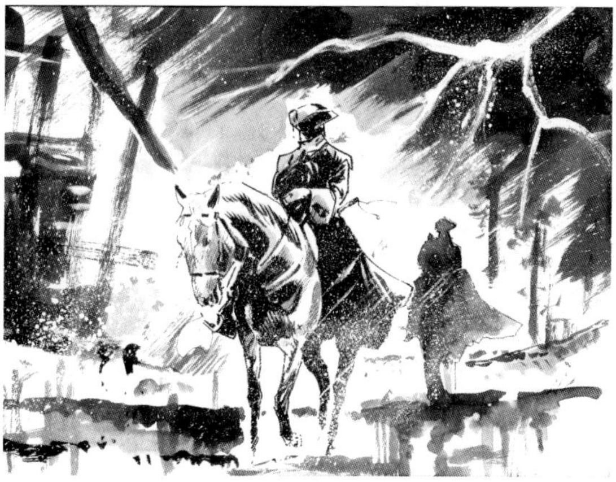

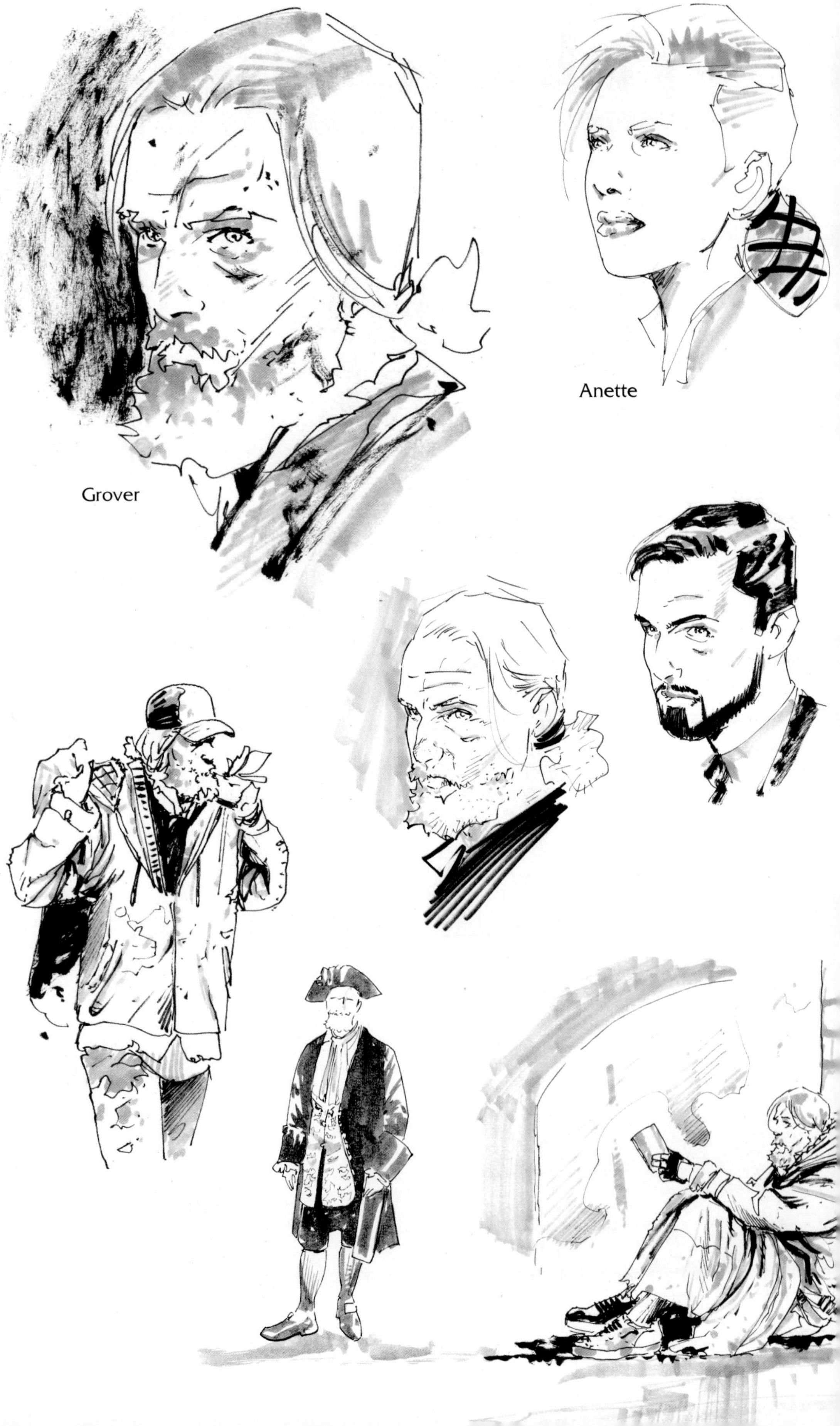
Anette
Grover

Leo (14–25 years old)

Anette

I tried to give the protagonists "ordinary" facial features—to show them as ordinary people who could be our neighbors . . . even for the bad guys I gave simple looks to show the simplicity of evil that hides behind false appearances.

Fenny

Maria (18–20 years old)

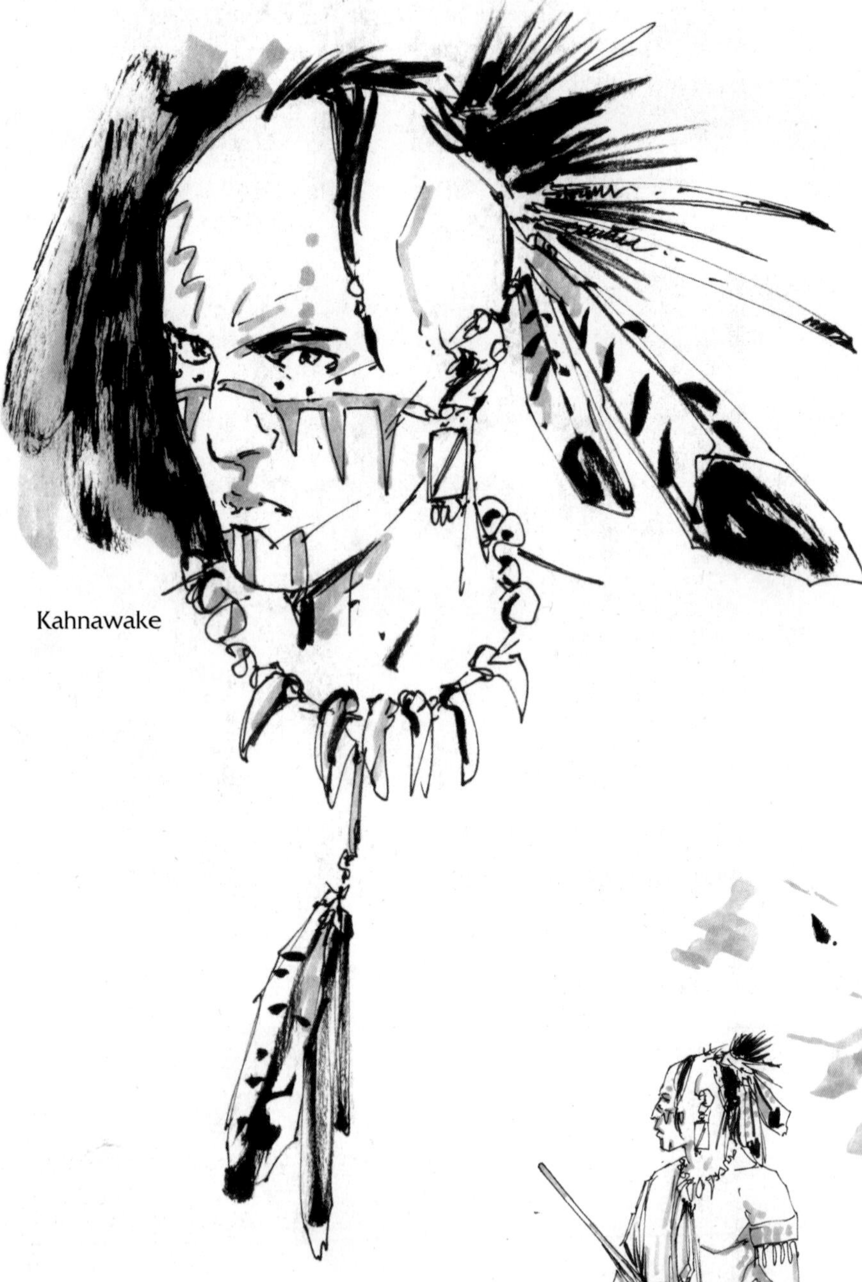

Kahnawake

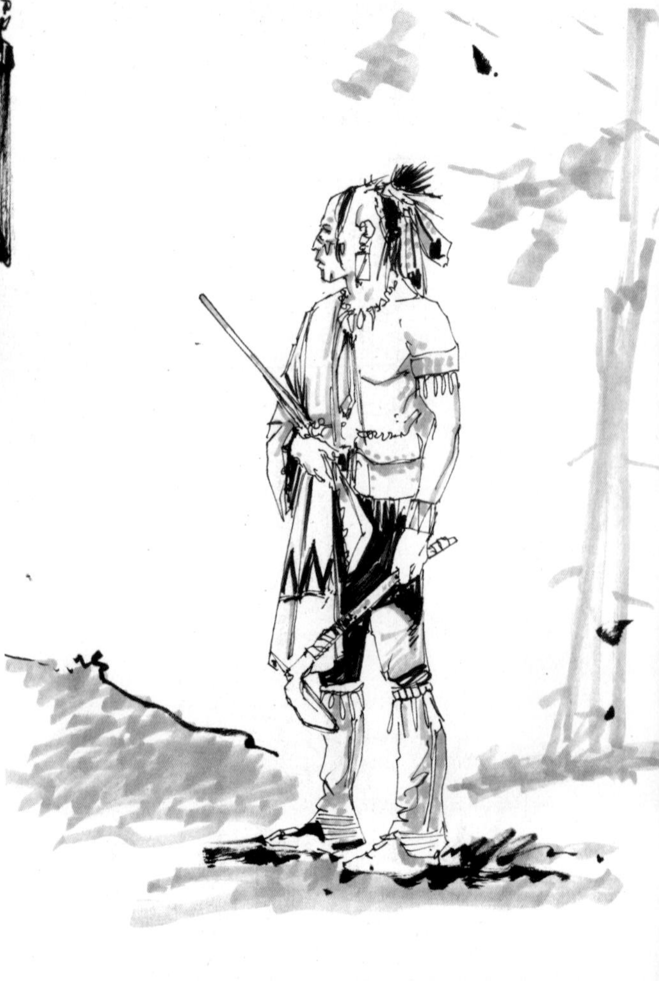

Kahnawake is indigenous, and I defined the character as a fusion of a Shawnee and a Mohawk . . . a man with a painted body, the war tattoos are more than him.

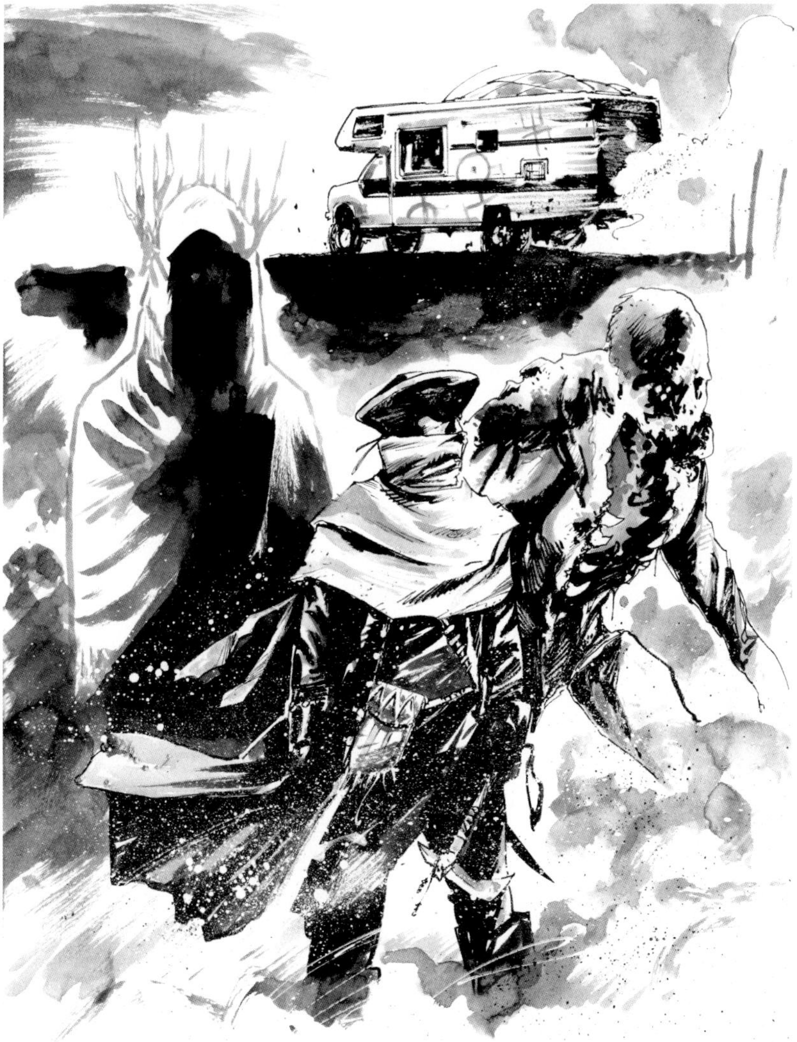

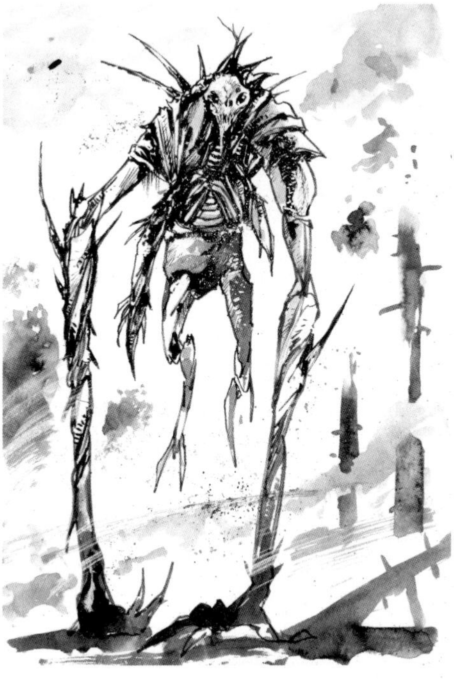

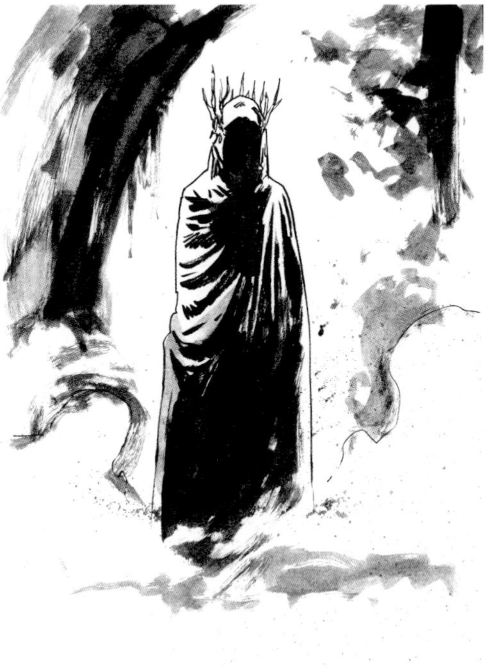

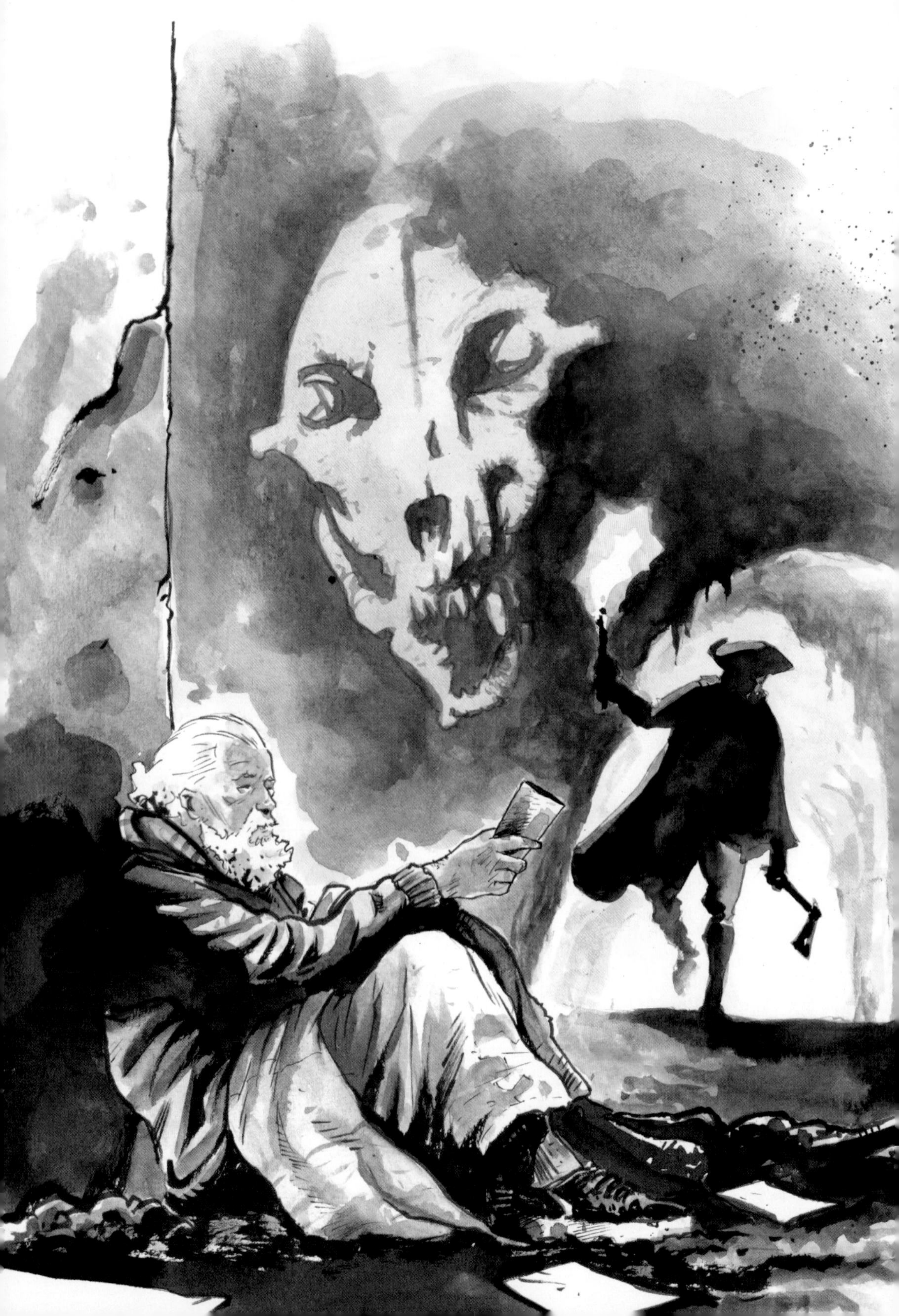

The nameless man corresponds to the classic character of the 1700s, with tricorn, sword, and muzzle-loading pistol . . . but I thought that a touch of color would be effective, and the red scarf lent itself very well to that purpose and gave a sense of fluidity to the movement during the action . . . a simple but always iconic touch.

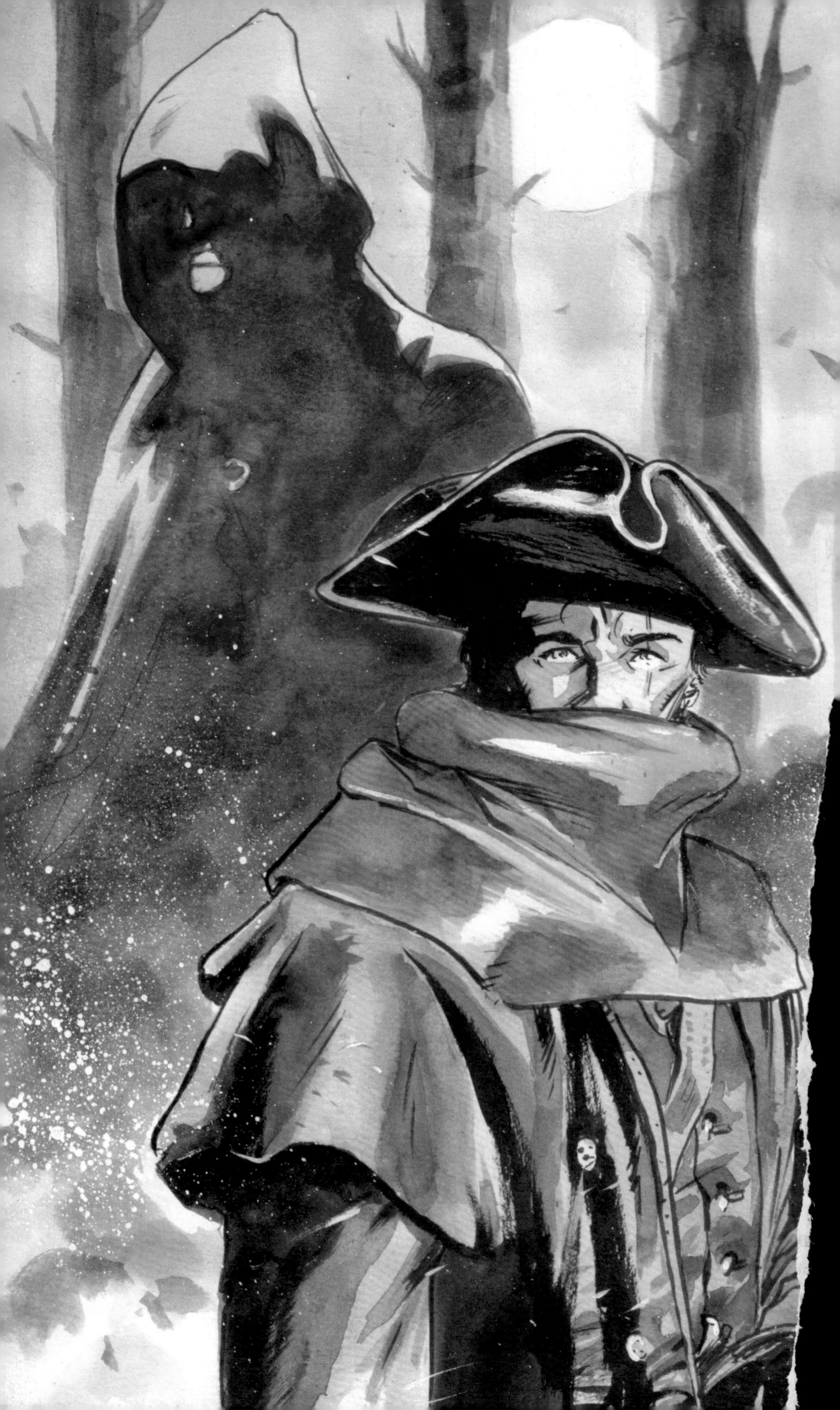